EXPLORING METHODS IN INFORMATION LITERACY RESEARCH

Topics in Australasian Library and Information Studies

Series editor: Dr Stuart Ferguson

This series provides detailed, formally refereed works on a wide range of topics and issues relevant to professionals and para-professionals in the library and information industry and to students of library and information studies. All titles are written from an Australasian perspective, drawing on professional experience and research in Australia, New Zealand and the wider Pacific region. Proposals for publications should be addressed to the series editor (sferguson@csu.edu.au).

Recent publications include:

Number 27
Libraries in the twenty-first century: Charting new directions in information services.
Edited by Stuart Ferguson

Number 26
Collection management: A concise introduction. Revised edition
John Kennedy

Number 25
The other 51 weeks: A marketing handbook for librarians. Revised edition
Lee Welch

Number 24
Archives: Recordkeeping in society
Edited by Sue McKemmish, Michael Piggott, Barbara Reed and Frank Upward

Number 23
Organising knowledge in a global society: Principles and practice in libraries and information centres
Ross Harvey and Philip Hider

Number 22
Computers for librarians: An introduction to the electronic library. 3rd edition
Stuart Ferguson with Rodney Hebels

Number 21
Australian library supervision and management. 2nd edition
Roy Sanders

Number 20
Research methods for students, academics and professionals. 2nd edition
Kirsty Williamson et al.

EXPLORING METHODS IN INFORMATION LITERACY RESEARCH

Edited by Suzanne Lipu, Kirsty Williamson and Annemaree Lloyd

Topics in Australasian Library and Information Studies, Number 28

Centre for Information Studies

Charles Sturt University
Wagga Wagga New South Wales

ISBN 978 1876938 61 1 (pbk.)
ISSN: 1030-5009

National Library of Australia cataloguing-in-publication data

---

Exploring methods in information literacy research

Publisher: Wagga Wagga, NSW: CIS, 2007
Series: Topics in Australasian library and information studies no. 28.

Bibliography
ISBN: 978 187 6938 61 1 (pbk.)

Information literacy--Research--Australia--Methodology
Information science--Research--Australia--Methodology
Library science--Research--Australia--Methodology

020.7094

Published in 2007

Series editor: S Ferguson
Production coordinator: M McNicol
Copy editor: R Crease
Cover designer: T O'Neill, CSU Print
Printer: On-Demand, Southbank VIC

Centre for Information Studies
Locked Bag 660
Wagga Wagga NSW 2678
Australia
Phone: + 61 (0)2 6933 2325
Fax: +61 (0)2 6933 2733
Email: cis@csu.edu.au
http://www.csu.edu.au/cis

Contents

Exploring methods in information literacy research

	Page
Acknowledgements	vii
Figures and tables	ix
Biographical notes on contributors	xi
Preface – Christine Bruce	xv
Chapter 1 The broad methodological contexts of information literacy research – Kirsty Williamson	1
Chapter 2 Introduction to the chapters – Kirsty Williamson	13
Chapter 3 Survey research – Natalie Cuffe	23
Chapter 4 Critical incident technique – Hilary Hughes	49
Chapter 5 Understanding information literacy in the workplace: using a constructivist grounded theory approach – Annemaree Lloyd	67
Chapter 6 Phenomenography: 'Follow the yellow brick road'! – Sylvia Lauretta Edwards	87
Chapter 7 Action research – Karen Visser	111
Chapter 8 Using focus groups in a mixed method approach to evaluate student learning in an information literacy embedding project – Lesley Procter and Richard Wartho	133
Chapter 9 Evidence-based practice and information literacy – Helen Partridge and Gillian Hallam	149
Chapter 10 The evidence-based model of information literacy research: a critique – Melanie Lazarow	171
Chapter 11 Alternative methods in information literacy research in Australasia – Suzanne Lipu	185

Contents

Acknowledgements

The idea for this book was first generated in 2004 in discussions by advisory members of the Australian and New Zealand Institute of Information Literacy (ANZIL). Dr Mandy Lupton (then chair of the research group) originally took on the editorial work, and invested a substantial effort into getting it off the ground and then passing it over for the current editors to complete. We greatly appreciate her work and also recognise the valuable identification of a need for this book by the ANZIIL advisory members.

The editors would particularly like to acknowledge the patience and cooperation of the authors throughout the book's journey. Your valuable pieces make a wonderful contribution to the information literacy field.

We would like to thank Rachel Crease (our copy editor) for her infinite attention to detail, promptness and especially her patience in dealing with our demands in getting the book to publication.

Finally the editors would like to thank the staff at the Centre for Information Studies whose expertise in publishing made the job of producing the final text as smooth as possible.

Figures and tables

		Page
Table 4.1	Example of plans and specifications (CIT)	54
Table 4.2	Example of data collection (CIT)	57
Table 4.3	Example of categorisation framework and sample categories (CIT)	60
Table 4.4	Example of categorisation process (CIT)	61
Figure 5.1	Example of category development (grounded theory)	72
Figure 5.2	Grounded theory process used in firefighter study	76
Figure 6.1	An illustration of phenomenography	89
Figure 6.2	Structure of awareness category 1 (phenomenography)	100
Figure 6.3	Structure of awareness category 2 (phenomenography)	100
Figure 6.4	The outcome space (phenomenography)	102
Figure 7.1	Lewin's action research cycle	112
Table 7.1	A triple helix (action research)	117
Table 7.2	Comparison between Rogers' criteria and College survey	122
Table 7.3	Product, process and function of learning (action research)	124
Table 7.4	Reflective evaluation for teachers (action research)	127
Table 7.5	Triangulation of reflection (action research)	127
Table 8.1	Focus group characteristics	138
Table 9.1	CriSTAL – critical appraisal checklist	157
Table 9.2	The ReLIANT instrument	158-159
Table 9.3	The six frames for IL education	160-161
Figure 11.1	Philosophical frameworks of research methods	186

Biographical notes on contributors

Christine Bruce is professor in the Faculty of Information Technology at Queensland University of Technology. She has extensive interests in higher education teaching and learning, and has developed the relational model for information literacy and information literacy education. Christine's long-term research agenda revolves around the perceptual worlds of information and technology users, including learning in the higher education context. Christine has addressed international conferences on information literacy and information literacy education. She has published more than 100 scholarly works and received awards from the American Library Association and American Association for Research into Education.

Natalie Cuffe is a lecturer in the Law Faculty at Queensland University of Technology. Prior to joining academia she worked in legal practice and as a law librarian. She teaches predominantly in the compulsory legal research and writing units in the LLB (Bachelor of Laws). Natalie enjoys being able to teach and research across the legal and information science domains. Her research interests include legal information literacy, legal education, legal skills, graduate capabilities and animal law.

Sylvia Lauretta Edwards is assistant dean teaching and learning in the Faculty of Information Technology at Queensland University of Technology. She has received ten teaching and performance awards including the prestigious Carrick Australian Awards for University Teaching, Award for Teaching Excellence in Physical Sciences and Related Disciplines in 2006. Sylvia completed a Masters of Information Technology (Research) in 1999 and her Doctorate in 2005. Sylvia's research interests include higher education, information literacy, information searching and evidenced-based librarianship. Sylvia has been an active executive member of state and national library associations, including two years as vice president and webmaster for the Queensland Library Promotions Council, and as a member of the Queensland State Council of ALIA.

Gillian Hallam is associate professor and faculty fellow in the Faculty of Information Technology at Queensland University of Technology (QUT). She is currently project leader for a national research study to investigate the development and use of eportfolios in higher education. Her teaching and research interests focus on the management and evaluation of information services, e-learning and on a range of professional and workforce issues in the LIS sector. Prior to joining QUT, she worked as a librarian in the corporate sector, managing business and legal information. Gillian was president of the Australian Library and Information Association (ALIA) in 2005-2006 and serves on both ALIA's Education and Professional Development Standing Committee and the Education and Training Standing Committee of the International Federation of Library Associations and Institutions. In 2005, Gillian served as chair of the 3rd International Evidence-based Librarianship Conference. She has won a number of university teaching excellence awards and is a fellow of the Higher Education Research and Development Society of Australasia.

Hilary Hughes is a lecturer in the Master of Learning Innovation (Teacher-Librarianship) program in the Education Faculty at Queensland University of Technology (QUT). She has extensive experience as a librarian/information literacy educator in academic, public and government libraries, most recently at Central Queensland University (Brisbane International Campus). Her teaching and research interests include information literacy, uses of information for learning in online environments, and cultural and linguistic diversity. Hilary is undertaking a PhD in the Faculty of Information Technology, QUT, entitled 'International students using online information resources for learning'.

Melanie Lazarow has been working at the University of Melbourne Library for eighteen years and is a senior information consultant. Previously she worked in the public library world and as a tutor and lecturer in librarianship. One of her roles is to teach qualitative software to research students for information analysis. She completed a Masters in History and Philosophy of Science at the University of Melbourne in 1998. Melanie serves on the Australian Library and Information Association Information Literacy Committee and the Australian and New Zealand Institute of Information Literacy Research Working Party as well as having twice been the vice president of the National Tertiary Education Union at the University of Melbourne. Melanie's concern is that evidence should not be seen as a value-neutral entity.

Suzanne Lipu is an associate lecturer in the School of Information Studies at Charles Sturt University (CSU). Suzanne's interests centre on information literacy in specific cultural contexts. She has published in the areas of developing information literacy programs in universities, teaching and assessment strategies in information literacy education, and lifelong learning for women in developing countries. She is currently working on her PhD in the Faculty of Education, CSU, entitled 'Information literacy – the social agenda: a feminist exploration of information literacy, personal empowerment and internationalisation'.

Annemaree Lloyd is a senior lecturer in the School of Information Studies at Charles Sturt University. Annemaree has extensive interests in information literacy in theoretical and applied settings. Her work focuses on workplace information literacy and she has published in the areas of information literacy in workplace contexts, the role of information literacy in embodied learning, information affordances and communities of practice. Her current research focuses on the relationship between information literacy and practice.

Helen Partridge is a senior lecturer in the Faculty of Information Technology at Queensland University of Technology and teaches in the areas of reference and information services, information retrieval, collection and access management, information literacy education and professional practice. Helen has published widely in the area of teaching and learning and has won a number of teaching awards. Helen is an active member of the Australian and international library community and in 2007 she was the recipient of the State Library of Queensland Award for her contribution to the library community. Helen has recently completed her PhD exploring the psychological perspective of the digital divide within communities. Her research interests include community information literacy, evidence-based library and information practice and library and information science education.

Lesley Procter was instrumental in establishing the sociology program at the University of Otago and currently teaches in the program. Her teaching and learning research interests include embedding information literacy in academic programs, learning support for first-year students, and communities of practice as learning contexts. She is the recipient of a New Zealand Qualifications Authority Tertiary Teaching Excellence Award, a Univeristy of Otago Excellence in Teaching Award, and a University of Otago Students Association Teaching Award.

Karen Visser has been a teacher, head of department and head of library in a number of high schools and colleges in the Australian Capital Territory. Her research, and the resulting programs described in this book, was undertaken as part of an MA (Information Management) completed at the University of Technology, Sydney. She is currently program leader for information services at the Australian National University which seeks to build a highly skilled information literate community in information technology, information management and information searching.

Richard Wartho is an information literacy specialist with experience at several university libraries in New Zealand and Australia. His chapter for this book was written when he was involved in a collaborative project with the Department of Anthropology at the University of Otago. Richard has also been a secondary school teacher and is currently a teacher librarian at St Joseph's College, Hunters Hill.

Kirsty Williamson is the director of the research group, Information and Telecommunications Needs Research, a joint initiative of Monash and Charles Sturt Universities in Australia. Since the early 1990s, she has undertaken many research projects, funded by a range of different organisations including the principal funding body of Australian universities, the Australian Research Council. Her principal area of research has been 'human information behaviour'. In recent years, she has also become involved in the related field of research, information literacy, which is the focus of this book.

Preface

Christine Bruce

Information literacy has been one of the most exciting and transforming concepts to have emerged in the last twenty years. Helping people to be effective learners and users in contemporary information environments is the cornerstone required to bring about learning for individuals, families and communities, learning organisations, learning cities and learning societies.

Underpinning our advocacy for information literacy, our information literacy programs and information literacy education must be a deep understanding of the concept itself, and the many and varied aspects through which people use information to learn, at home, at work and at play.

Exploring Methods in Information Literacy Research provides the conceptual tools for all of us who wish to explore new approaches to research in the information literacy arena, or who wish to revisit previously familiar methods. Each chapter has been written by someone who has worked with the method; some of the chapters have been written by authors who have recently gone through the experience of learning to use the method, positioning them as ideal contributors to this volume. Each author explores the key aspects of their chosen method and explains how it may be applied in practice. New researchers and early career professionals will appreciate the clarity of the introductions provided.

As with any introductory material, each chapter will also entice readers to go on to explore more detail in other places. We should remember that each chapter represents an author's view at a particular point in time, and that the methods they are describing are also represented at a particular point in time. Research methods are alive; they grow, and develop as they are used. Don't be afraid to experiment and explore, to mix and match, according to your needs.

An important note: all the chapters of the book have been peer reviewed (double blind), with the exception of the second chapter which introduces the other chapters.

CHAPTER 1
The broad methodological contexts of information literacy research

Kirsty Williamson

The contributions in this book, to be introduced in the next chapter, discuss rich and varied methods and techniques for conducting research about information literacy (IL). To set these contributions in the broader context of social sciences research methodology, the process I begin in this chapter, I start with a discussion of the key research philosophies and traditions. Included here is a section on philosophy and method related to 'mixed methods' research. Mixed methods research is not widely reported in the library and information studies (LIS) field, and so the contribution in this regard should be particularly useful.

My positioning of the chapters in a broader philosophical picture will be, to some extent, a personal conceptualisation based on extensive reading of the literature. There is a major problem in the field of research resulting from the fluid use of terminology. Thus, for example, what one researcher might label a philosophy, another might call a paradigm, yet another an epistemology. The fact that research approaches are dynamic and ever-changing also makes it difficult to categorise them in clearly defined ways. As I said in my research methods book (Williamson 2002a), where I discuss the issues of terminology, it is important 'to try to learn to accept, and deal with, the fluidity and rich diversity of terminology' (p.38). Case (2002, pp.131-155) also provides a useful discussion, highlighting the diversity and problems of terminology, as well as other conceptual issues. Nevertheless, I believe that the exercise of placing one's research into a broader research context is an important and rewarding one.

The two major philosophical traditions that begin this process are termed 'positivist' and 'interpretivist' (sometimes written as 'interpretive'). Another term sometimes applied to these traditions is 'paradigms'. The reason why these terms 'philosophy' and 'paradigm' are similar can be seen in the definition of the latter by Kuhn (1970, p.10), who said that a 'paradigm' is 'a set of interrelated assumptions about the social world, which provides a philosophical and conceptual framework for the systematic study of that world'.

Positivism

The term 'positivist' was first used in 1830 by the philosopher Comte, one of the founding fathers of sociology. Later, in the 1920s, a brand of positivism known as 'logical positivism' was developed by a group of scholars known as the Vienna circle, members of which moved to the USA in the 1930s. Proclaiming the values and benefits of science, this group began the movement to apply scientific research methods to the social sciences. Thus positivists consider that, as in the field of science, knowledge can only be based on what can be observed and experienced. Key positivist tenets are therefore 'measurement' and 'objectivity', resulting in a focus on quantitative data. The associated style of reasoning is 'deductive', where the argument moves from general principles to particular instances.

Positivist research usually begins with theories and models, defines variables for study and predicts their relationships through framing hypotheses which are then tested. Generalisations are eventually made. Common research designs are 'experimental design', with its emphasis on cause and effect, and 'survey', which must be carried out according to scientific principles. For example, the sample must be randomly selected according to the scientific definition: where each element in the sample must have an equal and independent chance of being included. Also important are the principles of 'validity' and 'reliability'. The former is concerned with accuracy of various kinds. For example, validity with measurement refers to the extent to which a research instrument measures what it is designed to measure. Reliability is concerned with obtaining consistent, stable research results with replication. Powell and Connaway (2004, pp.43-49) discuss these concepts.

Despite the rigour associated with positivism, discussed above, the label 'positivist' is used in this book wherever 'measurement' or 'testing' is the aim of the research, whether or not high standards in relation to sampling, validity and reliability are met.

Interpretivism

'Interpretivism' is a broad term which encompasses a number of different paradigms, all concerned with the meanings and experiences of human beings. Since the central tenet of interpretivism is that people are constantly involved in interpreting their ever-changing world, researchers who are interpretivists believe that the social world is constructed by people and is therefore different from the world of nature. They favour 'naturalistic inquiry' (where field work usually takes place in a natural setting), embrace an inductive style of reasoning and emphasise qualitative data.

Because of their belief that the social world is constructed by people, the key task of interpretivist researchers is to come to understand how the various participants in a social setting construct their world (Glesne & Peshkin 1992, p.6). As recognised by interpretivists, people invariably have different perspectives which means that researchers need to learn to deal with what are referred to as 'multiple realities'. Guba and Lincoln (1981) describe the latter as the layers of an onion, nesting within or complementing each other: 'Each layer provides a different perspective of reality, and none can be considered more "true" than any other' (p.57). These multiple realities are gauged through an exploration of the beliefs, feelings and interpretations of research participants, who are also sometimes referred to as actors.

To accommodate the need to be 'totally open to the setting and subjects of their study' (Gorman & Clayton 1997, p.38), interpretivist researchers are much less 'linear' in their approach than are positivist researchers. Their research designs tend to be iterative, with various elements in the research being interwoven and the development of one influencing decisions about the others. For example, data analysis is undertaken throughout the project, not just in the concluding stage. The literature review is still usually developed for background understanding of the topic; research questions are developed, although they will usually be less specific and more flexible than in a positivist study, allowing for adjustment as data are collected; and there is some planning of data collection but, once again, with flexibility in mind.

Good interpretivist researchers are aware that there can be difficulties in understanding fully the perspectives of others very different from themselves. They record the perspectives of participants as accurately as possible, often providing them with some opportunity to comment on what has been recorded about them. They then 'develop concepts, insights and understanding from patterns in the data' (Reneker 1993, p.499), attempting not to impose pre-existing expectations (Patton 1990, p.44). A rigorous process developed for this is 'grounded theory' where theory is built literally from the 'ground' upwards, that is, from the data of participants. Original proponents of grounded theory were Glaser and Strauss (1967).

Interpretivist paradigms and methods

A key interpretivist paradigm is 'constructivism', where the emphasis can be either on people developing meanings for their activities together, that is, socially constructing reality, as analysed in the famous book, *The Social Construction of Reality* (Berger & Luckman 1967); or on individuals making sense of their world on an individual basis, that is, personally constructing reality, as postulated by Kelly (1955). This latter process is encapsulated in Dervin's 'sense making' theory, which has had a major impact in the LIS field. See, for example, Dervin (1992); Dervin & Nilan (1986). A constructivist approach to grounded theory has now been developed. Charmaz (2003) says that, unlike the original grounded theory, constructivist grounded theory is not 'objectivist'. It 'recognises that the viewer creates the data and ensuing analysis through interaction with the viewed' and therefore the data do not provide a window on an objective reality (p.273). Thus, there is recognition that researchers' backgrounds will influence their interpretations of the data. They cannot avoid being influenced by 'disciplinary emphases' and 'perceptual proclivities' (p.259). This means that, although every effort is made to look at 'how "variables" are grounded – given meaning and played out in subjects' lives' (Dawson & Prus 1995; Prus 1996 cited by Charmaz 2003, p.272), there is acceptance that researchers shape their data collection and redirect their analysis as new issues emerge'(p.271).

Another interpretivist paradigm is 'critical theory', the proponents of which write value-laden documents aimed at redressing the balance where 'a history of repression determined by patriarchal, ethnocentric, ageist and other social stratification systems influences the ways in which people choose, and are able to construct, their own realities' (Denzin & Lincoln, 1998, p.187). Yet another is 'phenomenography' which is described in the relevant chapter in this book as 'an interpretive research approach' and, citing Marton (1986), as 'a research method adopted for mapping the qualitatively different ways in which people experience, conceptualise, perceive, and understand various aspects of, and phenomena in the world around them'(p.31).

'Ethnography' or 'participant observation' is a key method used by interpretivists. Originally developed by anthropologists for the study of culture, it has now been adapted by some researchers to encompass a range of techniques to enable rich description of the views, experiences and behaviour of research participants (Bow 2002). Techniques used by ethnographers include interviews – individual and focus group – observation, and examination of documents. However, interpretivist researchers will often simply use one or more of these ethnographic techniques without undertaking an ethnographic study per se, where a variety of techniques would usually be used. As Saule (2002, pp.184-5), citing Guba (1990, p.23) and Denzin and Lincoln (1998, p.4), states, ethnography is validated through triangulation – the use of multiple methods and theoretical constructs to add rigour, breadth and depth to a study. Lipu, in the final chapter of this book, refers further to ethnographic method.

Other conceptual approaches

Not everyone who favours either quantitative or qualitative methods (or a combination thereof) espouses, or may even be aware of, the philosophical approaches outlined above – at least not precisely as discussed. Researchers speak of quantitative, qualitative and mixed methods research. In addition to the terminology problem, there is a wide variety of views on how the landscape of research should be configured. This is particularly evident in the field of inquiry labeled 'qualitative research' which, because of the range of methods and techniques available, is particularly widely discussed in the literature. (See, for example, Patton 1990; Mellon 1990; Gorman & Clayton 1997; Denzin & Lincoln 2003).

Qualitative research

While Denzin and Lincoln (2003) emphasise the 'interpretive' nature of qualitative research, and would include the interpretivist paradigms and methods discussed above, theirs is a broad, historical conceptualisation and is not synonymous with interpretivist research. They say that 'qualitative research is a field in its own right' … crosscutting 'disciplines, fields, and subject matters' (p.3). Other comments are that 'it is difficult to define clearly', 'has no theory or paradigm that is distinctly its own' (p.9), and, historically, is surrounded by:

> a complex, interconnected family of terms, concepts, and assumptions … [that] include the traditions associated with foundationalism, positivism, postpostivism, poststructuralism, and the many qualitative research perspectives, and/or methods, connected to cultural and interpretive studies (p.3).

It is surprising to find positivism listed here, especially since Denzin and Lincoln critique the views about reality which underpin positivist research, making it seem at odds (as indeed it is) with the interpretive approach with its emphasis on the 'value-laden nature of inquiry'(p.13). They cite Huber (1995) in saying that positivist critics of qualitative research 'presume a stable, unchanging reality that can be studied using the empirical methods of objectivist social science' (p.12). But, viewed historically, the earliest ethnographers were positivist qualitative researchers who 'asserted that through a scientific and rigorous analysis, universal truths could be discerned that lay beneath the superficial diversities of different culture' (Saule 2002, p.179). Even recently Charmaz (2003) has labeled the original grounded theory (Glaser & Strauss 1967; and the later version Strauss & Corbin 1990, 1998) as 'objectivist', as noted above. Also, post-positivists particularly place an emphasis on qualitative research (Myers 1997; Denzin & Lincoln 1994). This is to enable them to capture as much as possible of a reality which they see as elusive but possible to approximate through using qualitative procedures 'that lend themselves to structured (sometimes statistical) analysis' (Denzin & Lincoln 2003, p.14).

Denzin and Lincoln (2003) talk of qualitative research as using 'a variety of empirical materials – case study; personal experience; introspection; life story; interview; artifacts; cultural texts and productions; observational, historical, interactional, and visual texts'(p.5). At another point they say that qualitative researchers 'draw upon and utilize the approaches, methods, and techniques of ethnomethodology, phenomenology, hermeneutics, feminism, rhizomatics, deconstructionism, ethnography, interviews, psychoanalysis, cultural studies, survey research, and participant observation, among others' (p.10). In other words, all forms, methods and practices of social inquiry can come under the banner of 'qualitative research'.

Not all writers, however, agree with Denzin and Lincoln's portrayal of qualitative research. Gorman and Clayton (1997), in their handbook of qualitative research for the information professional, for example, state that the qualitative approach 'lies within the interpretivist paradigm, which focuses on social constructs' (p.23). My view is that the terms 'positivist' and 'interpretivist' offer the best labels to distinguish two different epistemological views: first, of researchers who believe that there is a measurable reality and, second, of those who postulate that reality is constructed by individuals and groups. While data are most likely to be quantitative with positivist researchers and qualitative with interpretivists, this will not be exclusively the case. This approach allows for mixed methods in both quantitative and qualitative research and for the all-encompassing approach to qualitative research of Denzin and Lincoln (2003). It also enables researchers who place an emphasis either on the need to 'measure' the social world, or on the need to 'understand' the meanings made by people, to have distinctive niches. There also needs to be accommodation of those who postulate that there are some aspects of life, although not all, which are measurable, at least at a particular point in time, and who favour the use of quantitative or qualitative methods as appropriate.

Mixed methods

As with other research conceptualisations, there is a lack of agreement about what constitutes 'mixed methods' research. At the simplest level, it involves the use of quantitative and qualitative methods in the same study. The use of mixed methods is a popular approach with some researchers who believe that this is a good way to gain a deeper understanding of issues and experience. For example, Ford (1987) believes that it is possible for researchers to use either quantitative or qualitative approaches, or both, according to the research problem, or problems, under consideration. He makes a strong case for integration because the use of different kinds of thinking involved in positivist and interpretivist approaches make a full understanding of topics more likely.

Other writers, while appreciating the benefits of mixed methods research, urge consideration of the assumptions underpinning different epistemologies which constitute 'different ways of seeing, knowing, and valuing' (Greene & Caracelli 2003, p.107). One of these is Mellon (1990), who believes that methodologies can be profitably combined, but warns that great care needs to be taken because they '... are separate and distinct from one another, with different purposes, methods and outcomes' (p.5). Greene and Caracelli, in arguing that their readers should undertake mixed methods research 'in a thoughtful and defensible manner' (p.94), express particular concern about the nature and role of inquiry paradigms in mixed methods practice. They review a small sample of social research and conclude that 'inquiry decisions are rarely, if ever, consciously rooted in philosophical assumptions or beliefs' (p.107). In other words, much mixed methods research – and I would add, single method research – appears to be a-theoretical, although both myself (Williamson 2002a, p.58) and Greene and Caracelli (2003, p.95) argue that all researchers have some kind of mental model of the social world, whether or not they are consciously aware of it, or make it explicit. Greene and Caracelli lament this lack of philosophical underpinnings, postulating that:

> there is merit in different paradigmatic traditions in that each has
> something valuable to offer to our understanding of our complex social
> world. If such differences are not attended to in practice, then the full
> potential of mixed methods inquiry will remain unfulfilled (2003, p.107).

Morse (2003) discusses two kinds of approaches to combining research strategies 'to obtain a more complete picture of human behavior and experience' (p.189). First, quantitative and qualitative research strategies can be combined within a single project to answer a particular question – labeled 'mixed methods design'. Second, quantitative and qualitative methods can be used separately in projects which are then combined to form one research program – labeled 'multimethod design' (p.191).

In discussing the 'mixed methods' design, Morse takes a stronger stance than Greene and Caracelli, warning that we must 'remain aware that the ad hoc mixing of strategies or methods (i.e., "muddling methods" [Stern 1994]) may be a serious threat to validity as methodological assumptions are violated' (p.191). She advocates that the researcher first recognise the 'theoretical drive' of the project and that this should determine whether it will be basically quantitative or qualitative in approach.

> If the purpose of the research is to describe or discover, to find meaning, or to explore, then the theoretical drive will be inductive. The method commonly used with be qualitative … If the purpose of the research is to confirm (i.e., to test a hypothesis or a theory), or to determine the distribution of a phenomenon, then the method used is usually quantitative (p.193).

While this would appear to offer a useful way of determining the 'theoretical drive', the inclusion of 'to describe', as a purpose suited to qualitative methods only, needs to be called into question. The descriptive survey (basically quantitative in approach) is very common.

Different research goals, different methods

It is a cardinal rule among many researchers, excepting those who are purist advocates of particular approaches, that method should be matched to research goals (for example, the purposes determining the 'theoretical drive' of a project, outlined above) and the questions needing to be answered. Quantitative data are appropriate for straightforward factual information (for example, 'what', 'who' 'how many', 'how much', 'where', 'when' information), measurable at a particular point in time. An example of questions suited to a quantitative approach would be: What is the extent and purpose of computer use for information seeking among first-year Arts students? Complex questions which involve 'why' and 'how' lend themselves to qualitative exploration. Examples could be: Why do certain information seekers rely entirely on search engines such as Google to meet their information needs? How could they be helped to change this behaviour? An in-depth approach is needed to explore and discover all the various reasons and complexities involved in answering these questions.

In this book we have chapters by a range of researchers whose goals and research questions for IL research differ widely. The method described in the survey research chapter is underpinned, without question, by positivist philosophy and is well suited to the research questions that are posed. The constructivist grounded theory chapter, the phenomenology chapter and the action research chapter all use different methods but have in common an interpretivist approach, concerned as they all are with the meanings and experiences of the participants who were involved in their studies. While the chapter on the critical incident technique is labeled as 'qualitative research', it has most in common with the positivist style of qualitative research, discussed above. The focus group chapter discusses a key research method, or technique as it is also labeled (Williamson 2002b), which is appropriate for use on its own or to supplement another method such as a survey which is what occurred in this case. This can be viewed as an example of 'mixed methods' research. The next two chapters focus on evidence-based practice and a critique of evidence-based practice, both offering a discussion of methodological issues along the way. Finally, the last chapter draws the threads of all the chapters together. A specific introduction for each of the contributions appears in the next chapter.

References

Berger, P.L. & Luckman, T. (1967). *The social construction of reality: A treatise in the sociology of knowledge*. New York: Anchor Press.

Bow, A. (2002). Ethnographic techniques. In K. Williamson, *Research methods for academics, students and professionals: Information management and systems* (2nd ed., pp.265-280). Wagga Wagga, NSW: Centre for Information Studies, Charles Sturt University.

Case, D.O. (2002). *Looking for information: A survey of research on information seeking, needs and behavior*. London: Academic Press.

Charmaz, K. (2003). 'Grounded theory: Objectivist and constructivist methods'. In N.K. Denzin & Y.S. Lincoln (Eds.), *Strategies of qualitative inquiry* (2nd ed., pp.249-291). Thousand Oaks, CA: Sage.

Dawson, L.L. & Prus, R.C. (1995). Postmodernism and linguistic reality versus symbolic interactionism and obdurate reality. In N.K. Denzin & Y.S. Lincoln (Eds.), *Studies in symbolic interaction: A research annual*, 17, pp.105-124. Cited by Charmaz, K.

(2003). Grounded theory: Objectivist and constructivist methods. In N.K. Denzin & Y.S. Lincoln (Eds.), *Strategies of qualitative inquiry* (2nd ed., pp.249-291). Thousand Oaks, CA: Sage.

Denzin, N.K. & Lincoln, Y.S. (2003). Introduction: The discipline and practice of qualitative research. In N.K. Denzin & Y.S. Lincoln (Eds.), *Strategies of qualitative inquiry* (2nd ed., pp.1-45). Thousand Oaks, CA: Sage.

Denzin, N.K. & Lincoln, Y.S. (1998). Introduction: Entering the field of qualitative research. In N.K. Denzin & Y.S. Lincoln (Eds.), *The landscape of qualitative research: Theories and issues* (pp.1-34). London: Sage. Cited by Saule, S. (2002). Ethnography. In K. Williamson, *Research methods for academics, students and professionals: Information management and systems* (2nd ed., pp.177-193). Wagga Wagga, NSW: Centre for Information Studies, Charles Sturt University.

Denzin, N.K. & Lincoln, Y.S. (Eds.) (1994). *Handbook of qualitative research*. Thousand Oaks, CA: Sage.

Dervin, B. (1992). 'From the mind's eye of the user: The sense-making qualitative-quantitative methodology'. In J.D. Glazier & R.R. Powell (Eds.), *Qualitative research in information management* (pp.61-84). Englewood, CO: Libraries Unlimited.

Dervin, B. & Nilan, M. (1986). Information needs and uses. In M.E. Williams (Ed.), *Annual Review of Information Science and Technology* (ARIST), *21*, n.p.: Knowledge Industry Publications, pp.3-33.

Ford, N. (1987). 'Research and practice in librarianship: A cognitive view'. In B. Katz & R. Kinder (Eds.) *Current trends in information research and theory* (pp.21-47). New York: Haworth.

Glaser, B.G. & Strauss, A.L. (1967). *The discovery of grounded theory*. Chicago, IL: Aldine.

Glesne, C. & Peshkin, A. (1992). *Becoming qualitative researchers: An introduction*. White Plains, NY: Longman.

Gorman, G.E. & Clayton, P. (1997). *Qualitative research for the information professional: A practical handbook*. London: Library Association.

Greene, J.C. & Caracelli, V.J. (2003). Making paradigmatic sense of mixed methods practice. In A. Tashakkori & C. Teddue (Eds.), *Handbook of mixed methods in social and behavioral research* (pp.91-110). Thousand Oaks, CA: Sage.

Guba, E.G. & Lincoln, Y.S. (1981). *Effective evaluation*. San Francisco, CA: Jossey-Bass.

Huber, J. (1995). Centennial essay: Institutional perspectives on sociology. *American Journal of Sociology, 101*, pp.194-216. Cited by N.K. Denzin & Y.S. Lincoln, (2003). Introduction: The discipline and practice of qualitative research. In N.K. Denzin & Y.S. Lincoln, *Strategies of qualitative inquiry* (2nd ed.). Thousand Oaks, CA: Sage.

Kelly, G. (1955). *The psychology of personal constructs*, Vols 1 and 2. New York: Norton.

Kuhn, T.S. (1970). *The structure of scientific revolutions* (2nd ed.). Chicago, IL: University of Chicago Press.

Marton, F. (1986). Phenomenography – A research approach to investigating different understandings of reality. *Journal of Thought, 21*(3), 28-49.

Mellon, C. (1990). *Naturalistic inquiry for library science: Methods and applications for research, evaluation and teaching.* New York: Greenwood Press. User study: pp.116-123.

Morse, J.M. (2003). Principles of mixed methods and multimethod research design. In A. Tashakkori & C. Teddue (Eds.), *Handbook of mixed methods in social and behavioral research* (pp.189-208). Thousand Oaks, CA: Sage.

Myers, M.D. (1997). Qualitative research in information systems. *MIS Quarterly, 21*(2), June 1997, pp.241-242. *MISQ Discovery*, archival version, June 1997, http://www.misq.org/misqd961/isworld/. *MISQ Discovery*, updated version, February 24, 1999. [Online] http://www.auckland.ac.nz/msis/isworld/ Retrieved 23 June 2005.

Patton, M.Q. (1990). *Qualitative evaluation and research methods* (2nd ed.). Newbury Park, CA: Sage.

Powell, R.R.& Connaway, L.S. (2004). *Basic research methods for librarians* (4th ed.). Westport, CT: Libraries Unlimited.

Reneker, M.H. (1993). A qualitative study of information seeking among members of an academic community: Methodological issues and problems. *Library Quarterly, 63*(4), pp.487-507.

Saule, S. (2002). Ethnography. In K. Williamson, *Research methods for students, academics and professionals: Information management and systems* (2nd ed., pp.177-193). Wagga Wagga, NSW: Centre for Information Studies, Charles Sturt University.

Stern, P.N. (1994). Eroding grounded theory. In J. Morse (Ed.), *Critical issues in qualitative research methods* (pp.214-215). Thousand Oaks, CA: Sage. Cited by J.M. Morse, (2003). Principles of mixed methods and multimethod research design. In A. Tashakkori & C. Teddue (Eds.), *Handbook of mixed methods in social and behavioral research* (pp.189-208). Thousand Oaks, CA: Sage.

Strauss, A.L. & Corbin, J. (1998). *Basics of qualitative research: Grounded theory procedures and techniques* (2nd ed.). Thousand Oaks, CA: Sage.

Strauss, A.L. & Corbin, J. (1990). *Basics of qualitative research: Grounded theory procedures and techniques.* Newbury Park, CA: Sage.

Williamson, K. (2002a). *Research methods for students, academics and professionals: Information management and systems* (2nd ed.). Wagga Wagga, NSW: Centre for Information Studies, Charles Sturt University.

Williamson, K. (2002b). Research techniques: focus groups. In K. Williamson (2002a). *Research methods for students, academics and professionals: information management and systems* (2nd ed., pp.251-264). Wagga Wagga, NSW: Centre for Information Studies, Charles Sturt University.

CHAPTER 2
Introduction to the chapters

Kirsty Williamson

The purpose of this chapter is to place each of the contributions to this book into the broad framework of philosophies and methods outlined in the previous chapter. The first two chapters fit into the positivist paradigm, the next three into the interpretivist paradigm, and the focus group chapter into a mixed method approach. The two chapters on evidence-based information literacy look at method from a variety of perspectives and the final chapter draws the threads together as well as discussing some alternative methods not covered in this book.

Survey research (Chapter 3)

'Survey research involves the collection of primary data from all or part of a population, in order to determine the incidence, distribution, and interrelationships of certain variables within the population' (Tanner 2002, p.89). For this particular project, a descriptive survey was appropriate to meet the goals, and to answer the research questions, of the researcher. The author, Natalie Cuffe, labels the research as 'descriptive applied research', with the purposes being 'to describe the use of information and information technology by law students' (p.24) and 'to determine the implications for developing a law school curriculum' (p.25). In justifying the positioning of the research as having a 'positivist social science' approach, Cuffe, citing Neuman (2003), says that the study sought to use an 'organised method for combing deductive logic with precise empirical observations of individual behaviour in order to... predict general patterns of human activity' (p.71).

The chapter discusses the survey as both a method and a research technique. Cuffe gives generic information from the literature on the various components of a survey, that is, sample selection; developing, piloting and administering the questionnaire; analysing the data; and reporting the results. She then describes the components in terms of the particular survey which is the focus of the chapter.

The survey targeted all final-year law students from three Queensland universities, an approach to sampling appropriate to a positivist study. The questionnaire was carefully constructed and piloted, including a test to verify answers to questions in the 'nature of use' section, and the data collected and analysed in accordance with the principles discovered in the literature. As required by the positivist style, attention is also paid to validity and reliability in the conclusion.

Given that sometimes research is criticised as lacking practical outcomes, it should be particularly noted that an alternative curriculum model for legal information literacy (IL) education was adopted and implemented as a result of this project.

Critical incident technique (Chapter 4)

The critical incident technique (CIT) is an example of a research method which is labeled 'qualitative', but is not interpretivist. Hilary Hughes, the author of this chapter, emphasises the 'objectivity' and 'behaviourist approach' which are not part of the thinking of interpretivists whose focus is on the multiple meanings created by people. She cites the American researcher John Flanagan (1954, p.355), the original designer of CIT, as saying that 'rather than collecting opinions, hunches and estimates [CIT] obtains a record of specific behaviors' (p.63). However, Hughes cites a number of studies where there has been a shift in focus from purely behaviour aspects to a more holistic concern with individual experience by integrating cognitive, affective, cultural and environmental factors (p.52).

Hughes outlines the strengths and weaknesses of CIT. Among its strengths is the fact that it is simple to understand and conduct, is flexible and modifiable, and has been used effectively in previous Library and Information Science (LIS) research. But Hughes found the emphasis on binary relationships (effective/not effective, successful/not successful) also tends to impose unrealistic classifications on behaviours, which generally are more accurately represented in shades of grey rather than black or white (pp.63-64).

In terms of Hughes' research, her project focused on the IL needs of international students at the tertiary level, with a key objective of studying and evaluating individual students' use of online resources. She outlines the reasons for her choice of CIT, how she established the general aims of the project as well as the plans and specifications. She describes types of data collection used with CIT, as well as outlining her data collection, which included interviews and a set task.

Her interviews with twelve international students enrolled at Central Queensland University Brisbane Internal Campus, who were purposefully selected to reflect the cultural and linguistic diversity of the student population on the campus, reflected the CIT dichotomous approach, but she also collected background information about each student and asked questions that would explore 'thoughts and feelings about using online information resources' (p.60). She points out that categorising the data is perhaps the most challenging aspect of CIT (p.58) and provides explicit detail about her own analysis. The final sections of the chapter focus on 'interpreting and reporting the data collection and analysis processes' and the conclusion.

Constructivist grounded theory (Chapter 5)

This chapter is about research which is underpinned by interpretivist philosophy. The researcher wanted 'to understand what it actually meant to be information literate (outside an educational context) and how IL was experienced by people who were engaged in vocational practice'(p.68). Thus the use of the constructivist paradigm, and particularly constructivist grounded theory, was the appropriate approach for grounding the research in the real life engagement within the workplace (p.68). As Annemaree Lloyd, the author, says: 'The use of grounded theory method provides a flexible and iterative process for dealing with multiple and conflicting meanings, interpretations and constructions that emanate from the individual's real world engagement with information' (p.69).

The chapter reports research with a very strong theoretical base and outcome, as well as providing an innovative approach to IL research. Lloyd explains Charmaz's (2003) approach to grounded theory, described in the previous chapter, as well introducing other key tenets of her research, citing, for example, Pidgeon (1996, p.83) for the notion that data should fit and 'be recognizable and of relevance to those studied' (p.69). She outlines the key strategies of coding, constant comparison, theoretical sampling and memoing, giving examples from her own research. She then discusses some issues and ideas to assist researchers develop their own research design for a constructivist grounded theory: the role of the literature review, locating the field and gaining access, selecting participants, collecting data, piloting the questions, interviewing, and ensuring the trustworthiness of outcomes. She particularly emphasises the negotiation of the findings with the research participants.

The outcomes of inductive, grounded research are rewarding as they are often unexpected and bring a flavour of serendipity. This was the case with this research and Lloyd ends her chapter by discussing the outcomes of her study.

Phenomenography (Chapter 6)

As stated in Chapter 1, phenomenography is an interpretive paradigm which focuses on people's experiences and conceptualisations of phenomena. Uljens (1993) says that phenomenography was not originally derived from phenomenological philosophy. 'Early empirical [phenomenographical] studies on learning and related topics were based more on some kind of general assumptions and observations concerning the human mind than on any elaborated theoretical stance'. He adds that it seems quite natural that phenomenological ideas have been of interest to phenomenographers and these he explores in his article which has been reprinted online (see reference list). *Stanford Encyclopedia of Philosophy* (2003) defines phenomenology as 'the study of structures of consciousness as experienced from the first-person point of view', with famous names such as Husserl, Heidegger and Sartre being associated with it.

The research goal of the author of this chapter, Sylvia Edwards, was to study the phenomenon of web-based information searching, with the major research question focussing on the different ways students approach web-based information searching. Phenomenography, with its emphasis on the different ways that people experience a particular phenomenon, was thus an appropriate method. Edwards says that the method, to understand academic learning better, began in the 1970s and that this is still the most common phenomenon studied with this method. She also says that there is no prescriptive format to conduct research using the method (p.90). I would add that this is not unusual in interpretivist research where approaches tend to be more flexible than in positivist research. Edwards continues that the data collection begins in the way most common in qualitative research: with semi-structured interviews, focus groups, open-ended written surveys (p.93). It is the analysis of the data which sets the method apart. She cites Bruce (1997a, p.103) and Walsh (2000) in stating that it is 'both a process of discovery and construction'. In other words, the conceptions begin with the data but the researcher constructs the categories, defining their meaning, focus and structure (p.97).

Edwards provides explicit details about how her categories were developed, including diagrams portraying the 'structures of meaning' for categories (showing the differences within the structure of each category) and the 'outcome space' (showing how the categories interrelate to each other (p.100). Her concluding sections discuss the communication of results, the application of phenomenography to IL research, and how 'variation theory' can be used to enhance the design of the learning environment to encourage learning.

Action research (Chapter 7)

Action research is an interpretive method (Oosthuizen 2002, p.159), the key feature of which is a reflective, spiral approach (Kemmis & Wilkinson 1998, p.21). As in all interpretivist research, the focus is on meanings or viewpoints but in this case there is an emphasis on the development of understandings (IL). In action research, the triangulation of viewpoints is also important. In the action research, reported in this chapter, the views were of the educational institution, the practitioner/ researcher, staff, and students.

As the author of this chapter, Karen Visser, states, the method was well suited to her goal of developing an IL program for students, with an almost exact parallel program for teachers (p.114). As she points out, action research is particularly suited to research in the fields of education and IL. For her project, specifically, there were many advantages of action research: the provision of a stable, sustainable framework but also flexibility to respond to a rapidly changing information environment and to accommodate an evolutionary response to research findings; the opportunity for self-reflective enquiry for individuals and groups within organisations; and the concept of the researcher as part of this process (p.114). She emphasises that the salient point of action research is that it is both a process of change (the action) and the process of learning (the research). The core terms are 'cycle', 'reflective', 'practitioner', 'enquiry', 'process', 'learning' (p.129). Particularly appealing for her was the fact that action research allows the practitioner as researcher to be integral to all phases of problem-solving (p.129).

Visser's research involved three spirals of enquiry, action, reflection and learning, which she says together recognised that the IL competence of the whole learning community needed to be enhanced (p.116). The article concentrates on the professional development (PD) spiral for the teachers. The literature review therefore also focuses principally on the factors needed to prepare teachers to be involved in a student IL program. The evaluation of the PD is given particular emphasis in the chapter. It involved triangulation of perspectives (teachers, action researcher and the PD committee and executive) and included both formative and summative, as well as quantitative and qualitative approaches.

Focus groups (Chapter 8)

Although the emphasis in this chapter is on 'focus groups', this method/technique is used to supplement and explain the findings from two surveys, one carried out before the focus groups, the other after. The research, overall, is an example of the 'mixed methods' approach, with the survey providing the quantitative component and the focus groups the qualitative data, to provide 'a more comprehensive and detailed understanding of the results of the quantitative research' (p.144).

The research described in the chapter focuses on the evaluation of the effectiveness of embedding IL concepts into the curriculum of an undergraduate sociology programme. Specifically, it sought to investigate how the assessment tasks assisted with specific IL skill uptake; the extent (if at all) to which students' IL skills improved; and the extent to which students' discipline-specific competencies increased (p.135).

Early in the chapter, the value of the focus group method for evidence-based research is discussed, as well as the general characteristics of focus groups along with the characteristics applicable to the specific research under consideration. Another section focuses on the advantages and disadvantages of focus groups. Ethical issues which arise with the use of the method are thoroughly considered, with this section making a valuable contribution to the chapter.

The results of the study are not treated in great detail as they have been reported elsewhere. Those that are provided are used to show how the focus groups enabled explanation of some of the survey findings.

Evidence-based practice (Chapter 9)

This chapter is about the role of evidence-base practice (EBP) in the library and information services (LIS) profession and in the field of IL specifically. The authors, Helen Partridge and Gilliam Hallam, define EBP as 'the process of using formal research skills and methods to assist in decision making and establishing best practice' (p.149). Along with Melanie Lazarow, in the next chapter, they discuss EBP in the LIS field as emerging from the domain of evidence-based medicine. The role played by key people in adapting the evidence-based approach to the LIS profession is also an early focus of the chapter. With this comes a discussion of the introduction of 'evidence-based librarianship' and 'evidence-based library and information practice', as well as 'evidence-based IL' (EBIL).

In discussing why EBP is important to the LIS profession, Partridge and Hallam begin by discussion the role of research, in general, before proceeding to argue for the need for EBP as part of the process in an era where 'increased competence and accountability' are required.

The section focussing on 'how EBP is undertaken' introduces strategies as described in the literature. The role of critical appraisal is highlighted and here the checklist of Booth and Brice (2004) is included. The ReLIANT instrument of Koufogiannakis, Booth and Brettle (2006), is also reproduced in this context, as well as the 'six frames model', which is described as an excellent supplement to the latter. This is followed by a discussion of what constitutes quality evidence and the poor status often suffered by qualitative evidence. Arguments for pluralistic, diverse approaches are proffered.

The final section of this chapter focuses on EBIL. Here three examples are presented to reveal some of the diverse ways in which EBP has been applied to IL. The conclusion is that EBP has a significant part to play in the area of IL education and practice.

Critiquing evidence-based practice (Chapter 10)

The evidence-based model for information literacy (EBIL) is a recent development. As Melanie Lazarow says in her chapter, it is related to the also new movement towards evidence-based library and information practice. This, in its turn, owes its origins to evidence-based medical practice which began in the 1970s although, in the case of IL, there is more emphasis on filling the gaps in quality research availability rather than making more use of research evidence as is the case in the medical field.

While she acknowledges the importance of evidence to all fields, Lazarow raises issues about the EBIL model which she says 'draws in questions of qualitative versus quantitative research, how cultural meaning is produced, what constitutes evidence and the way the paradigm is used politically' (p.171) The research method perspective is important because evidence-based practice favours quantitative approaches giving precise answers. On the other hand, as Lazarow says, the EBIL approach tends to limit the questions that can be asked to pragmatic ones that are easily answered with measurement. Questions with greater social, cultural and political complexities tend not to be easily investigated using the EBIL model.

This is a thought-provoking chapter that also pays attention to philosophical relationships in the research landscape and therefore extends some of the discussion from earlier chapters in this book. It particularly reinforces the dictum that it is important to match the method to the research question or questions under investigation.

Alternative methods (Chapter 11)

The final chapter, after revisiting the framework discussed earlier in the book, discusses some key research methods that are not represented. The first of these is 'narrative research methods'. Suzanne Lipu, the author of this chapter, says that stories are a powerful source of information and communication for humans and play a significant role in most cultures. She postulates that 'narrative research opens up the possibility for IL researchers to collect rich and unique accounts of people's experiences with information' (p.188).

'Feminist research methods' are next in focus. Here Lipu discusses the fact that there is no single feminist theoretical perspective and that the commonality lies in the aim to make women's experiences central to any research undertaken and to try to redress imbalances of the past where men's lives have usually been centre-stage. She discusses three elements that are important to feminist researchers: reflexivity; care useful of language throughout the research process; and consciousness of power relationships.

Finally Lipu discusses 'cross cultural research methods', the three particular ones being 'ethnography/participant observation', 'participatory research' and 'collaborative research'. Ethnographic techniques are commonly used in the library and information studies field, having been used to study 'information-seeking behaviour' (e.g., Williamson 2006) and IL (e.g., Williamson et al. 2007). Lipu points out the value for IL research. Participatory research is well suited to cross cultural studies because of its focus on equity and the high level of participation it encourages, attempting to ensure that 'the participants' agenda or needs are not lost or replaced in favour of the researcher's agenda'. Collaborative research has some similarities but differs in that it is more likely than participatory research to have originated from the researcher, but similarly includes considerable input from 'collaborators'.

Conclusion

This chapter has sought to introduce and discuss each of this book's contributions in relation to the broad framework presented in the previous chapter. The chapters bring a rich array of methods for the study of IL which should be helpful to others who are interested in undertaking research in the field.

The key points to remember are that researchers need to match their research methods to the questions to be investigated and that the reasons for the choice of methods and underpinning paradigms should be seriously considered. I would encourage you to make these reasons explicit in the reporting of your research. This means that researchers need at least a basic knowledge of research philosophies and methods, obtained by undertaking a research methods course or reading a good research methods book. It is hoped that this book will provide some inspiration.

References

Booth, A. & Brice, A. (Eds.) (2004). *Evidence-based practice for information professionals: A handbook*. London: Facet.

Kemmis, S. & Wilkinson, M. (1998). Participatory action research and the study of practice. In B. Atweh, S. Kemmis & P. Weeks (Eds.), *Action research in practice: Partnerships for social justice in education*. London: Routledge.

Koufogianakis, D., Booth, A. & Brettle, A. (2006). ReLIANT: Reader's guide to the literature on interventions addressing the need for education and training. *Library and Information Science Research, 94*, pp.44-55.

Oosthuizen, M.J.H. (2002). Action research. In K. Williamson, *Research methods for students, academics and professionals: Information management and systems* (2nd ed., pp.159-175). Wagga Wagga, NSW: Centre for Information Studies, Charles Sturt University.

Stanford encyclopedia of philosophy (2003). Phenomenology. [Online] http://plato.stanford.edu/entries/phenomenology/ Retrieved 12 December 2007.

Tanner, K. (2002). Survey research. In K. Williamson, *Research methods for students, academics and professionals: Information management and systems* (2nd ed., pp.89-109). Wagga Wagga, NSW: Centre for Information Studies, Charles Sturt University.

Uljens, M. (1993). The essence and existence of phenomenography. *Nordisk Pedagog [Journal of Nordic Educational Research], 13*(3), 134-147. [Online] http://www.ped.gu.se/biorn/phgraph/misc/constr/phlo.phgr.html Retrieved 12 December 2007.

Williamson, K. (2006). Research in constructivist frameworks using ethnographic techniques. *Library Trends, 55*(1), 83-101.

Williamson, K. (2002). *Research methods for students, academics and professionals: Information management and systems* (2nd ed.) Wagga Wagga, NSW: Centre for Information Studies, Charles Sturt University.

Williamson, K., Bernath, V., Wright, S. & Sullivan, J. (2007). Research students in the electronic age: Impacts of changing information behaviour on information literacy needs. *Communications in Information Literacy, 1*(2), 47-63. [Online] http://www.comminfolit.org/index.php/cil/issue/current/showToc

CHAPTER 3
Survey research

Natalie Cuffe

Survey method is used to collect information directly from people about specific characteristics (for example, age, gender), past or current behaviour and activities, attitudes/beliefs/opinions, expectations, knowledge and self-classification (Neuman 2003, p.264). The basic premise of survey research is that by surveying a small group of people one can make generalisations about the larger group of people that the smaller group was selected from (Powell & Connaway 2004, p.83). An example would be surveying final-year law students about their experiences of information literacy (IL) learning and then making inferences about all law students' experiences. In IL practice a survey may be used to gather a diversity of data, such as students' learning experiences and evaluations of IL programs, that may then be used in a variety of ways, such as to assist in developing and improving policies or educational programs.

Survey method will be examined in the context of a survey undertaken of law students' experiences of legal research learning (legal information literacy) at three Brisbane universities, using a questionnaire, and the implications of this for legal education curriculum development (Cuffe 1999, 2001, 2002, 2003). The focus of this chapter will be on the use of questionnaires as a data-collection technique in survey research.

Articulating the research problem

One of the first tasks of a researcher is to determine the information area to be studied and to identify the type of data that is sought from the research (Graziano & Raulin 1997, p.144). Once background reading in the area has been completed, it is necessary to state the issues as researchable questions that will assist in identifying the data to be obtained. Researchable questions generally take one of two forms: hypothesis (to be tested) or research objectives (to guide research) (Bouma & Ling 2004, p.29). A hypothesis is a statement which asserts a relationship between concepts, and a concept is an idea that stands for something or represents a class of things (Bouma & Ling 2004, p.29). Not all research is best guided by hypotheses. There are situations where developing research objectives is a more desirable way of narrowing the focus of a research problem, particularly where the goal of the research is descriptive rather than explanatory (Bouma & Ling 2004, p.35). Much social science research is *descriptive* (providing a detailed picture of a phenomenon, a picture of the specific details of a situation, social setting or relationship, 'how' and 'who' questions) rather than *exploratory* (generating new ideas, conjectures or hypotheses for future research) or *explanatory* (examining the 'why' questions, building on exploratory and descriptive research to identify the reason something occurs) (Neuman 2003, pp.29-31). It is also important to clarify in your own mind at the beginning of your research the difference between the research problem and the research purpose. The *research problem* is what the research is about and the *research purpose* is why the research is conducted (Powell & Connaway 2004, p.28).

The legal information literacy research, discussed in this chapter, was indicative of descriptive applied research within a positivist social science perspective. It was descriptive because it sought to present a picture of the specific details of a situation, social setting or relationship (Neuman 2003, p.30) – to describe the use of information and information technology by law students. It was applied research because its purpose was to provide information that was useable in the resolution of problems and has some practical application in mind (Powell & Connaway 2004, p.53) – in this case guidelines for the development of legal curriculum for undergraduate law students. It took a positivist social science approach because it sought to use an 'organised method for combining deductive logic with precise empirical observations of individual behaviour in order to … predict general patterns of human activity' (Neuman 2003, p.71). The information sought from the legal information literacy research is best described in the following research objectives:

1. to reveal and describe the *extent* of use of information and information technology by undergraduate law students (in essence *access* to and *frequency* of use) [research problem].
2. to reveal and describe the *nature* of use of information and information technology by undergraduate law students (in essence their *experiences* and *successes*) [research problem].
3. to *analyse students perceived successes* with information and information technology using a research problem test [research problem].

4. to seek law *student views* on the place of IL *education* (in essence their experiences and perception of legal research training and skills) [research problem].

5. to determine the implications for developing a *law school curriculum* [research purpose].

The legal information literacy research sought primarily to obtain *quantitative data* – data collected in the form of numbers (Neuman 2003, p.35) because the number of respondents required to obtain an adequate sample would make the analysis of large quantities of qualitative data impractical. However, some *qualitative data* – data collected in the form of pictures or words (Neuman 2003, p.35) was gleaned from the 'comments' space in the questionnaire which provided further insight into the answers to the closed questions. Also it would be a practical impossibility to use a small sample of the large population under study and apply a research technique such as observation enabling the collection of qualitative data, because there would then be insufficient useable data to be able to reliably generalise from the small sample back to the large population group. Despite the position that 'qualitative research methods can be useful for gathering data about information users' behaviours and information needs' (Powell & Connaway 2004, p.59) the legal information literacy research sought primarily quantitative data to fulfil the research objectives.

Questionnaires as a data-collection technique in IL practice

Various techniques are available to the social science researcher to collect both quantitative and qualitative data. Neuman outlines experiments, surveys, content analysis and existing statistics research as suitable to gain quantitative data and field research and historical–comparative research as appropriate for qualitative data gathering (Neuman 2003, pp.35-39).

Given the need for quantitative data on characteristics, behaviours and beliefs relating to information and information technology use by law students, survey research seemed most appropriate for the legal information literacy research undertaken (Neuman 2003, p.264). As mentioned above, the type of survey was descriptive and had the purpose of describing characteristics of the population being studied, making specific predictions and testing relationships (Powell & Connaway 2004, p.87; Dillman 1978). A survey researcher asks people questions in a *written questionnaire* (mail-out, hand-out or electronic) or during an *interview*, then records the answers (Neuman 2003, p.35).

After considering the various methods of collecting data, it was decided that a *self-administered questionnaire* was the most appropriate and advantageous for the legal information literacy research undertaken for the following reasons:

- it would be cost-effective and practical to administer (Anderson 1993, pp.7-8).
- it would provide hard quantitative data that would be relatively easy to collect and analyse (Dillman 1978).
- a hand-delivered questionnaire results in a negligible response rate problem (Powell & Connaway 2004, p.143).
- it would allow for a significantly sized and representative sample which would improve the reliability of the conclusions to be made about the entire population under study – the general rule of thumb is the larger the sample the better (Powell & Connaway 2004, p.105).
- paper hand-delivered questionnaires rather than interviews were used because of the opportunity to sample significant numbers from the law school student population.
- questionnaires tend to encourage frank answers, largely because it is easier for the researcher to guarantee anonymity (Powell & Connaway 2004, p.143).

Hand-delivered, self-administered questionnaires were used to avoid some disadvantages that apply to other forms. Mail-out or email questionnaires have the common disadvantage of low response rates with participation perhaps needing to be promoted through incentives. There is also the inability of the researcher to control the conditions under which the questionnaire is completed or respond to a request for clarification of a question if needed (Neuman 2003, p.289). Interviews in person or on the telephone allow more probing of answers to questions and generally have a higher response rate, but increase the cost of the survey significantly, reduce anonymity and introduce the potential for interviewer bias where actions of a particular interviewer affect how a respondent answers (Neuman 2003, pp.290, 296-297).

Survey research, either by questionnaire or interview, can be used in a variety of ways in IL practice. As the survey method is a way of collecting information from people about characteristics, behaviours and activities, attitudes and opinions, expectations and knowledge, the survey method may be useful to gather data about the following in IL practice, for example:

- *students' needs in IL learning* – for example, asking about the type of IL education students have received and what learning needs are still to be met, self-assessment of IL competency through a test (a pre-test), teaching and assessment methods that most assist their IL learning (the 'research problem') [data useful to inform policies, curriculum review – the 'research purpose'].

- *students' experiences of IL learning* – for example, evaluating IL sessions in terms of appropriateness of content, structure, facilities, teaching method (the 'research problem') [data useful to inform unit curriculum review and IL program evaluation – the 'research purpose'].
- *the impact of IL learning on students* – for example, a survey questionnaire with a post-test that seeks to check the broader impact of IL learning (beyond a specific assessment task) to the ability to transfer and apply IL skills to new learning environments and tasks (the 'research problem') [data useful to inform holistic course curriculum review and IL program evaluation – the 'research purpose'].
- *the experiences of IL educators* (both academics and librarians) – for example, regarding their own IL abilities and experiences to reveal how this may impact on their teaching (the 'research problem') [data useful to inform staff development and resource allocation – the 'research purpose'].
- *national surveys of IL teaching objectives, methods and content, educator characteristics* – for example, surveying Australian law libraries about their IL programs (the 'research problem') [data useful to inform policies, IL program development, resource allocation, staff development – the 'research purpose'] (for example, see ALA websites).
- *the typical quantitative data gathering that libraries undertake* – for example, number of completions of web tutorial on information literacy.

Steps in survey research and key terms

A number of steps are required to undertake a survey. They are outlined below, along with a description of key terms. The references in the headings are to the legal information literacy survey, the discussion of which follows.

Survey research steps

The typical questions to be considered in designing and implementing a survey and reporting on survey results in a method section of a report are outlined below. Although they are described in a linear fashion, some earlier steps may need to be revisited after considering issues raised by later steps. For example, although populations and samples are dealt with after survey design, some consideration needs to be included from the beginning in terms of the objectives and feasibility of the research. The steps focus on questionnaires as a survey technique, but many of the considerations are similar where the interview technique is used. A discussion of the steps undertaken in the legal information literacy research follows as an example of how these broader considerations are refined for application to a particular research project that utilised a self-administered questionnaire.

Step 1: Overall survey design (see 'Articulating the research problem' and 'Questionnaires as a data collection technique' above)

- consider what is the research problem and research purpose.
- articulate the research objectives or hypotheses to be tested.
- reflect upon the purpose of survey research and why a questionnaire or interview is the preferred data collection technique for the research – advantages and disadvantages of survey research.
- consider whether you need quantitative or qualitative data.
- upon deciding survey research is appropriate, determine type of technique to be used – questionnaire (self-administered, mail, web-based) or interview (in person, telephone). See WSU Libraries Information Literacy Survey (Wichita State University 2004) for a web-based example.
- decide whether the survey is to be cross-sectional (data collected at one point in time) or longitudinal (data collected over time) (Creswell 2003, p.155).
- begin a draft of the questionnaire or interview schedule – what information is needed to test the hypotheses or answer the research objectives?

Step 2: The population and sample (see 'Population, sample and time dimension' below)

- identify the *population* (the group of people to be studied), their size and characteristics and consider how you might access them. You might need to consider the availability of *sampling frames* (lists that closely approximate the characteristics of the population) such as telephone lists, lists of students enrolled in a course if you wish to undertake probability sampling (Neuman 2003, p.216). *Probability sampling* is a mathematical approach where each person in the target population has 'an *equal* and *independent* chance of being included in the sample' (Williamson 2002, p.333).
- once you have decided upon the population you can decide upon the *sample* (a sub-group of the population that is representative of the population) and the *sampling technique. Sample size* should also be contemplated at this point. The appropriate size of a sample depends on the type of data analysis to be used, how accurate the sample has to be for the researcher's purpose and on the population characteristics (Neuman 2003, p.213). The general rule of thumb is

the bigger the better but this needs to be balanced with practical considerations such as time and money (Powell & Connaway 2004, p.105).

• appropriate choice of sampling technique is crucial for selection of a sample that is representative of the population under study. Researchers seeking qualitative data tend to use *non-random samples* or *non-probability sampling* – where the researcher cannot guarantee that any particular characteristic has any probability of being included in the sample (Powell & Connaway 2004, p.94) and the respondents are selected on their availability and convenience. Although this means that the researcher can only hope that those selected for study bear some resemblance to the larger population, qualitative researchers are often more concerned with the sample relevance to the research problem than their representativeness of the population in statistical terms (Neuman 2003, p.211). Non-random sampling techniques include:

- *accidental sampling*, where the researcher selects respondents at hand until the sample reaches a desired size;

- *quota sampling*, where the researcher selects respondents on the basis of set criteria that reflect the diversity of the population, in any manner that is convenient; and

- *purposive sampling*, where researchers use their own judgment, knowledge of the population and objectives of the research to select the most appropriate sample group to be studied (Neuman 2003, pp.211-215; Powell & Connaway 2004, pp.94-96).

• quantitative researchers tend to use a *population* (see below), if that is possible, or *random samples* as they are most likely to yield a sample that truly represents the population (Neuman 2003, p.218). Random sampling techniques include:

- simple random, where the researcher develops an accurate sampling frame (list of population) selects respondents from the sampling frame according to a mathematically random procedure and then locates the respondent that was selected to be included in the sample;

- systematic sample, where the researcher selects every 'nth' respondent on the list (sample frame) until the total list has been sampled;

- stratified sampling, where the researcher divides the population into subpopulations (stratas) and then draws a random sample from each subpopulation (Neuman 2003, pp.215-224).

STEP 3: Developing the survey instrument (see 'Developing survey instrument' below)

- the *questionnaire layout* is important. It should be clear, neat and easy to follow so as not to discourage respondents from answering (Neuman 2003, p.284). There should be a *cover sheet* with details about the survey, instructions for completion and the contact details for the researcher.
- there is no proper *length* for a questionnaire; it depends on the context of the survey and the characteristics of the respondents. Neuman suggests that a short three to four page questionnaire is appropriate for the general population, but that for specific groups on a specific relevant topic, questionnaires of ten to fifteen pages may be possible (Neuman 2003, p.282).
- consider the type of information you want from the respondents (for example, facts, opinions, behaviours) and what would be a *logical order for the questions.* A questionnaire has opening, middle and ending questions (Neuman 2003, p.282). Demographic information may be sought at the beginning, with the middle questions grouped into common topics and ending with an 'any other comments' question. All questions should be numbered.
- *closed* and *open questions* are the most common types of survey questions. Closed questions give respondents fixed responses from which to choose. Open questions allow a respondent to give any answer. Which type of question is appropriate depends on the research purpose and the practical limitations of the project. Closed questions are often used in large surveys because they are more time economical for the respondents and the researcher (Neuman 2003, p.277-278). Closed and open questions are commonly used together in the same questionnaire. *Skip* or *contingency questions* are two-part questions where the respondent's answer to the first part decides which of two different questions a respondent next answers (Neuman 2003, p.277).
- when using closed questions, the researcher has to make some decisions about the types of *response categories* that will be included and the number of choices to be available to respondents. Neuman suggests that two response choices may be too few, but more than five choices are rarely a benefit (p.279). The type of measurement scale adopted will depend on the level of detail the researcher is seeking in the response. For example, *nominal* scales are where the answer categories are names rather than numbers (for example, Excel, PowerPoint); *ordinal* scales have some meaning to the order of the answers (for example, first-year student, second-year student) and *interval* scales are where the distance between the measurement choices has real meaning (for

example, income brackets) (Anderson 1993, p.13). *Category* scales are those that require selecting one of a limited number of categories that are ordered on a scale (for example, strongly agree, agree, neutral, disagree, strongly disagree) (Anderson 1993, p.15).

- consider any *ethical issues* that may arise from the questions. Are there any risks for respondents? Have they consented? Will the answers remain anonymous? Do you need to complete ethical clearance forms for your organisation's ethics committee?
- plan how you are going to record the data – *coding* (reorganising raw data so it is machine readable) by numbering response categories assists in data entry.
- always *thank* the respondents at the end of the survey!

Step 4: Piloting the survey instrument (see 'Piloting the questionnaire' below)

- *pilot* or pre-test the draft questionnaire with a small number of people who are reasonably representative of the population group.
- a pilot gives the researcher the opportunity to ask the following questions about the survey instrument: Did each of the questions measure what they were intended to measure? Were all of the words/questions understood? Did all the respondents similarly interpret the questions? Did each fixed response (closed) question have an answer that applied to each respondent? Were some questions regularly skipped or answered unintelligibly? (Powell & Connaway 2004, p.140).
- finalise the questionnaire considering any feedback from the pilot – if necessary pilot again.

Step 5: Administering the questionnaire and collecting the data (see 'Data collection' below)

- questionnaires can be administered *in person* by the researcher, by *mail* or by *email/web*.
- if the questionnaire is administered in person (for example, to a group of students in a tutorial) non-response will be minimal. Mail and email distribution may require a follow-up mailing to receive an adequate *response rate*. (See further Powell & Connaway 2004, pp.143-147; Neumann 2003, pp.285-289).
- whichever collection method is adopted, the circumstances should be as conducive as possible to encourage the respondents to answer.

Step 6: Data input and analysis (see 'Data input and analysis techniques' below)

- before entering the survey data into a package for statistical analysis such as SPSS (Statistical Package for the Social Sciences), ensure that you have recorded how each answer is to be coded in a *code book* (for example, record that the answer 'Sometimes' to Q3 is a 2 and then you enter '2' into the SPSS spreadsheet).
- ensure that you are *storing* the survey results in an appropriate manner – *securely* so they can only be accessed by authorised personnel and *in the order* that you input them into SPSS in case you need to go back and check the data entry on a particular questionnaire.
- after all the data have been entered into the statistical package, you can begin some *statistical analysis*. Statistical analysis may be *descriptive* (describing numerical data) or *inferential* (testing hypotheses). Descriptive statistics are most commonly used in descriptive research such as that often undertaken by information professionals. Descriptive analysis generally begins with the generation of *frequency counts or tables* (computations of how many respondents answered in a particular way presented in numbers and percentages) and then progresses to *cross tabulations* as appropriate (tabulating the frequency counts of one variable/question by the frequency counts of another variable/question) (Anderson 1993, p.47).

Step 7: Reporting on survey research outcomes (see 'Use of survey results in IL practice' below)

- reporting on survey research outcomes requires a *description of the survey method,* to demonstrate rigorous method which includes the validity (whether the instrument measures what it is designed to measure) and reliability (whether consistent results would be obtained on replication of the survey results (Williamson 2002, p.334). The *findings of the research* and the conclusions to be drawn from them are then detailed.
- this seven-step outline of the survey method may be useful as a guideline for reporting on method. The research findings would include tables and graphs, generated from the frequency counts, summarising the data and a discussion of how the data fulfil the research objective and for what purpose it will be used. (See further Creswell 2003.)

The legal information literacy survey

This section provides examples from the legal information literacy survey, intended to illustrate the general principles of survey research, discussed above. It includes coverage of the population/sample, the development of the survey instrument including the piloting thereof, data collection, data input and analysis techniques, and the use of survey results in IL practice.

The population/sample and time dimension

Obtaining an adequate sample is one of the most important factors in conducting survey research. This is particularly so with a descriptive survey, such as the legal information literacy research, where information was being gathered about attributes, attitudes and skills. In most instances, the population about which information is sought is quite large and it is impossible to question every person in that population. In most surveys, a sample of the population is drawn and then the findings are generalised from the sample to the population by the process of deductive reasoning. The *population* in a survey is the group about whom the researcher wishes to obtain information (Graziano & Raulin 1997, p.147). The findings based on a survey of a subgroup or *sample* of a population should provide a reasonably accurate representation of the state of affairs in the total group provided appropriate attention has been given to the *sampling technique* (Powell & Connaway 2004, p.89; Anderson 1993, p.26).

Law students at Queensland University of Technology (QUT), University of Queensland and Griffith University were targeted for the legal information literacy survey. The three universities in Brisbane offer quite different undergraduate law programs in terms of substantive legal and skill content and it was valuable to survey all three to take account of the varying approaches and their impact on law students.

The *population* of law students at QUT, University of Queensland and Griffith University in Queensland at the time of the survey was approximately 4000. As a population group they were relatively homogenous in terms of academic aptitude and a smaller sample was appropriate in these circumstances (Graziano & Raulin 1997, p.149; Anderson 1993, p.28). *Final-year law students* could be considered as a *population* in their own right because, as the group exiting the legal education process, they were in the best position to reflect on legal education and were also most likely to be at the highest level of skills development. Using a population with specific parameters means that generalisations can be made to that population if there is a sufficiently high response rate. When the questionnaire was administered the final-year student groups at each institution numbered approximately 752: Griffith University (approximately 125), University of Queensland (approximately 217) and QUT (approximately 410). The survey was limited to students engaged in full-time and part-time modes of study. External students were excluded because it was not practical to access them as part of the survey. Final-year students from Bond University and James Cook University were not included in the survey because of time, cost, practical restraints, the natural limits of the project and a desire to examine public universities in the Brisbane and surrounding region. The curriculum of the three universities surveyed was also sufficiently diverse so it was unnecessary to seek access to more law schools.

Another dimension of social science research is the treatment of time. Different research treats time in different ways. The legal information literacy research adopted a *cross-sectional approach* because only one point in time was being observed. While this is the simplest and least costly alternative, its disadvantage is that it does not capture the social process or change that will occur with the development in technology and educational approach. However, this approach is consistent with the descriptive nature of the research (Neuman 2003, p.31).

Developing the survey instrument

The development of a good questionnaire is vital to the research process, particularly for ensuring the internal *validity* of the instrument. In the legal information literacy study, the principles espoused by Neuman (2003) and Channels (1985) were combined to aid instrument design. The questionnaire should begin with some *introductory remarks and instructions* and the writing style throughout should avoid confusion and keep the respondent's perspective in mind (Neuman 2003, p.268). The construction of questions should also take into account the risk of *social desirability bias* and *threatening questions*, which could pose a real problem with law students. In this situation respondents may try to present a positive image of themselves to researchers instead of giving truthful answers and provide instead what they believe to be the normative or socially desirable answer (Neuman 2003, pp.274-276). One method of increasing truthful answers is to guarantee confidentiality and by indicating that truthful answers are wanted and that any answer is acceptable (Neuman, 2003, p.275). These factors were all considered in designing the legal information literacy survey instrument.

Closed-ended questions formed the basis of the questionnaire with an 'any other comments' option at the end. Because of the large scale nature of the survey this was quicker and easier for both respondents and the researcher. Neuman suggested that there is no absolute proper *length of questionnaires* and they can vary according to the respondent group. For highly educated respondents and a salient topic, using questionnaires of fifteen pages may be possible (p.282). The questionnaire used in the legal information literacy study was six pages in length.

The *layout* of a questionnaire should always be professional, make good use of space, be clear and easy to follow (Dillman 1978). The question format utilised a 'check a box' approach and response categories varied according to the question. The *response categories* were predominantly *nominal*, where the answer categories are classifications and not numerical measures, for example, 'compulsory' or 'optional', and *ordinal*, where there is some meaning to the order of the answers, for example, daily, weekly, monthly measures (Channels 1985, pp.132-133). A number of the questions used the same response categories and the *matrix or grid question* was employed as a compact way to present a series of questions using the same response categories (Neuman 2003, p.285).

No appropriate survey instrument suitable for use in the legal information research was found in the information science or legal education literature and the questionnaire was prepared on the principles discussed above. The final survey instrument is attached as an appendix to this chapter (see also Cuffe 2003). The final legal information literacy questionnaire was followed by a test problem. The whole instrument comprised forty questions on six pages divided into the following sections:

- *cover sheet* – this explained, among other things, the purpose of the survey, instructions for completing it, assurances of confidentiality of data and a consent statement approved by the University Research Ethics Committee (one page).
- *demographics* – this sought details of gender, age group, enrolment status and GPA (grade point average) (5 questions).
- *extent of use of information and information technology* – this sought data on the extent of access and frequency of use of information and information technology, the nature of legal research training received and student views on the place of legal research education (13 questions).
- *nature of use of information and information technology* – this asked questions to ascertain the level of the survey respondent's experience in completing information and information technology tasks (such as whether the respondent is successful in listing keywords about a research problem) and nature of the respondent's attitude to legal research and IL. The questions were phrased in a style similar to that used in technological literacy projects at QUT using a

matrix or grid question because this appears to have been considered a
successful technique for gaining similar data (16 questions).

- *research problem* – this presented a basic problem on common legal research
  tasks involving Australian law that was designed to test the students'
  perceptions of their success rates in a range of information and information
  technology activities and to provide common information about student legal
  research ability that could not be provided by individual university assessment
  results. The discussion of survey instruments in the library literature on
  evaluating bibliographic instruction was reviewed in developing the
  questionnaire (for example, Bober et al. 1995; Daragan & Stevens 1996). This
  literature prompted the adoption of the format of part questionnaire and part
  test in the survey instrument. The purpose of the test was to verify answers to
  questions in the *nature of use* section of the questionnaire (6 questions).
- *any other comments.*
- *terminology guide.*

Piloting the questionnaire

It is important that once a first draft of a questionnaire is completed it is evaluated
by experts and then pre-tested or piloted (Powell & Connaway 2004, p.139-140).
The draft legal information literacy questionnaire was piloted with a group of
nineteen final-year students enrolled in the Advanced Legal Research and
Reasoning Unit from QUT. The pilot questionnaire was administered easily
through a tutorial group. Students completed it and then discussed its structure and
form with the researcher. A pilot sample should be reasonably representative of the
final study group or there is little value in conducting the pilot (Powell &
Connaway 2004, p.140). Nevertheless, any bias in not piloting at Griffith
University and University of Queensland was not overly detrimental as there was a
sufficient number of QUT students to test any problems with the general structure
and intent of the survey instrument (as opposed to feedback on the variation of
content answers that would have been gained from piloting with Griffith University
and University of Queensland as well).

The students who undertook the pilot survey commented that they found the
questionnaire easy to read and understand and that it was of an appropriate length.
They suggested that, in the *Nature of use* section which asked about student
experiences with information and information technology, an 'always successful'
category be included and this suggestion was incorporated in the final instrument.
Anecdotally, these students commented in the discussion about the pilot instrument

that they liked the idea of integrating legal research in subjects throughout the curriculum and one commented that 'it was frightening to get to fourth year and realise how much we don't know about research'.

The final instrument was also reviewed by a statistical consultant from the Statistical Consulting Unit, Centre in Statistical Science and Industrial Mathematics, QUT, prior to being administered. The statistical consultant found the design of the survey to be valid and made some suggestions about fine tuning the instructions for answering some of the questions. These were adopted in the final questionnaire instrument.

Data collection

Permission to undertake the legal information literacy survey was sought from the Heads of the Law Schools at QUT, Griffith University and University of Queensland. A contact person in each institution distributed the self-administered questionnaire in final-year professional unit lectures. The questionnaire was not administered in any legal research lecture because it was important to avoid a situation which may have led students to think they were evaluating a legal research subject rather than informing the researcher of the way they find and use legal information. As noted earlier, the general issue of obtaining an adequate response rate is virtually negligible with a hand-delivered, self-administered survey. As expected, there were minimal problems with response rates given that the survey was administered during lectures. The only final-year students not surveyed were those not in attendance at lectures.

It was never intended to separate survey results and publish them for a particular academic institution because this might compromise particular institutions. However, it was deemed pertinent and expedient to administer the questionnaires at the different institutions on different coloured paper and to collate these results by institution. These results were then forwarded onto the heads of school of the relevant institutions as the results would be useful for curriculum review and development purposes. An undertaking was provided to the heads of school that the results would not be published by institution but as a collation and generalisation of the three universities.

There were 226 responses to this self-administered questionnaire which is an acceptable response rate from the approximately 700 final-year law students studying internally in Brisbane for some fairly reliable conclusions to be drawn. Neuman states that a response rate of 10 per cent to 50 per cent is common for a mail survey (Neuman 2003, p.285).

Data input and analysis techniques

SPSS (Statistical Package for Social Sciences) is a widely used and available computer program for statistical analysis, report writing, tabulation and general purpose data management (Powell & Connaway 2004, pp.246-257). SPSS was used by the Statistical Consulting Unit, Centre in Statistical Science and Industrial Mathematics, QUT to input the raw data and generate frequency tables for the legal information literacy survey. The researcher also used SPSS to analyse and correlate the data and create graphical representations of the results. The frequency tables of survey results generated by SPSS were attached to the report of the research (see Cuffe 2003).

Only a limited attempt was made to analyse the results according to gender, enrolment status or GPA (grade point average) as no significant difference was discerned in analysing the results cross-tabulated with these variables. It was also not the aim of the research to undertake an analysis by these variables but rather to present a holistic picture of the experiences of final-year law students in three Brisbane universities.

Since the purpose of the legal information literacy research was to generate a basic picture of law students' experiences of information and information technology use in the legal education process and seek their perceptions of IL education, *descriptive statistical analysis* was chosen to generate this information. This is the predominant type of data analysis employed by researchers in library and information science (Powell & Connaway 2004, pp.231-232). Descriptive statistics can perform a number of functions including portraying a variety of characteristics of the population with regard to the variables measured, and measuring the relationship between different variables in the data (*correlational statistics*) (Powell & Connaway 2004, p.235). It is these two functions of descriptive statistics that were adopted in the analysis of the legal information literacy survey data. Frequencies measured by *nominal* and *ordinal* scales (all the data apart from the comments) were presented in percentages in tables and graphs. Statistical analysis involving mathematical equations such as means and standard deviations were not undertaken as it is not appropriate to describe data with nominal and ordinal scales in this way (Channels 1985, p.190). Similarly, *inferential analysis* was not attempted as the research did not seek to 'predict or estimate population parameters or characteristics from random sample statistics, and to test hypotheses using tests of statistical significance to determine if observed differences between groups are real or merely due to chance' (Powell & Connaway 2004, p.237).

In some instances, respondents to the legal information literacy survey left certain questions blank. After discussions with the statistical consultant it was decided to incorporate these non-responses by including a 'no answer' response category in the analysis where required. There was a small percentage of non-responses but it was considered important to record them given the absence of a 'don't know' response category on the questionnaire which would have been an appropriate inclusion for some questions. There is no adverse effect or bias on the conclusions drawn as a result of this – indeed this may have occurred if some adjustment for non-response had not been made (Channels 1985, pp.158-159, 186). The non-responses portray part of the picture of law students being unable to transfer their knowledge and skill to novel situations.

Use of survey results in IL practice

Survey results can be used in a variety of ways in IL practice. Results can be used to guide and improve policies, evaluate IL programs, and assist with faculty undertaking curriculum review (academics and librarians are a very powerful IL research partnership). They can also provide tangible evidence of need to direct resources to IL programs and initiatives. The fact that it emerged from the legal information literacy survey that final-year law students had difficulties answering a research problem test that academics and librarians would expect first-year students to easily answer was quite a powerful picture to present in discussions about the need for curriculum review. The results of the survey showed that, despite the rich information and information technology environment surrounding law students and existing skills training, legal curricula at the time did not seem to have succeeded in the task of educating students for the effective information problem-solving that is critical in legal practice. The answers to the research problem revealed that students had a base level of knowledge about legal research (information and information technology) tools but were unable to translate this content knowledge into demonstrating an understanding of legal research process that is critical for transferring their learning to new situations.

The results of the legal information literacy survey were used to develop a curriculum model for legal education that moves from legal research *training* (use of information tools) to legal information literacy *education* (the holistic process of critical information use). The alternative curriculum model fostering legal information literacy education includes:

- *legal information literacy principles* – general principles to inculcate IL in undergraduate legal education.
- *legal information literacy skills* – a set of relevant information and information technology skills for contemporary legal education.
- *legal information literacy curriculum practices* – curriculum directions for the application of information literacy principles and assessment to legal research courses and, more broadly, the law school curriculum.

The alternative curriculum model has been adopted and implemented and is now moving into a phase of examining how legal educators' experience impacts upon the delivery of the legal information literacy program.

Ethical considerations

As surveys seek information from people about characteristics, behaviours, expectations and opinions, a survey researcher needs to be conscious of ethical considerations such as a respondent's right to privacy. Respondents are more likely to reveal personal information if they believe the answers to the survey are needed for legitimate research and that their answers will remain *confidential* and *anonymous* (Neuman 2003, p.302). Survey researchers will need to seek clearance for their surveys from their organisations' ethics committees. They also need to seek the respondents' *consent* to participate in the research which may occur via a consent statement on the survey cover sheet. In most non-captive situations (where there is no pressure on people to participate, unlike in a classroom), most ethics committees consider that the filling in of a questionnaire is an indication of consent.

Conclusion

A survey is a research method used to collection information from people about characteristics, attitudes, behaviours, expectations and knowledge either by questionnaire or interview. The survey method and questionnaire tool utilised in the legal information literacy research were *valid* and *reliable*. The method/tool was valid because it measured what it was intended to (the results were appropriate) and was reliable because the tool, if administered repeatedly, would provide consistent results (as evidenced in the pilot and the large scale administration of the questionnaire), although subsequent iterations would be affected by the evolution of legal research curricula (Channels 1985, pp.136-138). Indeed, similar processes of asking students to reflect upon their success in completing a range of skill-based tasks was successfully employed by the researcher in a teaching and learning grant on graduate attributes – in order to gain data on student experiences for curriculum review purposes (see Cuffe 2001).

There are many uses for surveys in IL practice, particularly if you have a large population (for example, large cohort of students) and need to do the research economically. Surveys enable the researcher to describe a picture of current phenomena in current IL practice that can be used to inform curriculum development, policies, program evaluation and resource allocation among other things. What surveys do not easily address are questions of 'why' – why does an information user adopt a particular search technique? Few of us are fully aware of the causal factors that shape our beliefs or behaviour so as to be able to answer such 'why' questions in a survey (Neuman 2003, p.64). A quantitative picture may be developed of a particular group of people or activity by survey but a more qualitative 'why' picture is more appropriately developed from other research approaches such as ethnographic research using individual or focus group interviews, constructivist grounded theory or phenomenography. It would be very interesting to update the legal information literacy survey and administer the questionnaire again, thus charting the evolution of legal research training (information tools focus) and the holistic process of critical information use within legal information literacy education.

References

ALA National Information Literacy Survey (ACRL). Accessed 10 February 2005 at http://www.ala.org/ala/acrl/acrlissues/acrlinfolit/professactivity/infolitsurvey/ surveyintro.htm

ALA Report on the National Information Literacy Survey: Documenting progress throughout the United States. Accessed 10 February 2005 at http://www.ala.org/ ala/acrl/acrlpubs/crlnews/backissues2001/november3/reportnational.htm

Anderson, A. (1993). *A guide to conducting surveys*. Kew, Vic: VicRoads Bookshop.

Bober, C., Poulin, S. & Vileno, L. (1995). Evaluating library instruction in academic libraries: A critical review of the literature 1980-1993. *Reference Librarian, 51/52*, 53-71.

Bouma, G. & Ling, R. (2004). *The research process*. (5th ed.). Melbourne, Vic: Oxford University Press.

Channels, N. (1985). *Social science methods in the legal process*. Totowa, NJ: Rowman & Allanheld.

Creswell, J. (2003). *Research design – qualitative, quantitative, and mixed method approaches*. Thousand Oaks, CA: Sage.

Cuffe, N. (2003). Legal information literacy – student experiences and the implications for legal education curriculum development. Master of Information Technology (Research) (QUT) thesis.

Cuffe, N. (2002). Law students' experiences of information and information technology – implications for legal information literacy curriculum development. *Problematic futures: Educational research in an era of uncertainty*, International Education Research Conference, Australian Association for Research in Education, Brisbane, December 2002. Available at: http://www.aare.edu.au/02pap/cuf02169.htm

Cuffe, N. (2001). Embedding graduate attributes in law – reflections of a law librarian seconded to a teaching and learning grant. *Australian Law Librarian*, *9*(4) 314-322.

Cuffe, N. (1999). Information literacy and legal research. *Australian Law Librarian*, *7*(1) 57-58.

Daragan, P. & Stevens, G. (1996). Developing lifelong learners: An integrative and developmental approach to information literacy. *Research Strategies*, *14*(2), 68-81.

Dillman, D. (1978). *Mail and telephone surveys: The total design method*. New York: John Wiley & Sons.

Graziano, A & Raulin, M. (1997). *Research methods: A process of inquiry* (3rd ed.). New York: Longman.

Neuman, W.L. (2003). *Social research methods: Qualitative and quantitative approaches* (5th ed.). Boston, MA: Allyn and Bacon.

Powell, R. & Connaway, L. (2004). *Basic research methods for librarians* (4th ed.). Westport, CA: Libraries Unlimited.

Wichita State University (2004). WSU Information Literacy Survey. Accessed10 February 2005 at http://library.wichita.edu/ilsurvey.htm

Williamson, K. (2002). *Research methods for students, academics and professionals: Information management and systems* (2nd ed.). Wagga Wagga, NSW: Centre for Information Studies, Charles Sturt University.

Further reading

Dillman, D. (2000). *Mail and internet surveys: The total design method*. New York: John Wiley & Sons.

Research Methods Knowledge Base – Survey Research. (Accessed 10 February 2005 at http://www.socialresearchmethods.net/kb/survey.htm)

Appendix: final survey instrument

Queensland University of Technology

INFORMATION AND INFORMATION TECHNOLOGY USE

IN UNDERGRADUATE LEGAL EDUCATION

Natalie Cuffe
Master of Information Technology (Research) Student
School of Information Systems
Faculty of Information Technology
Queensland University of Technology
Telephone: 3864 5046
Email: n.cuffe@qut.edu.au

This questionnaire is being distributed as part of a Master of Information Technology (Research) thesis at QUT. The thesis is entitled *Information and information technology use in undergraduate legal education.* The results will be used to identify patterns of information and information technology use by final year law students.

This is not an evaluation of any legal research courses undertaken at law school. It is asking about the way you find and use legal information. This questionnaire is being distributed at QUT, UQ and Griffith University.

The questionnaire should take no longer than 10 minutes to complete. The questions can be answered by ticking the appropriate answer(s). Please answer truthfully. Any answer is acceptable.

A terminology guide is included on the last page of the questionnaire.

Only aggregate data will be published and all information provided by you will be anonymous and treated as strictly confidential. All records will be maintained in a secure environment accessible only to the researcher.

Participation in this research is voluntary and you are free to withdraw from the study at any time without comment or penalty. By completing this questionnaire you are deemed to have agreed to participate in this project.

If you have any queries I can be contacted on 3864 5046. If you have any concerns about the ethical conduct of this research please contact the Queensland University of Technology's Registrar, on 3864 1056.

Thank you for participating in this survey.

Demographics

1. Gender   □ Female   □ Male

2. Age group   □ 20 – 25   □ 26 – 30   □ 31 – 39
                □ 40 – 50   □ Over 50

3. Are you a   □ full-time student   □ part-time student

4. Is this your first degree?   □ Yes   □ No

5. What is your Grade Point Average (GPA)?

      □ 0 - 3   □ 3.1 - 4   □ 4.1 - 5   □ 5.1 - 6   □ 6.1 - 7

Extent of use of information and information technology

6. How often do you go to the law library?

      □ Almost daily   □ Once a week   □ Several times a month
      □ Several times a semester   □ Never

7. On the table below please indicate which of the following you have access to and where you have access. Please tick all appropriate categories. *(See back page for terminology guide)*

Computer	□ Home	□ University	□ Work	□ No access
World Wide Web	□ Home	□ University	□ Work	□ No access
E-mail	□ Home	□ University	□ Work	□ No access
word processor	□ Home	□ University	□ Work	□ No access
cd-rom	□ Home	□ University	□ Work	□ No access

8. On the table below please indicate the frequency with which you use each of the following:

computer	□ daily	□ weekly	□ monthly	□ occasionally	□ never
World Wide Web	□ daily	□ weekly	□ monthly	□ occasionally	□ never
E-mail	□ daily	□ weekly	□ monthly	□ occasionally	□ never
word processor	□ daily	□ weekly	□ monthly	□ occasionally	□ never
cd-rom	□ daily	□ weekly	□ monthly	□ occasionally	□ never

9. Did you receive legal research training at law school?

      □ Yes   □ No *(Please go to Question 19 below)*

2

10. Was the legal research training you received at law school:

☐ Compulsory   ☐ Optional

11. In what years of your degree did you receive legal research training? *(Please tick all appropriate years)*

☐ Year 1   ☐ Year 2   ☐ Year 3   ☐ Year 4   ☐ Year 5

12. Which of the following did your legal research training include? *(Please tick all appropriate categories)*

☐ Law library tour
☐ How to use the library catalogue
☐ Researching case law
☐ Researching legislation
☐ How to use cd-roms
☐ How to use the Internet
☐ Researching international law
☐ Researching law from overseas jurisdictions eg. US, UK
☐ Legal reasoning and writing, legal citation
☐ Researching secondary sources eg. journal articles, parliamentary debates/ hansard

13. Was the legal research training you received offered by:

☐ Lecturer   ☐ Librarian   ☐ Both librarian and lecturer

14. Which of the following teaching methods do you find currently assists you, or you think would assist you, in your learning legal research skills? *(Please tick all appropriate categories)*

☐ Lectures
☐ Small group tutorials
☐ Demonstrations
☐ Hands-on
☐ Web-based teaching materials and exercises
☐ Other_____

15. Which of the following assessment methods do you find assists in your learning legal research skills? *(Please tick all appropriate categories)*

☐ Short-answer exams   ☐ Multiple choice exams
☐ Library exercises   ☐ Essays requiring a structured research methodology
☐ Other_____

16. Where in the law school curriculum do you think legal research and information technology skills training best fits? *(Please tick all appropriate categories)*

☐ Separate first year subject   ☐ Integrated within another first year subject
☐ As an elective   ☐ Separate final year subject
☐ Integrated within one subject in each year of the law degree
☐ Other _____

17. Do you think legal research and information technology skills training in law school should be:

      ☐ Compulsory   ☐ Optional

18. Do you think legal research and information technology skills training in law school should be assessed by:

      ☐ Grading (ie. 1 - 7)   ☐ Pass/fail

Nature of use of information and information technology

Tick the option indicating your experience in the activities listed below.

19. Using a word processor to complete an assignment	☐ Always successful	☐ Usually successful	☐ Seldom successful	☐ Not used
20. Downloading a file from the World Wide Web	☐ Always successful	☐ Usually successful	☐ Seldom successful	☐ Not used
21. Using email to communicate with lecturers and students	☐ Always successful	☐ Usually successful	☐ Seldom successful	☐ Not used
22. Using legislation annotations to find reprints of legislation	☐ Always successful	☐ Usually successful	☐ Seldom successful	☐ Not used
23. Using AustLII to find unreported cases	☐ Always successful	☐ Usually successful	☐ Seldom successful	☐ Not used
24. Using case citators to find case citations	☐ Always successful	☐ Usually successful	☐ Seldom successful	☐ Not used
25. Using the library catalogue to find a book on a topic	☐ Always successful	☐ Usually successful	☐ Seldom successful	☐ Not used
26. Evaluating whether legal information found is current	☐ Always successful	☐ Usually successful	☐ Seldom successful	☐ Not used
27. Finding second reading speeches in Hansard	☐ Always successful	☐ Usually successful	☐ Seldom successful	☐ Not used
28. Listing keywords about your research problem	☐ Always successful	☐ Usually successful	☐ Seldom successful	☐ Not used
29. Finding out whether Australia is a party to a treaty	☐ Always successful	☐ Usually successful	☐ Seldom successful	☐ Not used
30. Searching full text cd-rom databases of cases	☐ Always successful	☐ Usually successful	☐ Seldom successful	☐ Not used

31. Overall how would you rate your law library skills?

☐ Excellent ☐ Good ☐ Average ☐ Poor

32. Overall how would you rate your computer and information technology skills?

☐ Excellent ☐ Good ☐ Average ☐ Poor

33. How important do you think legal research and information technology skills are to the study of law at university?

☐ Not at all ☐ Slightly ☐ Moderately ☐ Very

34. How important do you think legal research and information technology skills are to the practice of law as a solicitor or barrister?

☐ Not at all ☐ Slightly ☐ Moderately ☐ Very

Research problem

The following questions relate to this research problem:-

You are a solicitor in a law firm in Queensland. A client comes into your office with a problem regarding a breach of contract that occurred a couple of weeks ago and they want to know whether they can sue for damages.

35. What keywords would you use to start researching the answer to this problem? *(Please tick only one category)*

☐ damages   ☐ (sue and contract) not recent
☐ contract and breach and Queensland   ☐ contract law

36. Which source would you look at first to start researching this problem? Rank the choices 1 to 4.

#___ Internet
#___ Textbook
#___ Looseleaf service
#___ Journal index to find journal articles

37. Which of the following is the best cd-rom index to Australian legal journal articles? *(Please tick only one category)*

☐ AustLII   ☐ LegalTrac
☐ AGIS   ☐ ILP

38. How would you find out whether any legislation on the topic had been amended? *(Please tick only one category)*

☐ Case citators   ☐ The Laws of Australia
☐ Legislation annotations   ☐ Australian Treaty Series

39. What is the correct URL for AustLII?

☐ AustLII   ☐ austlii@austlii.edu.au
☐ http://www.austlii.edu.au   ☐ Don't know

40. What is the best process for locating up to date Queensland legislation? *(Please tick only one category)*

☐ Federal Statute Annotations, Australian Current Law Legislation, Queensland Reprints
☐ Queensland Legislation Annotations, Queensland Legislation Update, OQPC site
☐ Queensland Legal Indexes, Australian Legal Monthly Digest, Queensland Reprints
☐ Queensland Legislation Annotations, Queensland Legislation Update, Queensland Reprints

Any other comments?

_____

_____

_____

_____

_____

_____

_____

6

CHAPTER 4
Critical incident technique

Hilary Hughes

Introduction

What are the key attributes of an effective IL educator?
What difficulties do students encounter in using online
information resources?

These are the types of qualitative questions that critical incident technique (CIT) is
well suited to exploring. This chapter outlines the origins, ongoing development,
implementation, advantages and disadvantages of critical incident technique and its
potential for information literacy (IL) research. I draw on my current research into
international students' use of online information resources to demonstrate the
application of CIT in an information literacy context.

Overview of critical incident technique

Defining CIT

Critical incident technique is a well proven qualitative research approach that
offers a practical step-by-step approach to collecting and analysing information
about human activities and their significance to the people involved. It is capable of
yielding rich, contextualised data that reflect real-life experiences. Its creator, John
Flanagan, described CIT as:

> A set of procedures for collecting direct observations of human behavior
> in such a way as to facilitate their potential usefulness in solving practical
> problems and developing broad psychological principles. The critical
> incident technique outlines procedures for collecting observed incidents
> having special significance and meeting systematically defined criteria
> (Flanagan 1954, p.327).

The value and efficacy of CIT is attested by research studies in a widening
range of social science disciplines over fifty years. As its name suggests, critical

incident technique involves the study of *critical incidents* – or significant instances of a specific activity – as experienced or observed by the research participants. Detailed analysis of critical incidents enables researchers to identify similarities, differences and patterns and to seek insight into how and why people engage in the activity.

> People assign meanings to their experiences, and when we group together collections of such meanings in order to make sense of the world, we engage in a kind of research, a seeking of understanding. The critical incident technique provides a systematic means for gathering the significances others attach to events, analyzing the emerging patterns, and laying out tentative conclusions for the reader's consideration' (Kain 2004, p.85).

CIT findings generally support practical outcomes – often related to education or training – and provide a knowledge-base for further research.

Origins and ongoing development of CIT

Critical incident technique was developed in the nineteen forties by John Flanagan, an American researcher in the field of occupational psychology (Flanagan 1954). Its original emphasis on human behaviour reflects the prevailing positivist research paradigm. Flanagan devised it as a means to gather and analyse objective, reliable information about specific activities. He intended that the findings would underpin practical problem-solving in areas such as employee appraisal and performance enhancement.

The first CIT studies addressed military issues such as combat leadership, pilot disorientation and bombing raid failures and supported pilot selection and training. Since then it has been used in a range of social science disciplines, including psychology and counselling (Chell 1998; Woolsey 1986), management (Ellinger & Watkins 1998) and education (Christie & Young 1995; Kain 1997; Redmann et al. 2000; Tripp 1993). Notably CIT has provided a sound methodological basis for library and information research, including:

- library user studies (Andrews 1991; Radford 1996; Slater & Fisher 1969; Sullivan-Windle 1993),
- library systems and information use (Tonta 1992; Wilkins & Leckie 1997; Wilson et al. 1989), and
- library management and human resources (Fisher & Oulton 1999).

Flanagan regarded CIT as a 'flexible set of principles which must be modified and adapted to meet the specific situation at hand' (Flanagan 1954, p.335). Over the fifty years since its inception CIT has proved responsive to changing research approaches. Researchers have modified CIT in various ways, extending beyond 'scientific' behavioural analysis to more holistic investigation of aspects of human experience and meaning that people attach to activities. Researchers, including myself, are tending away from previous concerns about objectivity and generalisation towards individual perspectives and significance (Chell 1998; Kain 2004).

Defining 'critical incident'

In general usage 'critical incident' often implies a major crisis or turning point, such as the 9/11 terrorist attacks or the Boxing Day tsunami. Chance events may be catalysts for discovery and innovation. Real life incidents also provide the focus for CIT studies. While they are not necessarily dramatic, they still represent aspects of human experience that are significant to the individual concerned. Numerous incidents – instances of a particular activity – are purposefully collected in the course of a CIT research project.

According to Flanagan (1954 p.338) 'an incident is critical if it makes a 'significant' contribution, either positively or negatively to the general aim of the activity' and it should be capable of being critiqued or analysed'.

Critical incident technique in practice

This section outlines the five-step CIT process established by Flanagan (1954). It also presents my doctoral study as an example of CIT modified and applied to IL research.

Background to the study

My study is entitled *International students using online information resources for learning*. It stemmed from my experiences as a librarian/IL educator in Australian tertiary institutions. From my professional practice and reading I am aware of the diversity of international students' personal, cultural and educational experiences and the associated challenges they often encounter while living and learning in Australia. However, empirical data about their IL needs is still quite limited.

This exploratory study involved twenty-six international students from two Australian universities. It sought insight into their experiences of using online information resources for study, as expressed through their actions, thoughts and feelings. My aim was to identify associated IL learning needs and so to support evidence-based development of IL strategies that respond to these needs.

Selecting CIT

I selected CIT as the research method for this study because:

- it supports a straightforward qualitative approach;
- it offers well-proven, clearly defined guidelines for data collection and analysis;
- it focuses on real-life human experiences;
- it enables the development of practical outcomes;
- it is relatively flexible; and
- it has successfully supported other library and information science and education studies.

However, in common with other researchers I have developed a modified approach to CIT. Since this study is based on a holistic understanding of IL and online information use (Bruce 1997; Hughes 2006) I widened the CIT behavioural focus to integrate behavioural, cognitive and affective responses and cultural and linguistic influences. As Chell (1998, p.60) comments:

> The unit of analysis may be the individual, the group or the team, but the CIT allows for the focus to shift, for example to the organisation, the industrial sector or the location – region or community, country or nation. Thus, for example, one may explore overarching concepts like 'climate', 'culture, 'style', by examining the categorical data across the sample as a whole.

A five-step process

Critical incident technique offers a clearly defined, systematic and sequential research process. As envisaged by John Flanagan (1954) it consists of the following steps:

1. establish the general aims.
2. establish plans and specifications.
3. collect the data.
4. analyse the data.
5. interpret and report the data.

In the following paragraphs I outline each of these steps as specified by Flanagan (1954). I also explain the ways in which I followed and adapted these guidelines in my study.

Step 1: Establishing the general aim

The first essential CIT step is to define the *activity* to be studied and establish its *aim*. This supports the development of the research questions and provides direction for the data analysis and presentation of the findings. The aim is encapsulated in a brief, clear statement – a 'functional description' that indicates the objective of the activity and what someone engaging in the activity is expected to accomplish. Flanagan recommended that researchers consult experts in the field to ensure that the aim is relevant and widely acceptable to other researchers and practitioners. In the IL context, sources of expert opinion might include: academics, Library and Information Science (LIS) colleagues or managers, organisations such as Australian and New Zealand Institute of Information Literacy (ANZIIL) or Australian Library and Information Association (ALIA), research and practitioner literature.

I determined that the activity at the heart of my study is *using online information resources for study*. Consequently, as experts in the field I identified eight academic librarians with extensive reference and IL experience and asked them: 'What do you consider to be the aim of using online information resources?' Their responses enabled me to compile the following collective aim:

> *The aim of using online information resources for study is to gather information, develop understanding, widen experience, overcome challenges, adopt critical perspectives, construct knowledge, create new meanings and achieve learning outcomes.*

Step 2: Establishing plans and specifications

This step involves developing a detailed and defensible plan of attack for data collection. Importantly this includes the identification of *critical incidents* and the recording of *critical behaviours*. Flanagan suggested that these details should be carefully documented to ensure consistency and objectivity in data collection, especially in large-scale studies involving more than one researcher. The four key considerations in this process are described below, accompanied by a brief explanation of their application to my study (summarised in table 4.1).

1. *situation* – the researcher specifies the location, conditions, research participants and the activity. In my study the situation was represented as: *Where?* – two Australian universities, *Who?* – twenty-six international students, *What?* – using online information resources for study.

2. *relevance* – the researcher specifies both the types of *critical incidents* and the nature of *critical behaviours* that are relevant to the study and therefore worthy of being recorded. In my study *critical incidents* were represented as *recent*

assignments that involved the use of online information resources. I rationalised this on the basis that assignments generally involve some active engagement with online resources. In addition they often have a significant impact on students' study experience and so are likely to be vividly remembered. In place of Flanagan's term *critical behaviours,* I used the more expansive term *critical interactions.* This recognises the complex nature of using online information resources that involves not only actions, but also a variety of inter-related critical and creative processes such as planning, managing and reflecting. I also introduced the notion of *dimensions* as an additional qualitative layer. These encompassed students' cognitive or affective responses to the use of online information resources for study, as well as cultural or linguistic influences on this use.

Table 4.1 Example of plans and specifications

Activity	Using online information resources for study purposes.
Aim of the activity	To gather information, develop understanding, widen experience, overcome challenges, adopt critical perspectives, construct knowledge, create new meanings and achieve learning outcomes.
The situation	Who? Twenty-six international students in their first year of study in Australia; undergraduate or postgraduate. Where? Two Australian universities. What? Using online information resources to complete assignments.
Critical incidents	Recent assignments that involved the use of online information resources.
Critical interactions	Any/all instances and actions involving the use of online information resources for study.
Dimensions	Any/all cognitive or affective responses to – cultural or linguistic influences on – the use of online information resources for study.
Sole researcher	Ensured consistency in data collection. Professional experience afforded familiarity with the activity. No training or recruitment of additional researchers was required.

3. *extent* – the researcher specifies criteria for collecting critical incidents based on their significance, in terms of the extent of their positive or negative effect on the general aim. In my study I took a broad approach here, in considering that all aspects of the online information use experience (behavioural, cognitive and affective responses, cultural and linguistic influences) are potentially significant and capable of having a positive or negative effect.

4. *observers* – the researcher ensures that all data collectors are familiar with the activity being studied and receive thorough instructions and training in the data collection process. I considered that my professional experience as librarian/IL educator ensured my familiarity with the activity. As sole researcher, no further selection or training of observers/interviewers was necessary.

Step 3: Collecting the data

This step involves collecting critical incidents that relate to the activity being studied. Flanagan provided detailed instructions concerning the means of collection, required sample size and composition of the questions.

Preferred means for data collection are individual interviews or direct observations. Group interviews are acceptable where participant numbers are large. Written responses or questionnaires may also be used, although they might be less effective since they tend to lack the immediacy of observations and interviews. Flanagan stressed the importance of informing the interviewees about the purpose of the study, the basis for participant recruitment and preservation of their anonymity. To minimise ambiguity and bias he also recommended careful wording of questions and the use of pilot interviews.

To enable full and accurate responses, participants are requested to focus on incidents that they have recently taken part in or observed first-hand. They may describe one or several incidents that represent positive and/or negative aspects of the activity being studied. They are also encouraged to provide factual reports, rather than interpretations, of what happened.

CIT seeks contextualised examples of the activity and its significance and questions typically follows a binary positive/negative pattern. For example:

*   think of a time that a colleague presented an effective/ineffective IL session.
*   describe the circumstances and nature of this incident.
*   explain why you consider this incident to be significant.
*   what did this person do that was effective/ineffective?
*   why was it effective/ineffective?
*   describe the outcome(s) or result of the incident.

Flanagan stated that there are no firm rules about appropriate 'sample size' for CIT. The determining factors relate to the complexity of the activity and variety and quality of the critical incidents, rather than the number of participants. He also suggested that data collection and analysis should be carried out concurrently. Incidents should continue to be collected until redundancy occurs – that is, when no new *critical behaviours* appear. Thus the optimum number of critical incidents for a CIT study can range anywhere between 50-100 to several thousand.

Table 4.2 outlines the data collection strategy that I developed for this study. It varies from standard CIT in two ways. First, the interviews were more expansive than many CIT studies. As explained previously, rather than focusing purely on behavioural aspects they were based on a holistic understanding of online information use which integrates actions, thoughts, feelings and influences. Second, I adopted a dual approach to data collection by supplementing the usual semi-structured interviews with observations of students carrying out a practical task. While the interviews focused on *how* and *why* participants used online information resources, the observed set task examined *how well* they used them. The advantage of this dual approach is that it allowed me to draw on both the participants' personal accounts of their online information use and my more objective assessment of the effectiveness of their use. This allowed for 'triangulation' and provided alternative perspectives on the activity, thus enriching the picture of the students' online information use.

The interviews were semi-structured and conversational, with a view to encouraging the students to speak freely about their experiences. I used a set of open questions as an interview guide, but did not always address them in sequence. I also used casual prompts to help elicit or clarify information. In the initial stages of the interview, to develop confidence and provide context, the students were invited to talk about their personal, educational, cultural and linguistic experiences and their previous library and information use. Next I requested them to focus their attention on a critical incident – a recent assignment that required the use of online information resources. My subsequent questions related to this experience. They had a characteristic CIT flavour and a positive/negative structure, for example: *What resources did you use / not use for this assignment? Why?*

The practical task represented another critical incident and sought examples of effective/ineffective uses of online information resources. I observed students using three online tools (the library catalogue, a journal database and an internet search engine) to select online information resources on the topic: *Compile an annotated bibliography on effective public speaking techniques in business.*

The participant group of twenty-six international students was relatively small for a CIT study and it produced only forty-eight *critical incidents* – one from each interview and set task. However, the expansive nature of the interviews and set task yielded over one thousand *critical interactions (*which correspond with Flanagan's *critical behaviours).* It is unrealistic to claim that I reached a point of redundancy in data collection given the complexity of the activity. However, the analysis process, which is described in the following section, reveals significant patterns and variations in the students' experiences.

Table 4.2 Example of data collection

Participants (reflected the culturally and linguistically diverse student populations)	Twenty-six international students enrolled at CQU Brisbane International Campus & QUT. Ten undergraduates and sixteen postgraduates. Studying a range of disciplines, mainly, Business and IT. Fifteen different countries of origin: Japan, Malaysia, Taiwan, China, Singapore, Indonesia, Thailand, Vietnam, India, Israel, Jordan, Mexico, Poland, Sweden, England.
Data collection activities	Semi-structured interviews. Observed set task involving the use of three online information tools (library catalogue, journal database and internet search engine).
Interview (focused on *use* of information resources)	Initial conversation about the student's personal, cultural, linguistic, educational experiences and previous library and online information use. *What online information tools and resources did you use /not use for this assignment? Why? How did you use them? What did you find hard/easy about using these online resources and tools? Why? What makes it hard/easy for international students to use online resources? Why? What could be done to make online information use easier for international students? Why? Overall was using online information resources for this assignment a positive experience/not a positive experience? Why?*
Observed set task (focused on *effectiveness* of students' use of online information resources)	Participants were requested to: *Imagine that you have been set an assignment with the topic 'Compile an annotated bibliography on effective public speaking techniques in business'. Please show how you would search for and select information on this topic using the library catalogue, a journal database and an internet search engine.*

Step 4: Analysing the data

This step involves an inductive data analysis process that aims to classify *critical incidents* and identify *critical behaviours*. These are arranged into a series of well defined, mutually exclusive categories and sub-categories of decreasing generalisability/increasing specificity. The analysis process recommended by

Flanagan is outlined below, followed by a description of its practical application to my study.

Frame of reference

The researcher develops a *frame of reference* – a set of broad categories for classifying the critical incidents. These main categories and their headings should reflect the aim of the activity and relate to the intended application of the data.

Category formulation

The researcher sifts the critical incidents, identifies critical behaviours and sorts them into categories and sub-categories. This might entail a trial and error approach since the categories are not pre-determined; rather the researcher allows them to emerge (or suggest themselves) during the process. Flanagan (1954, p.344) considered this to be the most challenging analysis aspect, since it depends on the 'insight, experience and judgment' of the researcher.

The following guidelines for constructing categories and creating the classification structure are adapted from Flanagan.

To construct the categories:

- sort a relatively small sample of critical incidents into broad (main) categories;
- create tentative names and brief definitions for the main categories;
- sort the remaining incidents into the main categories – create additional main categories and definitions, or modify existing ones, as necessary;
- divide main categories into sub-categories as finer similarities and differences become apparent;
- continuously re-examine the main categories and sub-categories – revise categories and reallocate critical incidents, as necessary; and
- continue this process until all critical incidents have been appropriately classified.

Aim for:

- a clear-cut and logical organisation;
- meaningful headings for sub-categories, without need for accompanying definitions;
- neutral headings – expressed in active terms; and
- comprehensive coverage of all critical incidents

Specificity

The researcher determines the appropriate level of analysis, according to the aim of the activity and intended use of the data. This involves balancing the relative merits of specificity against generality. The former affords greater complexity and detail, while the latter results in a simpler, broader overview.

Trial, error, persistence, logic and intuition all contributed to my data analysis approach. This involved continuous examination – and re-examination – of interview transcripts and observation records to ensure salient, consistent coverage of the participants' online information use experiences.

Note: seeking to retain a close connection between the participants' comments within the context of the whole interview I worked mainly with the transcripts using colour-coding and margin notes to identify categories and I used spreadsheets to organise the categories. Alternative approaches to CIT data analysis include manually sorting critical incidents on index cards and using a data analysis program such as *QSR NVivo*.

CIT underpinned the analysis process, although my analytical approach extended beyond purely behavioural concerns in also addressing cognitive and affective responses and cultural and linguistic influences. As explained in Step 2, the key data elements – *critical interactions* – were a more expansive version of Flanagan's *critical behaviours*. The *dimensions* were my addition.

Working inductively with the data, I identified categories and developed the *categorisation framework* that is outlined in table 4.3. In line with CIT specifications this related directly to the aim of the activity – *using online information resources for study* – and its intended application to IL. The *categorisation framework* comprised four levels of categories of differing types. Level 1 and 2 categories could stand alone, while level 3 and 4 categories needed to be attached to individual level 2 categories.

- *level 1 online sources* – these were the six main categories. They corresponded to the different types of online tools and resources that participants interacted with (or used) for their assignments, namely: *online sources (general), online catalogue, online journal databases, internet search engines, university/library online sources, specialist online sources.*
- *level 2 critical interactions* – these sub-categories were the most numerous and varied. They comprised the *critical interactions* and so represented the many ways in which participants interacted with particular online sources, for example: *developing a search strategy, searching a journal database, evaluating a web resource.*
- *level 3 CIT descriptors* – these sub-categories described the nature of particular *interactions*. One or more of these descriptors could be attached to an interaction. They were grouped in four pairs and so reflected the standard CIT binary pattern, as follows:
  - U/NU (used/not used) – instances of a student's interaction or non-

interaction with a particular online source;

- E/IE (effective/ineffective) – instances of a student's effective or ineffective interaction;
- EA/H (easy/hard) – instances of a student experiencing ease or difficulty in their interaction with a particular online source; and
- P/N (positive/negative) – instances of a student reporting positive or negative responses to their interaction.

- *level 4 dimensions* – these sub-categories represented qualitative *dimensions* that overlaid *interactions*. They related to:
  - cognitive and affective responses – the students' reactions, their thoughts and feelings about using online information resources; and
  - cultural and linguistic influences on their interactions.

Dimensions were further subdivided into *aspects* (level 4a). One or more of these dimensions could be attached to a particular interaction. Table 4.3 offers a snapshot of my *categorisation framework* and some sample categories.

Table 4.3 Example of categorisation framework and sample categories

Level 1 **Online sources**	Using online sources (general) Using online catalogue Using online journal databases Using internet search engines Using specialist online sources – ABS, AUSTLII etc. Using university/library online sources – course readings, IL tutorials, e-prints
Level 2 **Critical** **interactions**	Selecting catalogue, journal database, Google etc. Searching catalogue/database/Google etc. Evaluating results Selecting resources Processing results – printing, saving, bookmarking etc. Synthesising information and so on
Level 3 **CIT descriptors**	U/NU (used/not used) E/IN (effective/ineffective) EA/H (easy/hard) P/NP (positive/not positive)
Level 4 **Dimensions**	CR – cognitive responses AR – affective responses CI – cultural influences LI – linguistic influences
Level 4a **Dimensions –** **aspects**	Cognitive responses – critical comments, suggestions Affective responses - exciting, pleasing, frustrating, boring etc. Cultural influences – literary, historical, political allusions, humour etc. Linguistic influences – vocabulary, jargon, academic style etc.

Table 4.4 demonstrates the categorisation process applied to an interview excerpt. This brief statement is rich in information about the student's use of the online catalogue and reveals some language-related difficulty but also positive development. Note: It is all too easy to lose sight of the fact that categorisation is a means rather than an end in itself. Its purpose is to allow the manipulation and grouping of data in different ways, enabling researchers to identify the similarities, differences, relationships and patterns and so leading to new understandings and practical outcomes.

Table 4.4 Example of categorisation process

Interview excerpt: *I searched the online catalogue. It was helpful. For international students it's basically easy – easier for Australian students because they know the right words. At first it was hard for me – now I've got used to it.*				
	Level 1 **online sources**	**Level 2** **critical interactions**	**Level 3** **CIT descriptors**	**Level 4** **dimensions**
I searched the online catalogue.	Using online catalogue	Searching catalogue	U	
It was helpful.			P	
For international students it's basically easy – easier for Australian students because they know the right words.			EA	LI – vocabulary
At first it was hard for me – now I've got used to it.			H – EA	

Step 5: Interpreting and reporting

This step involves interpreting and reporting the data, in line with the intended application of the findings. CIT does not require a specific report format, but the results often include a set of *critical behaviours* that define the activity studied. In order to establish the credibility of the findings, Flanagan emphasised a need to carefully explain and justify how the four preceding steps had been carried out and to specify precisely the circumstances in which the findings could be said to apply.

The findings of the study were presented as thematic narrative, recommendations, tabulations and graphics. The separate parts highlight various inter-related aspects of international students' online information use. In combination they create a practical and conceptual knowledge-base with potential to inform, support and promote IL development. In accordance with CIT principles, the findings of this study offer a research-based approach to developing students' IL learning and practical problem-solving.

Ethical and intercultural considerations

CIT requires close attention to ethical practices, since it involves interaction with human participants who entrust researchers with information about their personal and professional lives. Consequently as researchers we have a responsibility to: preserve the participants' confidentiality and respect their dignity; take care to explain the purpose of the study, the exact nature of the participants' involvement and the ways in which their responses will be handled; assure them that their participation is voluntary; avoid any kind of coercion and allow participants to discontinue their involvement at any time; and heed any signs of distress, anxiety or embarrassment. In addition, the diverse nature of our society calls for a high degree of social, cultural and linguistic sensitivity. While this is not unique to CIT, it was an important consideration in the design and implementation of my study involving international students (Hughes 2004).

Advantages, disadvantages and IL applications of CIT

Advantages

CIT lends itself to exploratory research that seeks context-rich, first-hand perspectives on human activities and their significance. The focus on recalled and observed incidents brings an immediacy and authenticity (Ellinger & Watkins 1998). This insight into real-life individual experiences assists the identification of broader patterns and understandings (Chell 1998), whereby the study of unique experiences can illuminate 'shared reality' (Kain 2004, p. 82). CIT also might enable the identification of key research issues, develop a knowledge-base for further investigation and support conceptual modelling (Woolsey 1986).

CIT interviews allow 'linkage between context, strategy and outcomes' (Chell 1998, p.68). Critical incidents provide a powerful research focus. They help define the aims and boundaries of the study and ground it in reality. In interviews they provide direction and can prompt participant recall. Data analysis procedures are structured, yet flexibly allow both fine-grained and more general approaches depending on the intended application of research findings. While CIT is considered to be a qualitative method, it admits some statistical description. Where required it enables relatively high levels of objectivity, for as Flanagan (1954, p.355) observed: 'Rather than collecting opinions, hunches and estimates (CIT) obtains a record of specific behaviors'.

From the practitioner's perspective, CIT is practical and relatively straightforward to implement. According to Christie and Young (1995, p.7), CIT is 'grounded ... in common sense procedures'. The technique can be applied to research projects of varying sizes and locations and can be implemented on an individual or team basis. It is capable of collecting and analysing large amounts of interview and observation data. Extensive theoretical knowledge and statistical expertise are not essential, although CIT does call for a well developed critical sense and attention to detail.

Although CIT procedures are quite precise, they are proving amenable to modification, especially with regard to data collection approaches (Ellinger & Watkins 1998; Shirey n.d; Woolsey 1986). In particular, as evidenced by my approach, CIT perspectives are tending to widen from purely behavioural concerns to more holistic conceptions of human experience that encompass 'the conscious reflections of the incumbent, their frame of reference, feelings, attitudes and perspective on matters which are of critical importance to them' (Chell 1998, p.68). Moreover, some researchers are finding useful compatibilities between CIT and other research methods such as case study or grounded theory (Chell 1998).

Disadvantages

On a conceptual level, CIT lacks the strong theoretical underpinnng of some other qualitative methods such as phenomenography or participatory action research. However, this can be advantageous for studies that aim to develop a conceptual frame or follow a 'grounded' approach. Also I have found CIT's behavioural emphasis somewhat constrictive since binary descriptions (effective/not effective, successful/not successful) are not always adequate for dealing with the nuances and gradations of human experience. Again, this may be compensated by CIT's modifiability.

On the practical level, the categorisation process for CIT data analysis is painstaking and time consuming. CIT's reliability as a method is sometimes challenged with regard to: limited generalisability of the findings; subjectivity of analysis; selectivity or lack of accuracy of critical incident data, due to its personal recalled nature (Chell 1998; Kain 2004). In common with other qualitative research approaches these aspects can be mediated by close attention to context-specific analysis and description in terms of 'a careful explanation of the process followed and attention to rich descriptive detail, providing the reader with a basis to judge the applicability of the research' (Kain 2004, p.78).

Information literacy applications

Critical incident technique offers a promising approach for some types of IL research. As mentioned previously, CIT already has a proven track record in the education and LIS fields. For example, Fisher and Oulton comment:

> We would argue that the technique has much potential value for
> researchers in library and information management in, for example,
> studies of the professional–client interface; understanding organisational
> cultures and management styles; and, of course, identifying real training
> needs (1999, p.124).

The *Encyclopedia of Library and Information Science* notes that CIT 'can provide information that is objective as well as valid and is a tool of great potential for the researcher interested in the human element of the information problem' (Shirey n.d, p.291).

CIT is particularly useful where evidence-based performance appraisal and development are required. Thus, in an IL context CIT might be used, for example, to evaluate teaching strategies, learners' IL capabilities, or online information services. The results of such research might then be applied to enhancing professional development, IL curriculum planning and implementation, learner-responsive information services, and ICT interfaces. It is significant also that the potential of critical incidents as stimuli for learning and reflection has been recognised (Chell 1998; Tripp 1993) and might be worth pursuing in IL education.

Conclusion

Critical incident technique is a robust research method that has proved effective in numerous studies in a wide range of social science disciplines, including library and information science. Its well defined set of principles and procedures ensure that it is a relatively simple method to master and apply. CIT is best suited to exploratory research that seeks understanding of specific human activities or as an information base for further research. In the context of information literacy, CIT has potential for research that aims to support practical problem-solving, performance enhancement and learning.

References

Andrews, J. (1991). An exploration of students' library use problems. *Library Review, 40*(1), 5-14.

Bruce, C.S. (1997). *The seven faces of information literacy*. Adelaide: Auslib Press

Chell, E. (1998). Critical incident technique. In G. Symon & C. Cassell (Eds.), *Qualitative methods and analysis in organizational research* (pp.51-72). London: Sage.

Christie, M.F. & Young, R.M. (1995). *Critical incidents in vocational teaching: A Northern Territory study*. Darwin: Northern Territory University.

Ellinger, A.D. & Watkins, K.E. (1998). Updating the critical incident technique after forty-four years. Advances in qualitative research. In *Academy of Human Resource Development Conference Proceedings*. ERIC Document Reproduction Service No. ED428234. Retrieved October 11 2002 from http://www.edrs.com/logon.cfm

Fisher, S. & Oulton, T. (1999). The critical incident technique in library and information management research. *Education for Information, 17*(2), 113-125, June.

Flanagan, J.C. (1954). The critical incident technique. *The Psychological Bulletin, 51*(4), 327-358.

Hughes, H. (2006). Responses and influences: A model of online information use for learning. *Information Research 12*(1), paper 279. Retrieved June 18 2007 from http://InformationR.net/ir/12-1/paper279.htm

Hughes, H. (2004). Researching the experience of international students. In P.A. Danaher, C. Macpherson, F. Nouwens & D. Orr (Eds.), *Lifelong learning: Whose responsibility and what is your contribution? Refereed papers from the 3rd International Lifelong Learning Conference,* June 13-16, 2004, Yeppoon (pp.168-174). Rockhampton: Central Queensland University Press.

Kain, D.L. (2004). Owning significance: The critical incident technique in research. In K. deMarrais & S.D. Lapan (Eds.), *Foundations for research: Methods of inquiry in education and the social sciences* (pp.69-85). Mahwah, NJ: Lawrence Erlbaum.

Kain, D.L. (1997). Critical incidents in teacher collaboration on interdisciplinary teams. *Research in Middle Level Education Quarterly, 21*(1), 1-9.

Radford, M.L. (1996). Communication theory applied to the reference encounter: An analysis of critical incidents. *Library Quarterly, 66*(April), 123-37.

Redmann, D.H., Stitt-Gohdes, W.L. & Lambrecht, J.J. (2000). The critical incident technique: A tool for qualitative research. *Delta Phi Epsilon Journal, 42*(3), 132-53.

Shirey, D. (n.d.). Critical incident technique. In A. Kent, H. Lancour & W.Z. Nasri (Eds.), *Encyclopedia of library and information science,* Vol. 6 (pp.286-91), New York: Marcel Dekker.

Slater, M. & Fisher, P. (1969). *Use made of technical libraries.* ASLIB Occasional Publications no. 2. London: ASLIB.

Sullivan-Windle, B. (1993). Students' perceptions of factors influencing effective library use. *Australian Academic and Research Libraries, 24*(2), 95-104.

Tonta, Y. (1992). Analysis of search failures in document retrieval systems: A review. *Public-access computer systems review, 3*(1), 4-3.

Tripp, D. (1993). *Critical incidents in teaching: Developing professional judgment.* London: Routledge.

Wilkins, J.L.H. & Leckie, G.J. (1997). University professional and managerial staff: Information needs and seeking. *College and Research Libraries, 58*(6), 561-74.

Wilson, S.R., Starr-Schneidkraut, N. & Cooper, N.D. (1989). *Use of the critical incident technique to evaluate the impact of MEDLINE. Executive summary.* United States National Library of Medicine. Retrieved June 18 2007 from http://www.nlm.nih.gov/od/ope/citexsum.txt

Woolsey, L.K. (1986). The critical incident technique: An innovative qualitative method of research. *Canadian Journal of Counselling, 20*(4), 242-254.

Data analysis software

QSR NVivo. Retrieved June 18 2007 from http://www.qsrinternational.com/

CHAPTER 5
Understanding information literacy in the workplace: using a constructivist grounded theory approach

Annemaree Lloyd

The aim of this chapter is to introduce practitioners to the grounded theory approach I employed in my doctoral studies which focused on exploring the meaning of information literacy (IL) in a specific workplace – a fire station. This chapter is not intended to be a 'how to' guide which you need to follow slavishly, but it will introduce you to the basic strategies and issues found in a grounded theory approach and will illustrate the elements by describing my own research. At the end of the chapter is a list of readings which you should explore before deciding on this method for your research. The objectives of this chapter are that you should:

- understand the grounded theory method,
- be able to describe key strategies which are used in a grounded theory method, and
- understand this process in the context of a research program.

Why did I choose a grounded theory approach to exploring information literacy in the workplace?

I selected this approach because I wanted to begin to understand what it actually meant to be information literate (outside an educational context) and how IL was experienced by people who were engaged in vocational practice (an area where IL research is just emerging). I was interested in whether being information literate meant more than developing a set of information-related skills, and I was curious about whether information-literacy practices would differ in other contexts. The important factor in my selection of this approach was that I wanted to develop a framework that related strongly to the experiences of the participants, which could subsequently be used by researchers to explore other workplace contexts. The substantive theory and model which were developed using this approach therefore needed to be grounded in the real world experiences of the community of practice, as its members engage with information. Grounding the research in real-life engagement within the workplace:

- broadens our understanding of IL as it is experienced outside the educational context,
- develops a baseline study for further research into workplace IL, and
- provides educators and trainers with a conceptualised framework which will inform training and education practices.

What is a constructivist grounded theory? An overview

Grounded theory is a method that enables you to collect and analyse data systematically and to construct a framework which will explain the data and the relationships among concepts which have emerged from your study (Charmaz 2003, p.250). Grounded theory approaches do not actually prescribe a method for data collection so the approach taken is up to you. I would advise you to explore a number of data collection techniques as each has its own benefits (Minichiello et al. 1995; Williamson 2000). In my own project, I used a qualitative framework which employed a series of semi-structured interviews and observations, but other grounded theory approaches have used a quantitative approach and data collection techniques may differ.

A constructivist approach to grounded theory method acknowledges the multiple realities of everyday life and recognises that knowledge is constructed among individuals and, in the case of research, between the participant and the researcher. The aim of a constructivist grounded theory approach is to develop an understanding of the participant's underlying experiences and to conceptualise it in a way that remains recognisable to the participant.

If we take as our starting point that information is 'any difference which makes a difference' (Bateson 1972, p.459), then we need to adopt a holistic approach to our exploration of IL. We need to explore and clarify the meaning of IL in the context of participants' beliefs, values, ideologies and situations, rather than just the overt 'acts and facts' (Charmaz 2003, p.275). We must accept that reality will differ, and will be influenced by context and situations which locate the individual in place and time.

Constructivists claim that:

> We invent concepts, models and schemes to make sense of experience, and we continually test and modify these constructions in light of new experience. Furthermore, there is an inevitable historical and sociocultural dimension to this construction. We do not construct our interpretations in isolation but against a backdrop of shared understandings, practices, language and so forth (Schwandt 2003, p.305).

Researchers who employ a constructivist framework as a focus for their research are concerned with the construction of meaning and actions which locates the 'data in time, place, culture and context but also reflects the researcher's thinking' (Charmaz 2002, p.677). Constructivist grounded theories are not concerned with positivist validation or replicability as the grounded theory study is localised, particular and consistent with studied life (Charmaz 2003). Data should fit and 'be recognizable and of relevance to those studied' (Pidgeon 1996, p.83). In constructivist grounded theory research, transcripts, analysis and journal articles and presentations about the research should be discussed between the participants and the researcher to ensure they remain consistent with the lived experience of the participants. Throughout my own study, a common comment made by the more senior participants was '*when will you tell us something that we don't already know*', and really this is the basic point of constructivist grounded theory method: to represent the meaningful experiences of the participants in a way which is recognisable to those participants.

The use of grounded theory method provides a flexible and iterative process for dealing with multiple and conflicting meanings, interpretations and constructions that emanate from the individual's real world engagement with information. The researcher's understanding of participants' experience emerges from the coding and is developed through shared understanding between the researcher and the participants. Coding (discussed in the next section) allows the researcher to sort similarities and differences in lived world engagement. In support of grounded theory, Pidgeon (1996, p.77) states that it 'leads to a model for research that is flexible, that is carried out in everyday contexts and that has as its goal the (co) construction of participants' symbolic worlds and social realities'.

Grounded theory method provides an avenue for the researcher to engage with the participants in the construction of meaning in context and acknowledges the complexity and multiple dimensions of interactions with phenomena in the lived world. This enables the analysis to be constructed from the data through active engagement, rather than simply 'applying it to new data, problems or context' (Pidgeon 1996, p.83). This approach also centralises the relationship between the researcher and the participant in the negotiation and construction of meaning about the role of information within the group context. The theoretical perspective which is used by the researcher also provides a store of sensitising concepts, in addition to the researcher's own views and experience. Acknowledging the dynamic and mutual relationship between the researcher and the participant allows the research to progress towards understanding the meaning of IL in the workplace community.

Some key things you need to know before you start: strategies of grounded theory

Grounded theory method has evolved into three distinct variations. These variations are described in the literature as the original Glaser and Strauss (1967) method, the Strauss and Corbin version (1994; 1998) and constructivist grounded theory (Charmaz 2003; Goulding 2002). The Glaser and Strauss method and the Strauss and Corbin version are distinguished from the constructivist grounded theory method on the basis that the two earlier versions advocated an objectivist position in relation to the discovery of meaning, the distancing of the researcher from the participants and the nature of reality. Objectivist grounded theorists deal with overt, explicit data, while constructivist grounded theorists are more concerned with the underlying assumptions and experiences of meaning making (Charmaz 2003; also see Bryant 2003 for an interesting discussion about these differences). Even though there are a number of distinct approaches to grounded theory, all methods have a number of common features, which distinguish a grounded theory approach from other approaches.

The next sections outline the common strategies of coding, constant comparison, theoretical sampling and memoing which are used to analyse data. These strategies are fundamental to all the variations and distinguish a grounded theory approach from other methods. In my own research, I found it useful to think about these strategies as thinking work, busy work and building work.

Coding (thinking work)

Coding your data is thinking work. Developing grounded theory is not a 'single shot process' (Charmaz 2002, p.682), in which interviews are conducted only once before the researcher leaves the field, never to return. The role of coding in the analysis is to move the 'researcher from description towards conceptualisation of that description' (Charmaz 2002, p.683). Coding is a two-step process. The first step, open coding, occurs during the first round of interviews and initiates the development of codes which are later transformed into analytical categories from which further questions will be drawn and used in the second data gathering phase. These initial categories are used by the researcher to 'discover participants' views rather than assume that researcher and participant share views and worlds' (Charmaz 2002, p.684). Coding occurs line-by-line, which means that as you read each line of a transcript you ask yourself questions such as 'What is going on in this context? What meanings are emerging? What influences this process or experience?'

For example, in the coding for phase 1 interviews, a central theme which emerged (and later became the major category) was the concept of *safety*, both in the *practice of fire fighting* and in the *maintenance of the culture of fire fighting*. This central category could be explained by other categories which I named *acting as a fire fighter*, *being a fire fighter* and *knowing the information universe*. The analysis which supported these categories related to the differences in the use of information. Probationer fire fighters developed a conceptual view of fire fighting practice through access to textual sources of information. This was an important part of their initial training that involved learning about safety and the formation of their own identity as fire fighters. Experienced fire fighters had greater access to information that could be drawn from textual, social and physical sources of information. The central category of *safety* became the driving information need which underpinned the nature of information access in all other categories. An example of my category development is illustrated in figure 5.1 (note that this is not the total category listing).

Example of primary category development

In the second step of the coding process, the researcher selects the most frequently appearing codes in order to synthesise and draw together an emerging picture of participants' experience (Charmaz 2002, p. 684). From this emerging picture, further questions are developed which are used in the second round of data gathering to check whether or not the interpretations fit with the participants' view (Charmaz 2002, p. 684).

Constant comparison (busy work)

The process of constant comparison begins the moment you begin to gather enough data. I like to think of it as the busy work of theory building. Constant comparison involves the comparing of data with other data from your transcripts to identify similarities and differences in the range of views, actions, situations, accounts and experiences (Charmaz 2003). Patterns and themes, emerging from the data-collection phase are then discussed between the researcher and individuals, and between the group and the researcher, to ensure that they are recognisable to those who participated in the study. The emerging patterns and themes form the basis for further exploration through theoretical sampling (which will be discussed in the next section).

In the present study, as the researcher I constantly compared the narratives, stories, actions and situations of the cohort in order to identify similarities, which led to the development of codes and categories for the first analysis and provided the framework with which to develop further questions for phase 2. Questions in phase 2 enriched and further explained the initial categories identified in phase 1. Through constant comparison, the dissimilarities were also revealed, which led to the further exploration of areas, which explained why a negative response or insight was provided. The use of constant comparisons leads to the conceptualisation of the processes which both facilitate information literacy and contest the practice of that literacy. In all variations on grounded theory, category saturation occurs when no new data emerge to inform or underpin the developing theory (Goulding 2002, p.70).

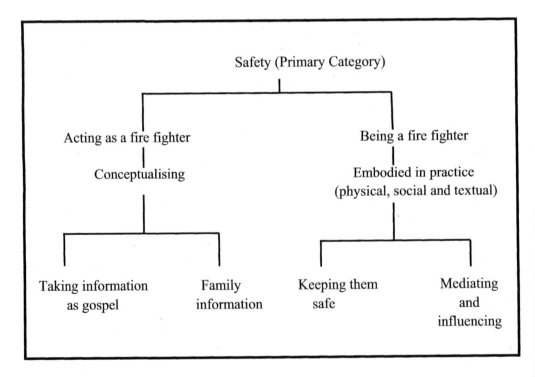

Figure 5.1 Example of category development

Theoretical sampling (putting it all together, constructing a picture)

Theoretical sampling is the purposeful selection of a specific sample for analysis, which will illuminate the emergent theory (Charmaz 2002; Pidgeon 1996). The theoretical sample is drawn once the categories, which form the phase1 analysis, have been saturated and no new categories emerge. The emergent theory is then used to develop a further set of questions which is then taken back out into the field. These questions are used to elaborate the researchers and the participants' negotiated view of the emerging theory and to deepen the researcher's emergent understanding (Charmaz 2002; Pidgeon 1996, p.78). This is highlighted by Goulding, who states that 'theoretical sampling should direct the researcher to individuals, situations, context and locations and the theory should only be presented when all core categories are saturated' (2002, p.70).

In my own research, to explore further and to deepen the emerging conceptualisations I returned to the original platoon of fire fighters that participated in the pilot study and the first round of interviews. This group acted as key informants who were able to elaborate on the themes and issues which emerged from the phase 1 analysis. In my research I needed to know more about how fire fighters' bodies acted as an information source in learning to develop fire sense, how experienced fire fighters mediated the information environment for novices, and how they influenced the transition from novice to expert. I needed to refine my ideas and understandings, not to increase my sample. In order to do this, I went back to the original group who acted as my key informants and selected experts and novices who could elaborate on these themes.

Memo writing (reflective work)

The act of memo writing allows the grounded theorist to elaborate 'assumptions, processes and actions' (Charmaz 2003, p.261) which emerge during the processes of constant comparison in the development of categories and theoretical sampling (Charmaz 2003). Memo writing is an active process for the researcher and aids in linking the analysis with observations and interpretations derived from the interview (Charmaz 2003). Throughout the fieldwork and analysis stages of my research, I wrote memos to myself which I later used to 'jog' my memory. For example, a memo that I had written immediately after an observation session at the fire station described how some information-related practices among permanent fire fighting groups were not always shared with other groups who support the permanent fire fighters in times of danger and risk. This memo was later expanded and used in my thesis to illustrate the concept of IL as a contested practice.

When you write a memo, you should do it in one sitting. Don't worry about sentence construction or grammar – just write, so that the memo captures your thoughts at the time. You will find that throughout the whole process of analysis and writing up the research you will go back to your memos time and time again. In my own research, I also used memos as a method of illustrating a particular point – of course these memos were tidied up before being presented in reports.

So how did I do it? Pulling it all together

If you use constructivist-influenced grounded theory, then you must be prepared to get involved with the everyday experiences of the research group with whom you are working and you need to develop a relationship with your participants. It also means that you need to expect and accept the unexpected!

Grounded theory emerges from the research data; it can not be forced and you may be very surprised at the direction your research heads after the first phase of coding and category building. This may seem frightening at first, but remember that the codes and themes which emerge relate to the experiences and reality of the research group with whom you work. Your job is to use the data to locate the similarities and differences in those experiences and to work with the research group to develop a negotiated view about what their experiences with information mean (that is, a view that you both understand).

A constructivist approach should focus on negotiated meaning, which enables rather than limits interpretive understanding. The strategies of grounded theory can be adopted without embracing a positivist leaning and recognise that the researcher creates the data and the subsequent analysis through interaction with the participant. Charmaz (2000) states that:

> [the] discovered reality arises from the interactive process and its
> temporal, cultural and structural contexts. Researcher and subjects frame
> that interaction and confer meaning upon it. The viewer then is part of
> what is viewed rather than separate from it (p.524).

Constant comparison and theoretical sampling enable the building of theory and provide conceptual analysis. Constant comparison engages the researcher in comparing elements (instances, cases, emergent categories, theoretical propositions) and enables the researcher to become sensitised to the similarities and differences and the full complexity of the data (Pidgeon 1996). It also allows the researcher to interpret and compare the individual's interpretation and subsequent representation in the creation of categories.

Theoretical sampling is the active sampling of categories which have emerged from the first sample. The researcher purposively selects theoretically relevant categories from the first sample with which to extend and develop the emerging categories (Bartlett & Payne 1997; Pidgeon 1996). The aim of theoretical sampling is to refine ideas, to identify conceptual boundaries and to locate the fit and relevance of categories (Charmaz 2000). Maines (1993) observes that data are narrative constructions, reconstructed from the original experience; they are not the experience themselves. In acknowledging this, the researcher comes to a construction of meanings which have been mutually agreed upon by the viewer and the viewed.

Constructivist grounded theorists develop categories which are consistent with studied life (Charmaz 2000). Coding is active and questions may be concrete or abstract, allowing researchers to ask further questions of and about the data. Data may be viewed again and again, and may be conceptualised and reconceptualised through the continuing interaction of the viewer and the viewed with the data. The analysis is rendered through reflective writing which encapsulates the perceptions of the viewed and the viewer, through narratives which evoke experiential feeling (Charmaz 2000). Figure 5.2 outlines the strategies and processes that I used in my research.

Developing your research design: some issues and ideas

I have discussed the key strategies of grounded theory method and I have outlined my own approach. My research aimed to explore and illuminate the experience of IL in the workplace and the processes and strategies that the participants employed in order to become information literate in the context of learning about work and learning to work. In this next section, I want to focus briefly on some issues and ideas which should help you when you develop your research design.

1. Do I do a literature review in a grounded theory?

Yes, but it should only sensitise you to the field. Research that adopts a grounded theory approach does not always start with a literature review. In the writing up of your research results, the literature may be dispersed throughout the study. This is because (as many grounded theorists argue) engaging with the literature at a very early stage of the research may result in the construction of artificial categories, or the forcing of preconceived ideas, which did not emerge from the actual research. The point of grounded theory is to focus on what emerges from the data, not what has emerged from the literature. The literature should provide you only with a store of sensitising concepts to use as background ideas. The literature provides you with a starting point for your analysis, not an end point (Charmaz 2003).

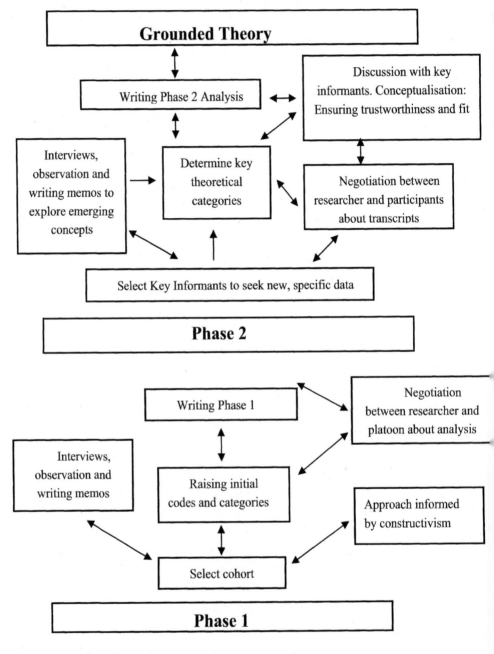

Figure 5.2 Grounded theory process used in firefighter study, adapted Lloyd-Zantiotis (2004,

In my version of this approach, I would suggest that you engage with the literature in order to understand what has gone before. Engaging with the literature will also help you to develop and refine your phase 1 questions. In this case, you should look only for original research, rather than conceptual or conjectural pieces which have been influenced by the original empirical research. As you proceed with your analysis, you will naturally begin to engage with the literature that relates to your own findings (you may even find as I did that you need to move away from the literature in your own discipline and explore other areas). Such findings are incorporated at a later date, most probably in your discussion when you compare your own findings with other research literature.

2. Is anybody out there? Locating the field and gaining access to a workplace

If you are planning to study a workplace, you need to identify a suitable industry or business. If you are employed as a special librarian, then you will probably find that you already have a workplace on tap. If not, then don't despair! You just need to do a bit of homework first. This will involve some preliminary research which can be done by locating homepages, finding the type of internal research which has been done (if any) and locating a contact person who can assist with getting your research proposal to the person with the authority to approve it. This should not be a problem, as most workplaces are interested in ways of improving their work practices and IL is increasingly being recognised as an important component of learning about workplace practice. Start with a phone call and then follow up with a specific research proposal which outlines the study, why you are interested in it and if possible the benefits of the study to the employer. You also need to outline confidentiality requirements and what provisions will be made to provide counselling for your participants if they require it. Make sure that you ask that a contact person be appointed who can provide you with information and help to facilitate the research process.

3. Whom do I choose?

The selection of participants for a grounded theory study is purposeful. This means that you will select people who will help to inform your study. In my own study there were twenty participants (fourteen in the phase 1 study and six in phase 2). The phase 1 study participants were located in two different places, which ensured that issues of bias were addressed. The second phase of the study was conducted to elaborate on the themes and perspectives from phase 1. A cohort of the original interview group was selected. This group acted as key participants through the remainder of the study.

4. How do I collect the data?

Permission has been granted; you have identified participants, prepared an information sheet which outlines the study and received their written consent. Now you are ready to start. Earlier in this chapter, I identified that grounded theory method is not really concerned with how you collect the data, just what you do with it afterwards. The nature of your approach (is it qualitative or quantitative?) will dictate the nature of data collection. Qualitative theoretical frameworks which advocate a holistic approach influence my research process. I need to engage deeply with the participants in my study in order to learn about how they connect with information in their work practices and how they construct meaning through their relationships. Therefore I used semi-structured interviews for both phases, group conversations which occurred through the fieldwork, the analysis and writing-up phases and observations of practice. I became a regular visitor to the fire station when the platoons involved in my research were on duty; this gave me the opportunity to develop a relationship with them. Many an interesting conversation was held about the research and findings during this period (always keep your tape recorder handy). This method and the questions were tested prior to undertaking the full study and are further discussed below.

It is important to keep your selection of participants to a manageable level. Unless you have funding, your study will involve you transcribing the data and if you use a grounded theory approach there will be a lot of this! This is an important process and I would encourage you to do this as it helps in the analysis by keeping you close to the study, allowing you to become immersed in the data from the very beginning. As a general rule, I found that it took between four and seven hours to transcribe each interview (which lasted between one and one-and-a-half hours or sometimes longer, depending on whether the platoon needed to rush off to a fire). Group conversations take a lot longer (anywhere from four to ten hours for the untrained typist) and it takes a fair bit of practice to deal with lots of voices. A good way to manage this is to ask the participants to 'name' themselves (as you might in a teleconference) and to avoid talking over the top of one another. Transcribing is never a straightforward process and you will find that you will have to wind and rewind the tapes and then read and listen to your transcription when you have completed to ensure accuracy. You will also need to incorporate any notes you took during or after the interview.

5. Piloting your questions (avoiding tears before bedtime!)

You have developed a set of questions which will help you explore your research focus. Now you have to test them. This process is often called a pilot stage and it is a critical stage of the process, so do not ignore it and do not rush it!

During the pilot stage of the study, you will test your questions with a selected group of participants. In my own study, I tested the questions and then I asked for feedback from the participants about the questions. This led me to rewrite a question which related to the use of information in critical situations because the pilot study participants felt that they did not really understand the question. It is advisable at this point to discuss the responses and your initial analysis with another person (preferably an experienced researcher who can provide you with an objective view of your process). Once you have tested your questions, and are satisfied that they will facilitate your exploration, you should proceed with the study.

6. Interviewing

The interview process for grounded theory research is often more like a conversation. You may start with your pre-determined questions, but will follow up with further probe questions to help participants to draw out and enrich their response. Remember that views, assumptions, beliefs and values will emerge that you could not have foreseen and you need to understand these, so it is important to follow these through to ensure that your developing codes and categories are rich and dense. Through this conversation the researcher is aiming at ensuring that they understand the meaning of the response.

In the first phase of fieldwork, I asked an experienced practitioner about how they learnt about fire fighting once they came to the fire station. The fire fighter's response listed a range of sources, including the physical senses. At this early stage I had not even considered the body as an information source. This response led to further questions about the relationship between the body and information and how this relationship facilitates the development of 'fire sense'. The role of the body as an information source was a common response by all participants. This led to further questioning in the second phase of the study about how the body acts as an information source, which led to its inclusion as a major category which supports the central category of *safety*.

In my study, the objectives for using a semi-structured interview technique were to:

- enable the researcher to grasp the importance of information and its use as it is understood and experienced by participants;
- allow participants to describe the affective dimensions of information use and information seeking in a particular context;
- enable the researcher to become sensitised to possible categories that may otherwise have been left undiscovered; and
- provide an avenue for the examination of the researcher's assumptions related to IL which sensitise this research.

The questions in phase 1 acted as the catalyst for subsequent probe questions, which enabled the researcher and the participant to negotiate understanding of the participant's experience. Initial questions related to the following topic areas:

- the value to the participant of information in the context of the workplace;
- the use of information in the workplace;
- affective dimensions of seeking information in the workplace;
- sources of information in the workplace;
- uses of information in routine and critical situations;
- the development of strategies (defining, locating, selecting and accessing) for finding information; and
- workplace barriers that hinder the information-gathering process.

The criteria underpinning the development of the interview schedule (series of questions) were that:

- interview questions were open-ended;
- interview questions were independent of the participants' understanding of what the term 'information literacy' means. This is particularly important, as this term has its provenance within the library and education sector and the use of the term may create confusion in non-educational sectors;
- questions were reflective of the IL process; and
- questions were able to provide a platform for participants to explore meaning and to allow the researcher to develop an understanding of the way in which information is used within a group to construct a framework for practice which is meaningful to all members of that group.

7. How can I ensure the trustworthiness of my outcomes?

The outcome of constructivist grounded theory 'tells a story about people, social processes, and situations' (Charmaz 2003, p.271). The contextualised and localised nature of the research focuses on the interpretation of 'a reality' as it has been negotiated through the researcher's and the participants' experiences of the interview process and rendered through the writing of those experiences (Charmaz 2003). Therefore, claims for the trustworthiness of the portrayal of people's experiences must be evaluated against claims for credibility, transferability and confirmability (Denzin & Lincoln 2003, p.35).

Claims for the trustworthiness of the collection, coding and analysis of research data were attended to by engaging the research cohort in all stages of the process, through discussion of the coding and analysis among the cohort, which led to confirmation of the data. Reading the transcripts while listening to the interview tapes verified the accuracy of the transcription process. This is really important even if you are doing the transcribing yourself.

The research material was also presented at conferences in which stakeholders (librarians and trainers involved in working with fire fighters and emergency services) provided useful feedback. A copy of a conference paper was also sent to a senior fire fighter within the New South Wales Fire Brigades service with requests for comment. Locating the research in two fire stations ensured that any bias that might have resulted from locating the research in only one fire station was minimised.

What can practitioners actually do with all this new knowledge?

For practitioners, the type of research approach that has been described in this chapter and the knowledge that it produces will help them to conceptualise IL in relation to their own settings (work, community or education). It does this by enabling them to understand how IL is experienced, how it is manifested and what its role is. In a workplace this is especially important because IL is not only made manifest through access to text or through digital sources but is also evident as social process among people, which facilitates learning about work and work practices (Lloyd-Zantiotis 2004).

The knowledge that can be gained from this type of research will enable practitioners to develop information-literacy programs which are relevant to the needs of the workplaces or communities that they support. These programs may not only focus on text, but may well include communication components or the highlighting of observational practices (as part of the information-seeking process). In developing an understanding of what information is valued in the workplace and how it is accessed, interrogated and used, librarians can tailor programs which specifically meet the needs of various workplace cohorts. For example, newcomers to the workplace need to engage with administrative and training sources of information in order to learn about the formal requirements of work. Experienced practitioners, who already have a deep understanding of the workplace and its practices, may need to move out of their own settings to search for and to connect with different types and levels of information and knowledge in order to deepen their knowledge and to enhance their ability to solve difficult workplace problems.

The knowledge that you gain will also help you to improve your own practices in delivering information-literacy programs. As a result of my own study, I now understand the importance of observation as part of information-literacy practice (observing the body in practice helps to identify information gaps in practice). I am also more aware of the way in which opportunities to access information are afforded by experienced practitioners, and would now consider IL sessions which include critical listening and story telling by experts as an important way of illustrating to students the range of information sources which exist within the workplace.

Your new found knowledge can also be employed by knowledge or information managers in the design of knowledge networks or systems. Knowledge is not always available in text form. Your research may reveal how information is located in the workplace, the types of sources which are used to learn about practice, what types of information are valued by practitioners and the way in which such information is accessed. You will come to understand the processes and practices that people use to locate, access and interrogate information in order to solve workplace problems in a specific context. In understanding how a person becomes information literate, you can work with knowledge managers to develop 'knowledge maps' to connect people in the workplace to information sources that may be physical, social or textual and which are relevant to their learning needs.

Learning about information from my own research

My own study had an explicit purpose: to explore the nature, meaning and manifestation of IL in the workplace. I did not find what I expected to find (a librarian's conception of information literacy related to skills, text and ICT), and for some time I struggled with what this all meant. What I did find deepened my understanding of what information literacy actually is, what it means to be information literate in the workplace and how the processes which underpin information literacy are made manifest in the workplace.

As a result of this research, I identified that IL not only acts as a connector and a catalyst for learning but can also be thought of as learning. The importance of social relationships, processes and practices within context were highlighted in this research. Information literacy in the workplace is not viewed as an individual process, but as a collaborative process between experienced practitioners and novices. In effect, IL is a cultural practice which is dependent on the development of social relations within the workplace. Information literacy acts as a connector between conceptual knowledge (accessed via text) and physical and social knowledge (accessed by the community of practitioners and through the body).

In coming to know how information is located within the workplace landscape and how to access and engage with it, probationer fire fighters begin the process of learning about practice and profession. Over time, as their relationship with information deepens, fire fighters become embodied in their practice and profession. Experienced fire fighters play a significant role in this learning by mediating and influencing access to information. The primary sources of the fire fighters' information universe are divided into social, physical and textual sources. Therefore the nature of information literacy and information practices differs from those that we see when the relationship with information is constituted through textual domains, as we see in the library and education context. When learning about practice and profession, the body and the workplace community become critical sources of information. This was highlighted throughout the study and directed me to consider the contextualised nature of IL.

So what do I do with this?

The concept of workplace information literacy that has emerged from my study may now be compared against other theories or frameworks for information literacy. In comparing different frameworks, I will now work towards locating the similar themes and processes of IL in a variety of contexts and attempt to answer questions about transfer. I am interested in the relationship between information literacy and embodied learning (how the body acts as an information source) and I have questions which relate to the community as information sources and the role that others play in facilitating IL. These new areas are drawn from the research data; I was not expecting them, but was delighted when they emerged!

This agenda for research will eventually enable those who have an interest in IL to develop understandings of the complexity of information, and to recognise that IL is not just a textual practice, but also a way of knowing the specific contexts of work.

Conclusion

This type of research approach will help you to improve and expand your provision of information-literacy programs, by allowing you to understand the way that information is used and experienced in a particular setting. The use of grounded theory method provides a suitable platform for research into what it means to be information literate and how information literacy is made manifest in a community of practice. Grounded theory method enables the researcher and participants to develop a shared understanding of the dynamics and real-life engagement of a community as they use information in the course of their work and workplace relations. The development of a shared understanding informs and enables the development of an interpretive framework, created through mutual construction and interpretation of the studied world.

References

Bartlett, D.P.S & Payne, S. (1997). Grounded theory – its basis, rationale and procedures. In G. McKenzie, J. Powell & R. Usher (Eds.), *Understanding social research. Perspectives on methodology and practice* (pp.173-195).Washington DC: Falmer Press.

Bateson, G. (1972). *Steps to an ecology of the mind.* San Francisco, CA: Jason Aronson.

Bryant, A. (2003). A constructivist response to Glaser. *Forum Qualitative Social Research, 4*(1). Retrieved April 20 2003 from http://www.qualitative-reseaarch.net/fqs-texte/1-03/2-03bryant-e.htm

Charmaz, K. (2003). Grounded theory: Objectivist and constructivists methods. In N.K Denzin & Y.S. Lincoln (Eds.), *Strategies of qualitative inquiry* (2nd ed., pp.249-291). Thousand Oaks, CA: Sage.

Charmaz, K. (2002). Qualitative interviewing and grounded theory analysis. In J.F. Gubrium & J.A. Holstein (Eds.), *Handbook of interview research: Context and method* (pp.675-694). Thousand Oaks, CA: Sage.

Charmaz, K. (2000). Grounded theory: Objectivist and constructivist methods. In N.K Denzin & Y.S. Lincoln (Eds.), *Handbook of qualitative research methodsy* (2nd ed., pp.509-536). Thousand Oaks, CA: Sage.

Denzin, N. & Lincoln, Y.S. (2003). Introduction: The discipline and practice of qualitative research. In N.K. Denzin & Y.S. Lincoln (Eds.), *The landscape of qualitative research: Theories and issues.* (pp.1-45). Thousand Oaks, CA: Sage.

Glaser, B. & Strauss, A. (1967). *The discovery of grounded theory: Strategies for qualitative research.* Chicago, IL: Aldine.

Goulding, C. (2002). *Grounded theory: A practical guide for management, business and market researchers*. London: Sage.

Lloyd-Zantiotis, A. (2004). Working information: A grounded theory approach to information literacy in the workplace. Unpublished Doctor of Philosophy thesis, University of New England, Armidale, NSW.

Maines, D.R. (1993). Narrative's moment and sociology's phenomena: Toward a narrative sociology. *Sociological Quarterly, 34*, 17-38.

Minichiello, V., Aroni, R., Timewell, E. & Alexander, L. (1995). *In-depth interviewing: Principles, techniques, analysis*. Melbourne, Vic: Longman.

Pidgeon, N. (1996). Grounded theory: Theoretical background. In J.T.E. Richardson (Ed.), *Handbook of qualitative research methods for psychology and the social sciences* (pp.75-85). Leicester, UK: British Psychological Society.

Schwandt, T.A. (2003). Three epistemological stances for qualitative inquiry: Interpretivism, hermeneutics and social constructionism. In N.K. Denzin &Y.S. Lincoln (Eds.), *The landscape of qualitative research: Theories and issues* (pp.292-331). Thousand Oaks, CA.: Sage.

Strauss, A. & Corbin, J. (1998). *Basics of qualitative research: Techniques and procedures for developing grounded theory*. Thousand Oaks, CA: Sage.

Strauss, A. & Corbin, J. (1994). Grounded theory methodology. In N.K. Denzin & Y.S. Lincoln (Eds.), *Handbook of qualitative research* (pp.273-285*)*. Thousand Oaks, CA: Sage.

Williamson, K. (2000). *Research methods for students, academics and professionals: Information management and systems*. Wagga Wagga, NSW: Centre for Information Studies, Charles Sturt University.s

Further reading

Below is a list of other references you might like to consult. These references provide information on the philosophical approaches to constructivism and on grounded theory method.

Berger, P. & Luckmann, T. (1967). *The social construction of reality: A treatise in the sociology of knowledge*. New York: Anchor Press.

Bryant, A. (2002). Re-grounding grounded theory. *Journal of Information Technology and Application. 4*(1), 25-42.

Corbin, J. & Holt, N.L. (2005). Grounded theory. In B. Somekh & C. Lewin (Eds.), *Research methods in the social sciences* (pp.49-55). London: Sage.

Crotty, M. (1998). Constructionism: The making of meaning. In M. Crotty (Ed.), *The foundations of social research* (pp.42-65), Sydney, NSW: Allen & Unwin.

Dey, I. (1999). Grounding grounded theory: Guidelines for qualitative inquiry. San Diego, CA: Academic Press.

Gergen, K.J. (1999). *An invitation to social construction*. Thousand Oaks, CA.: Sage.

Gergan, K.J. (1994). *Realities and relationships: Soundings in social construction*. Cambridge, MA: Harvard University Press.

Glaser, B. (1998). *Doing grounded theory: Issues and discussions*, Mill Valley, CA: Sociology Press.

Glaser, B. (1992). *Emergence vs forcing: Basics of grounded theory analysis*. Mill Valley, CA: Sociology Press.

Glaser, B. (1978). *Theoretical sensitivity*. Mill Valley, CA: Sociology Press.

Kendell, J. (1999). Axial coding and the grounded theory controversy, *Western Journal of Nursing Research. 21*(7) 43-757.

Kirk, J. (1996). 'Managers use of information: A grounded theory approach'. In *Information seeking in context, Proceedings of the International Conference on Research in Information needs, Seeking and Use in Different Context, 14-16 August*. Eds P. Vakkari, R. Savolainen & B. Dervin, Tampere, Finland, Taylor Graham, London, pp.257-267.

Lloyd, A. (2004). 'Working (in)formation: Conceptualizing information literacy in the workplace' in *Proceedings of 3rd International Life Long Learning Conference, 13-16 June*, Central Queensland University Press, Rockhampton, Qld, pp.218-224.

Marshall, D.E. & Rossman, S.B. (1989). *Designing qualitative research*. Newbury Park, CA: Sage.

Schwandt, T. (2001). *Dictionary of qualitative inquiry*, (2nd ed.). Thousand Oaks, CA: Sage.

Schwandt, T. (2000). Three epistemological stances for qualitative inquiry: Interpretivism, hermeneutics and social constructionism. In N.K. Denzin & Y.S. Lincoln (Eds.), *Handbook of qualitative research*. (2nd ed., pp.189-213). Thousand Oaks, CA: Sage.

Spradley, J.P. (1979). *The ethnographic interview*. New York: Holt, Rinehart & Wilson.

CHAPTER 6
Phenomenography: 'Follow the yellow brick road'!

Sylvia Lauretta Edwards

Phenomenography is an interpretative research approach. Its roots stem from attempts in the 1970s to better understand academic forms of learning (Marton 2000), and this remains probably the most common phenomena studied using this approach. Phenomenography is a qualitative approach to research. Interviews are the primary research method used, with most phenomenographic studies interviewing between twenty to fifty participants.

Phenomenography as a term is derived from two Greek words; 'phainemenon' which means appearance and 'graphein' which means description (Pang 2003). Put simply then, phenomenography is a description of things, objects, experiences, facts, events or trends as they appear to us. At the heart of the research approach is an attempt to describe the qualitatively different ways the phenomenon is experienced by the group.

The aims of phenomenography

Let me start with a simple phenomenographic example. Imagine a person and that the person is holding a half-glass of red wine. Now, truthfully answer the following question: Is the glass half-empty or is the glass half-full? If I asked this question in a room full of people, some would say the glass is half-empty and others would say the glass is half-full. 'Of course!' you are thinking, 'we all know that old adage'. Yet consider for a moment; is there another answer to the question? … Some people may say, 'Actually, I see a half-full glass of fine merlot!' and others may say, 'Wine! Never touch the stuff! I don't care how full it is, I wouldn't be holding it!'

This simple example is a useful way to explain phenomenography to non-phenomenographers. The wine glass example can be restated as 'what are the varying ways of experiencing (or seeing)' holding a wine glass.

In any group, large or small, there is only a finite number of ways of seeing, or experiencing, any phenomenon; and in this example this finite set of ways comprises at least three categories. In a larger roomful of people we may identify more than these three categories, but for our example the above paragraph has identified three worldviews of this phenomenon. They are:

- category 1: the glass of wine is seen as half-full.
  - category 1, sub-group A: the glass of wine is seen as a half-full glass of fine merlot.
- category 2: the glass of wine is seen as half-empty.
- category 3: the glass of wine is seen as something never to be touched!

The aim of phenomenography, then, is to determine the finite number of ways the phenomenon may be experienced by the participants of the research. One of the founders of the research approach, Ference Marton, when describing the approach, states: 'phenomenography is about the relations between human beings and the world around them' (Marton 1988, p.179). So next time you read a phenomenography article that states something like: 'The glass is seen as ...', you will understand that this is one of the ways this phenomenon is experienced by people in the reported study.

Now the only problem with the 'wine glass' example is that it may reinforce a common misunderstanding; that a phenomenographic category explains how one individual views a phenomenon. This is not true. What each individual sees is actually not important in a phenomenographic study. While the above three categories explain the different conceptions to you, the individual's personal experience is not important. Instead, the collective experiences of the group are considered in an attempt to find the distinctly different ways of seeing the experience. Again, Marton explains phenomenography as a way to understand the variety of human experiences of a phenomenon, by describing or mapping how these different experiences relate to each other, how they are similar in certain aspects of the experience, and how, where and why they are distinctly different.

> Phenomenography is a research method adopted for mapping the qualitatively different ways in which people experience, conceptualise, perceive, and understand various aspects of, and phenomena in, the world around them (Marton 1988, p.179 & Marton 1986, p.31).

In phenomenography it is important to understand that when I asked you the original question, I was not considering 'the glass' on its own, nor was I considering your view alone. I was looking for the way 'the glass' is experienced by all the different people holding or viewing the glass. Because the remainder of this chapter will use a teaching and learning example, I will rephrase this in teaching and learning terms. As the researcher I must look for the relationship between the learners and the object of their learning. In fact, as any individual being interviewed could express more than one way of experiencing, or understanding, the phenomenon, the individual is not what we consider. To borrow from an illustration presented by Berglund (2002, p.17), figure 6.1 may help you understand this perspective. The researcher's task is to consider the internal relationship between the subject, or the participants, and the object they are interacting with.

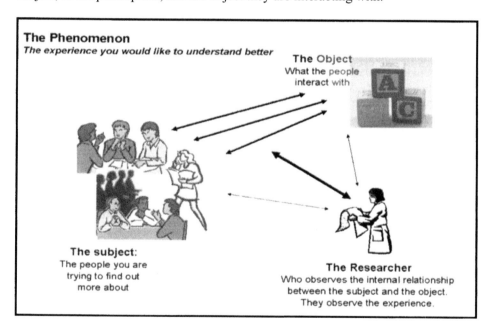

Figure 6.1 An illustration of phenomenography (Berglund 2002, p.17)

> Phenomenography rests on … a more reasonable idea [that] the object [may be seen] as a complex of the different ways in which it can be experienced (Marton 2000, p.105).

In the mid nineties, Bruce and Gerber (1995) identified the variety of phenomenographic studies in an annotated bibliography, which was subsequently updated (Klaus & Bruce 1998). These two compilations documented hundreds of studies conducted using this approach. Within the Australian and New Zealand regions, the most widely known phenomenographic studies are those of Christine Bruce, *Seven Faces of Information Literacy* (1997a, 1997b), Bowden and Walsh (1994, 2000) and Joyce Kirk (2004).

It is important to note that there is no prescriptive format to conducting phenomenographic research. When phenomenography is used, therefore, the procedure adopted is expected to be well documented and the individual variations in the approach used explained (Bowden 1994). Readers of phenomenographic studies may therefore be confused by the maze of methodological variations in the different studies. While this may seem unusual, some argue that this methodological variation is not only inherent but may be of value (Bowden 1994; Cope 2000, p.76).

> Phenomenography is not a method of itself. Although there are methodological elements associated with it ... Phenomenography is rather a way of – an approach to – identifying, formulating, and tackling certain sorts of research questions, a specialisation that is particularly aimed at questions of relevance to learning and understanding in an educational setting (Marton & Booth 1997, p.111).

In order for you to understand how to apply this research approach, you now need to understand the terms used to explain research findings from phenomenographic studies. After this explanation of terms, the remainder of the chapter will provide you with a step-by-step approach that will enable you to apply a pilot-sized phenomenographic study to your own work environment.

Phenomenographic terms

To return to the wine glass example, when we aim to describe to others the experiences we have identified, we are considering the glass, its contents, as well as the person's attitudes and their reactions to the glass. Therefore, the **conception** (or the different descriptions of the way the phenomenon is experienced) involves both the object and the people; it is the experience that is being investigated. People will do different things when they interact with the object in different contexts, so the use of conceptions may change in different contexts.

In phenomenographic studies, the findings are usually described as a set of **categories** and these categories describe the conceptions. In using the term conceptions here, it is important to note that some phenomenographers refer to conceptions, while others may use the term experiences, or even the term perceptions. These terms and their derivatives are often used interchangeably.

After completing a study, the researcher provides detailed descriptions of each category, so that the reader will understand what the category means, and which aspects are the central **focus** of each categories 'way of looking at the world'. That is, when you think about the distinctly different worldviews of the phenomenon that has been talked about by participants during interviews: What are the different things that this group tends to hone in on, talk about, and maybe even fixate upon? What are people focusing on when they interact with the object? Also, what is in the boundaries of their awareness, or even what are they not aware of? What critical element of the experience is understood or not understood? The descriptions of the categories then show you the primary focus of each experience, and explain the **structure of awareness** (Marton & Booth 1997).

Marton explains that phenomenography aims to describe the distinguishing characteristics of the variety of experiences identified in the research. It is this description process that enables us to define a finite set of categories that explain the essentially different experiences of the phenomenon, and provide our final set of categories explaining how and why they are interrelated.

> It is necessary to establish what are the critical attributes of each group and what are the distinguishing features between the groups. In this way we develop the set of 'categories of description', characterised in terms of the variation in which a certain phenomenon is experienced, conceptualised, and understood. There are logical relations to be found between the categories of description and, as they represent different capabilities for seeing the phenomenon in question in relation to a given criterion, a hierarchy can be established. This ordered complex of categories of descriptions has been referred to ... as the outcome space (Marton 1994, p.4428).

Having described the categories, then, we not only understand the distinct differences between each one of the set of categories, but we understand how the categories are related to each other, where the similarities in the description appear, and how and why they are distinctly different. In the wine glass example, for instance, two of the three categories focus on the contents of the glass. The third category focuses on both the glass and its contents as a whole, as well as on their lack of (or distaste of) the experience of drinking wine. So, after describing the categories, phenomenographers usually explain how the categories are related to each other, in the **outcome space**. This outcome space can be displayed as a diagram, image, a table, or in whatever way the researcher feels is appropriate to display how the categories map to each other.

Follow the yellow brick road: a phenomenographic case study

To illustrate this, I am going to provide you with a series of steps, or yellow bricks[1], to follow. For each step I will use examples from my own research into university students' experiences of web-based information searching (Edwards 2000, 2004, 2006a, 2006b; Edwards & Bruce 2002, 2004). The examples should explain some of the basic definitions and the research approach, providing you with the steps you need to undertake your first phenomenographic study. Please remember that this is a basic description; you will have to follow up the references to fully understand this method and apply it in practice.

Yellow brick 1: Identify the phenomenon you wish to study

Your first step is to identify what you wish to research. I began my study with a question. I wanted to know the different ways in which the students approach web information searching. This question was actually multifaceted; what I really wanted to know was:

1. what were the different ways students approach information searching when using the internet and/or the web-based library databases?
2. what are the different ways students learn to search for information when using these web-based resources?
3. if there were different ways of approaching web-based information searching, are there any levels of sophistication, or other differences, in information-searching behaviour approaches?
4. if levels did exist, are there any triggers to move from one level of searching sophistication to another level?

If you think about these questions the key to each of them is the word 'different'. If I wanted to know the different ways students approached or learnt about information searching, and identify any 'triggers' for moving to different levels, then the only method that could really provide me with the answers to the question was phenomenography, because it provided a way to identify any variation in the students' experiences, and in their searching behaviour. You see in phenomenographic studies the research goal is to investigate the **variation** in the way people conceive of or experience a phenomenon (Bruce 1999).

---

[1] The phrase 'the yellow brick road' comes from the children's book *The Wonderful Wizard of Oz* (Baum 1900). It refers to the instruction given by the Good Witch of the North to the main character Dorothy (a lost girl from Kansas). She is told to follow the yellow brick road to Emerald City to meet the Wizard of Oz who can help her get home.

Yellow brick 2: Design your strategy for gathering data

Having chosen your phenomenon and your method, you must now design your data-gathering process in some depth. The phenomenographic approach uses a series of standard research methods, such as semi-structured interviews, focus groups, and transcripts of these. Phenomenographers may also use open-ended written surveys. As we aim to identify the conceptions of each phenomenon, most interview questions are decided upon after a pilot study has been undertaken to test whether the questions will elicit the type of answers required to identify the possible categories. The main driving factor should be to keep in mind that the primary purpose of each interview is to draw out the interviewee's experience and understanding of the phenomenon.

Given people can express their conceptions of the world in different ways, your study must aim to develop a series of opportunities for the subject to show their different conceptions of the world. So, it is important to enable a dialogue between you and the subject to develop, a dialogue that helps them to explain their own conceptions of their world to you. As the interviewer you must probe to get to the real meaning of what the person is saying; what do they really mean when they make that statement? You have to get them to 'unpack' what they say. That is, you need the participants to carefully think about and explain what they do, and why they do it.

In many previous studies, like mine, the opening questions require either a pictorial or written response. This helps get the participant's mind focused on the phenomenon being researched and the pictorial and written sections allow you, as the researcher, to see the spontaneous association by the respondents with a later found category of description. Requiring participants to explain what they have drawn or written, as the first step in the ensuing interview, enables you to probe further to attempt to understand the experience from the respondent's perspective. It gives you both something to start talking about easily together.

Your remaining questions should be aimed at focusing the respondent to carefully explain their thinking, and carefully explain their individual experiences. You are expecting the participant to reflect on their real experiences, so you need to probe to find them. Asking questions like 'Can you explain what you meant by …?' should help.

In the period where you design the interview questions, and any other steps in the design of the data-gathering process, do not be tempted to rush the process. Phenomenographic studies really benefit from a number of small scale pilots running before the main study in order to try another way of formulating the questions, or to try another example of an exercise, and so on (Dahlgren 1993). My study used one pre-pilot and two pilot exercises. Furthermore, I used a series of data gathering rounds after the multiple pilots. The results from the first round of interviews, with third-year and postgraduate university students, were analysed in Semester 2, 2001. These preliminary findings provided the first categories of description (see yellow brick 4) and the outcome space (see yellow brick 6). The preliminary findings were then tested and verified during 2002 with a similar group of students, and tested again in 2003 with first-year university students. This was part of the original design. My intention was to ensure that when I finally had results, the findings could be confirmed and validated, and I could argue they held true across a range of university year levels and disciplines.

At this design point you should apply through your organisation for ethical clearance for the research about to be undertaken. This process is different in each institution, so you will have to make sure you understand your institution's progression for this very early on. Allow yourself plenty of time in the design process for ethical clearance. Once you have been ethically cleared to proceed, you can start collecting the data. You may also find some of the questions asked in the next section helpful for this second step design process.

Yellow brick 3: Collect and transcribe your data

Having designed your interviews, you now need to collect the data. Each participant should be welcomed to the interview, and the purpose of the research briefly explained. As the researcher you must emphasise to the participant that there is no correct nor incorrect response, but that you are genuinely interested in their individual experiences.

During my research interviews, I ensured that students were audio-taped, by two recorders. A research assistant was present during the interviews to help me to keep track of time and ensure the recording was completed successfully. The interview room was equipped with a computer with internet access, and this also had connections to the QUT Library and its databases. I asked the respondents to complete the written questions first, and then asked them to tell me about the answers that they had written. As they explained, I drew out further information on each aspect of interest. This was to check, and double check, that I understood the experience from their point of view, rather than from mine.

The reflective questions I asked during the interview required the participants to explain their information-searching behaviour by using a recent search topic that was familiar to them. That way they provided examples to me of what they did as they searched. By asking them about a recent searching incident, the 'experience' they reflected upon was fresh in their minds, so the data I gathered was clearly focused on recent events. It was also more likely that the participant would reflect upon everything of likely relevance. In addition, they were asked to explain how they learnt to search for information, and how they would go about learning what they needed to learn to search a new library database.

It is important to note that while my students were asked to comment on a recent search experience, that is, to talk about a recent phenomenon experience that they would remember, what they chose to reflect upon was their own decision. Most talked about a recent search for information for an assignment they were in the process of completing or had just completed. A small number talked about a recent social information need they were attempting to solve.

For example, in the following quote the student is remembering her unsuccessful search for marriage celebrants.

> **Int 1: 2 (p.1)** Ok. My recent search was on some information that I wanted to find, some very personal information. On civil marriage – I wanted to find out, because I don't know who to talk to, like to find out how does marriage work, registry marriage – so I went to the search engine Yahoo.com. I tried three different ones. First I tried … yahoo, I typed in different search engines – sorry, different key words, one was civil marriage, weddings, registry marriage, and simply marriage. But it didn't really give me the right answers because it just came up with … my results were like civil courts, registration of births and marriages, and … wedding photographers, wedding planners and florists. And there was a right one, but that was for NSW and Melbourne. But I wanted the one in Brisbane. I tried Brisbane as well but it just didn't work, so my search was unsuccessful.

The student later talked about how the search had taken twenty to twenty-five minutes when she decided to abandon the search. The next written instrument question follows below with her verbal answer included.

> **Question 2:** If you had to do a search for information how would you go about it? Using a topic familiar to you, provide examples of what you would do to find information? That is, please describe what you would do to search for information.

> **Int 1: 2 (p.2)** Exactly the same way I did in question 1.

In this example, as the interview progressed the student's searching technique appeared to be the same for both her social needs as well as her university/assignment needs.

After the interview, I asked each student to search for a specific information topic while they were filmed by a video camera. While they were filmed I asked them to talk through each thing they did, explaining why they choose each action, and what its purpose was (this is called a 'think-aloud protocol'). I found my role as the researcher in this particular aspect of data gathering difficult. I had to be careful not to influence the searching technique, and to only interrupt to ask for clarification when required, for example, 'You just selected a limit to Australia, why did you select that limit on the search engine?' It was really important that my voice and mannerisms did not in any way influence how they searched. So do not forget that as an observer you must ask for further information when needed. You must not be tempted to offer your participant help in how to complete something.

Finally, the participants were asked if they had any further comments or questions themselves, and they were then thanked for their time and efforts. They were also asked if they could be contacted for further information if required.

If you ensure that your interview reflection sections are voice-recorded and the searching exercise is video-recorded for research purposes, it is easy to have these reproduced. In my research, each of the interviews was approximately one hour's duration. The majority of the audio tapes and video tapes were transcribed by a research assistant into interview transcripts ready for analysis. It was then my task to manually check each transcript against the tapes to ensure accuracy.

Yellow brick 4: Analyse your data for significant differences in meaning

Once you have your transcripts, the next step is the analysis of the data. This is the hard part, and you may wonder where to start. You start at your transcripts and either use a series of different coloured 'post-it' notes or highlighter pens, or you can grab sections of text and add them to various statistical analysis tools. There are a variety of software packages that may be employed here (for example, Nudist or NVivo or other software equivalents). I have tried these but found that I lost sense of the whole if I broke transcripts down into insignificant parts in order to analyse them. I wanted to ensure I did not view the students as individuals, but kept the sense of the whole group. You will have to investigate this aspect yourself, and consider what works best for you.

In my case, I used different coloured highlighters, a few post-it notes in different colours and sizes, and I found using an MS Excel spreadsheet was also valuable for summarising this process. I reviewed the transcripts initially to identify the similarities and the core differences between the interviewees. Each respondent had their own way of approaching things, with some similarities and some differences in how they went about the learning process. Identifying the similarities and the differences is the first step in identifying categories; you are identifying the variation found in the phenomenon. From this, a preliminary set of categories was then drawn up based on the first round of interviews. I could then test it against future rounds and adjust it as necessary. Analysis, therefore, involved an iterative process of seeking meaning and structure.

> Commonly the following activities would be involved: becoming familiar with the data, identifying relevant parts of the data, comparing extracts to find sources of variation or agreement, grouping similar segments of data, articulating preliminary categories, constructing labels for the categories and determining the logical relationships between the categories (Bruce 1999, p.43).

From the analysis of the transcripts, I then developed the categories of description of the phenomenon. Over time, the categories were carefully considered, looking for any similarities within the categories. So, the analysis process is both a process of discovery and of construction (Bruce 1997a; Walsh 2000). The conceptions of each category are revealed through the data, in that way it is discovered; but at the same time, as the researcher, you construct the categories and define them all in terms of their meaning, their focus and eventually their structure (Bruce 1997a), so in that way they are constructed. The purpose is to clearly define each group's way of looking at the world. This careful analysis reveals any small similarities within the categories and is important to ensure that the categories truly reflect critical differences with regard to variation in the way of experiencing a phenomenon (Cope 2000).

From my analysis, a framework of four categories emerged which captured the variation in the students' different ways of searching for information. I found it easy to describe each of the categories using the words the students themselves used during the interviews, as they described their information searching experiences (Edwards 2004, 2006a). These spontaneous statements about information searching, made at some point in an interview, really captured an image of the experience, so I decided they were the simplest way to describe the experience to others.

- category 1: *information searching is seen as looking for a needle in a haystack.* If you consider the image described, a haystack has no structure and no form. It is not designed in anyway to make it easy to search. In fact, its absolute bulk and mass make it very difficult to search when looking for a small needle.

Students see it as imperative to understand the topic or they will 'never find it out there'.

- category 2: *information searching is seen as finding a way through a maze.*
  Students see information searching as the process, or the planning, of a search. They still focus on the topic, but there is a strong emphasis appearing on the choice of terms and synonyms. The image of the haystack is replaced by the image of a maze. If you consider a maze, it has both structure and a way out. That is, there is a feeling that if they persist through all the dead-ends they find, eventually the searcher will find the way out of the maze and achieve their required results.
- category 3: *information searching is seen as using the tools as a filter.*
  The imagery here is of a filter that will sift through the junk and provide them with a smaller set of results. Searchers tend to use the tools to help them understand the topic as well as to find the required information. The tools, therefore, can be used to enhance the understanding of the topic.
- category 4: *information searching is seen as panning for gold.*
  Students see information searching as similar to those above using the tools as a filter, or sieve, but this time they focus on limiting their results to higher quality resources during the search process (or, if you prefer, panning by the edge of the river for gold). While this category is similar to the previous category, their focus is on using the appropriate tools to find the primary resource for information. In this experience students actually talk about requiring primary rather than secondary sources of information.

Yellow brick 5: Analyse your data for significant differences in structure

Having identified your basic categories, by identifying the different meanings, now look deeper into your data and identify the differences within the structure of each category. This is an important step in the analysis process which should be reported in the findings. It is called identifying the **structure of awareness**.

Recently phenomenographic studies have begun to portray the structure of awareness for each category using an inner and an outer circle (Bruce 1997a; Cope, 2004; Edwards 2004, 2006a, 2006b). I should point out that previously the structure of awareness has only been described in words and tables (Marton 2000. Marton & Booth 1997; Marton et al. 1993). I think the image approach is a useful way to explain your different category findings to others.

To understand this idea, consider the mental image of the inner and outer circles in figures 6.2 and 6.3 (overleaf). These two circles, rimmed with the words 'internal horizon' and 'external horizon', are the limits of what is perceived within each category. These figures are over-simplified structure-of-awareness charts from my own research. The focus for each category is shown in the central white circle. The focus, very simply, is a way to describe what the participant's spontaneous centre of attention is in this experience. Around that, there are two circles, the inner circle is called the internal horizon, and the outer circle is called the external horizon.

In category 1 (figure 6.2) the internal horizon shows you that very little about the information environment, the various information tools, and the way they are constructed is understood by those in this experience. They focus simultaneously on the search topic, the search window, people who may be helpful to them, their favourite search engine, and they rely on consulting books (encyclopaedias, dictionaries, and so on) for further information to understand their topic. That is, they are keenly 'aware' of these things, and therefore in this experience these things are within the limits of the internal horizon.

There are also a few elements in the outer circle, the external horizon, but these elements are a little vague and hazy in this experience. They know there are other search engines, but they rarely use them, and they sort of know they are supposed to have a basic search strategy, but they do not usually think about preparing one before they search. The search strategy is more 'hit and miss', rather than prepared.

The large white area outside the two circles shows the confused and probably unremembered elements of this experience. Anything in this area, like information quality, wildcard use, Boolean use, and so forth, may have been heard of at some time by the student, but these aspects are not remembered and not used when they actually search.

In comparison, if you look at figure 6.3, the category 2 experience shows some of the elements from the external horizon circle have now moved into the internal horizon limits, and some of the elements outside, or beyond the external horizon limits have now moved within its limits, so they are now vaguely remembered and occasionally used in this experience.

So, put very simply, the outer and inner circles show you the limits of what is focused upon in the internal horizon, and what is vague and fuzzy in the external horizon. These images are charts that show what structural elements in each experience the group is aware of which is why they are referred to as the structure of awareness. It is important that you develop the structure of awareness for each

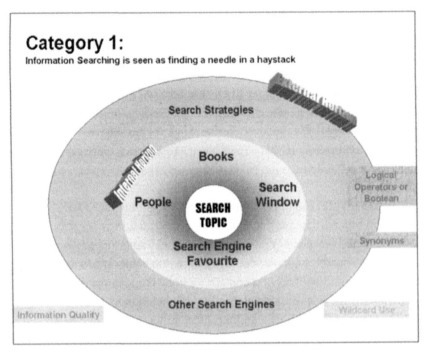

Figure 6.2 Structure of awareness category 1

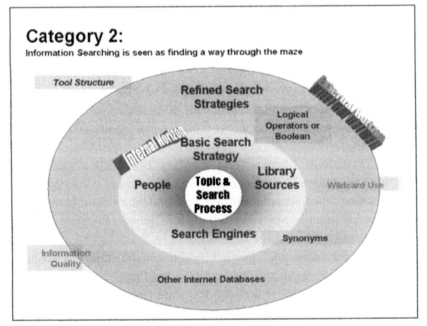

Figure 6.3 Structure of awareness category 2

category. Whether you use an image or words to explain your description of that awareness is up to you, but the structure must be described to others somehow. One point to remember is that if you do use the image idea, you must further describe the categories in words.

For my research, the final categories of description provided an opportunity to determine what may make web information searching approaches different. The structure of awareness highlighted the levels of sophistication that existed within these approaches, and, particularly important, whether curriculum design could be improved based on managing the students' experiences. It became clear what the different ways of seeing this phenomenon were, and where the evidence could be found for this worldview. Using phenomenography as a method, a clear understanding of the differences in the ways students approach web information searching, and in the ways of learning to search for web-based information was found.

Yellow brick 6: Develop an outcome space

You have seen from the previous two steps that the first output of phenomenographic research is the categories of description and their structure of awareness. The final output from the research approach is where you develop an outcome space to show the world your findings. According to Bruce (1997a, p.87), 'Outcome spaces are diagrammatic representations of the logical relationships between the different conceptions of a phenomenon. So, using my study as the example again, having identified the four categories, I then drew a picture of the hierarchical relationship between them. In simpler terms, I mapped them into an outcome space (see figure 6.4).

The outcome space is a way to show readers how the categories interrelate. If they are connected in any way, how are they connected? Is there any framework that makes it easy for the reader to understand any connections or lack of them?

> each category is a potential part of a larger structure in which the category is related to other categories of description. It is a goal of phenomenography to discover the structural framework within which various categories of understanding exist (Marton 1986, p.34).

In my study, the categories were in a hierarchical relationship (figure 6.4). In the first category, described briefly above (see yellow brick 5), the phenomenon experienced has no structure and no form (the haystack), and the experience described has no predetermined method to make the searching experience straightforward. The experience described appears to be frustrating for the students.

For instance, one of the students talked about people reinventing the wheel with every new database.

> **Researcher 1:12 (p.4):** So, how would you describe everything that's out there in regards to information. How would you paint that picture?

> **Int 1:12 (p.4):** [long pause] Oh it'd be pretty messy. It'd be a bit of a dog's breakfast. ... Like, because I say that in ... in ... in that you're chopping and changing all the time. Like, you know every time you go to a different database it's different truncation and it's different this and there's a different setup and you're reading ... so, databases have been on this planet for a really long time in some form and I just think why is there not a standard? Like why do people keep reintroducing this wheel ... and

> **Researcher:** reinventing the wheel with every new database?

> **Int 1:12 (p.4):** and a different wheel and I mean, well why?

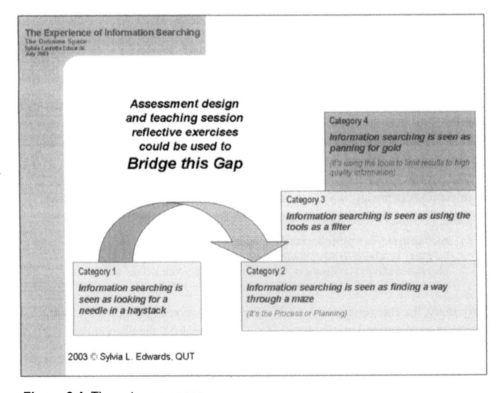

Figure 6.4 The outcome space

While this student perceived some structure in the tools she was using, she did not perceive any structure in the overall information environment. Which is a shame, as knowing this may have helped to make the experience easier for her.

In the remaining three categories, students described using the environment structure and the tool structure to help in the searching process. The categories can, therefore, be divided between those who perceived an experience with structure and those that did not. The next quote demonstrates how the experience is no longer frustrating. In this experience, it is both an understood process and an understood environment.

> **Int 1:6 (p.1)**: I had to search Internet definitely, but I also had to search some library to get a general information about (topic), and I also had to find the recent updates because the issue had to be current. So I had to search many many many fields, so I went to Internet first because it is the easiest way to get information that is Internet connected. … I prefer to go to Metacrawler because it is a metasearch engine. … Then I would probably go to the library and find books about (topic) and (sub-topic), because it is needed for general definitions.

This critical difference, perceiving environment and tool structure, forms the basis of the two columns in the outcome space. On the left-hand side, the student experiences do not perceive structure and therefore the environment is seen as unhelpful. On the right-hand side, the student experiences perceive the information environment as having a structure that is both helpful and, in the higher level experiences, proves to be a productive way to help compile their searching approaches.

The right-hand side of the outcome space also shows a step, or stairs, image. The outcome space displays the three categories on the right-hand side with each step being an enhancement on the previous experience. In this way, the image shows that the latter experiences include the previous step's experiences, which have been built upon and improved upon as the searching experience progresses. As I thought about what the students were describing, I realised that you could almost say that as the searching experience grows, the step drawn for that experience in the outcome space should be smaller, as the experience is much more focused for this group. They really understand the information environment; they are very 'balanced' in their approach to searching, so they don't need a 'big-sized step' to spread out on.

This step and stair image also shows that in many cases an individual who is capable of searching in the highest category level experience may instead choose to search at a lower level of searching abilities. That is, an individual capable of a more sophisticated search may begin searching by using one or two terms in the search window. Their ensuing set of results number in the thousands, so the individual decides to refine the search, using the environment structure and the search tool's structure to assist in the process. Something many of us should be able to relate to: you start searching, find thousands of results, so you decide to 'switch your brain back on' and start searching seriously!

Yellow brick 7: Communicate your results

It is now all over, 'bar the shouting'! So now you shout your results to the world. Other than getting your name published out there, there is another reason to do this. It has been suggested that phenomenographic outcomes can be said to be reliable and sound if:

- there is a demonstrable orientation towards the phenomenon ...
  through the process of discovery and description
- they conform to the knowledge interest of the research approach
  [and]
- they are communicable (Bruce 1997b, p.106).

Bruce suggests that the trustworthiness of the study can be established if the research meets each of these criteria. Ultimately, though, the only way to assess the value of the research is to report the results. If categories are not understandable and not able to be interpreted by other researchers, practitioners, and possibly the educators for whom the research is intended to enlighten, then the research will not be communicable, and a major flaw in the approach will be evident (Bruce 1997b). So telling the world your results is a way to demonstrate the trustworthiness of the outcomes. This type of communication of results was ongoing throughout my research, with numerous accepted journal and conference papers (Edwards 2000, 2004, 2006b; Edwards & Bruce 2002, 2004, 2006).

I decided to name my model for the final published work the Net Lenses Model, because I felt the outcome space electronic model (Edwards 2006a, 2006b) identified the *different lenses* through which the experience of web information searching (*net searching*) is seen (or viewed). Each student can search the net using any or all of the available four lenses.

So that is it, your seven steps up the yellow brick road are now complete! The next section gives you a few ideas about how the method may be applied in practice.

How can the research technique/method be applied to information literacy research?

Bruce has previously proposed four general directions for possible phenomenographic research (Bruce 1999, p.44). I suggest these are still relevant today. They are:

1. the study of ways in which people experience information and its role in society; such as the effect of technology on information roles and use.
2. the study of varying understandings of LIS concepts and principles; such as information literacy, leadership, and competence in the field of LIS.
3. the study of qualitative variation in the experienced meaning of LIS processes; such as indexing, abstracting, information retrieval and professional practice.
4. the study of qualitative variation in the experienced meaning of LIS elements; such as information centres, libraries, librarians and other information professionals.

Look at the list above, think about which statement lights a fire inside of you, or sparks a little bit of interest, and start researching!

Applying phenomenography in practice by using variation theory

There is, however, one more complicated concept which should be explained in this chapter: that is, variation theory. I believe this to be a central concept to understanding how phenomenographic research may be applied in practice. Using my own research as an example, after doing the phenomenographic research to understand the variation in the ways of experiencing web information searching, I then needed to extend my work and apply it in my teaching practice. To do this, I applied variation theory to my phenomenographic research findings to enhance the design of the learning environment in the unit I originally studied in order to encourage learning. So what is variation theory?

To explain, let us consider what teaching and learning research has found to date. Research now suggests that ways of experiencing something are essential to what learning takes place (Shulman 1986). In fact, Marton and Booth (1997) contend that qualitatively changed ways of experiencing something is the most advanced form of learning. Therefore, if we can describe learning as coming to experience something in a qualitatively changed way, we should also acknowledge that experiencing something must require the ability to detect or discern a new way of experiencing something. Discernment, then, is a significant attribute of learning

(Runesson 1999). However, that means if we are able to discern a difference, we must have experienced a difference, or a variation, from our previous experience.

Let me bring this back to a simple real-life example. A friend of mine, many years ago, suspected her three-year-old son was deaf, as he did not talk, he never reacted to noises, and he did not appear to hear when he was spoken too[2]. Cutting a long story short, the child was eventually operated on to insert grommets[3] in his ears to clear extensive blockage. After the young boy woke in recovery, he sat up in bed with a very puzzled look on his face. His eyes darted around the room a little, and then he put his hands up to cover both of his ears. He sat there covering his ears, and then uncovering them, and his eyes grew wider! The boy experienced something new; for the first time in his young life he could hear things he had no memory of ever hearing before.

Prior to this day, to this boy, everything in the world was quiet, and he never experienced a variation in sound. He probably had no concept of what the word 'sound' meant or, for that matter, what the words 'quiet' or 'noisy' meant. In those first few post-operative hours, the *focus* of his experience was to cover and uncover his ears. His central focus was on his hands and his ears, and in whatever way he then reasoned, his thinking focus would have been – 'I can hear'.

At the same time he discovered sound, this child would have found himself at the bottom of a very steep learning curve. During the next few weeks, his central focus gradually, and probably more than once, changed. Once shown sound, he began to perceive differences in the sound he heard. He learnt to distinguish between quiet, noisy or loud. He began to notice music, the noise that comes with wind and rain, traffic sounds, and even animal noises from his pet dog; but the biggest thing to perceive, and eventually learn to focus on, was language. He had to learn to distinguish the different tones and phonetics of speech, and how these tonal changes meant different words, or even different moods, on the part of the person speaking. He had to learn to distinguish between sounds and thereby recognise language, and from that recognition he could learn all the other social skills he had never known before. He then, and only then, could learn to talk himself.

This boy experienced a variation and discerned a difference in what he had previously experienced. He also experienced, during those first few weeks and

---

[2] This is a true story. The boy in the story is now in his early twenties. You will be pleased to know he leads a normal life and has normal hearing. The story has been used with the permission of the 'boy' and his parents.
[3] A grommet is a tiny tube inserted into the eardrum to allow air to enter the middle ear, see http://www.mydr.com.au/default.asp?Article=3205

months, a series of different elements or aspects to focus on. The boy slowly learnt to speak, and to catch up on the years he had missed in language development because of deafness. He began school a year later than most children, which gave him the time he needed to develop the language and social skills he required for school.

What does all this mean to you as the reader? Why have I related this long story? Variation is the primary factor that is needed for discernment, which in turn will lead to learning (Bowden & Marton 1998). In the above example, the boy noticed that sound had levels and tones. He also noticed that sometimes these are background sounds and other times they were sounds carrying language. From this example, we can see that to discern a difference, then, it is necessary to experience the variation from a previous experience (Runesson 1999). He simultaneously discerned other aspects of this experience (or phenomenon) against all the possible variations in the experience. He also changed his central focus throughout his experiences, and each of these experiences would show us a series of categories with a central focus that is essentially different in each experience. If we had studied these experiences as they happened, we could then use his experiences to understand learning to speak, and learning to hear, and so forth. We could use them to identify the variation in the experience of the phenomenon of learning to hear, or the phenomenon of learning to speak. We could then use those identified variations to understand what to do to help other children in similar circumstances to learn to hear or speak.

Variation, therefore, is a primary factor in encouraging learning. If we want to use variation to encourage learning, what do we need to do? In order to understand what should be varied in an environment to encourage learning, it is first necessary to understand the varying ways of experiencing something. Which brings us right back to where this chapter began – phenomenography, which is a research approach aiming to uncover the variations in an experience, and describe these variations as a finite set of categories.

In research terms, the identified categories reveal the space of the variation. To use the example from my research, the varying ways of seeing web information searching. They also reveal the central focus of each experience and the different dimensions within the experience that are simultaneously noticed, or ignored. Having found the variations, I could then use the research identified variations to develop exercises or change approaches in my teaching that will encourage people to discern another aspect of the experience, an aspect they have previously not discerned. I can now structure the learning environment to ensure students experience all the possible variations of the information-searching experience, and having experienced them, to also then discern the differences in those variations. By doing so, I am now able to design an environment that encourages learning how to search more effectively.

So the long story, and chapter, now ends. In case you are wondering why I used the yellow brick road analogy, on her travels, Dorothy learnt quite a bit about her travelling companions, and about herself. Most important, she learnt that there was 'no place like home'. I was hoping that as you travelled the road with me, and later with your own participants, you would find phenomenography felt like home! That's why I used this analogy. Good luck out there and I do hope you enjoy following the yellow brick road.

References

Baum, L.F. (1900). *The wonderful wizard of Oz*. Chicago, IL: George M. Hill.

Berglund, A. (2002). *On the understanding of computer network protocols*. Uppsala: Uppsala University, Department of Computer Systems, Information Technology.

Bowden, J. (1994). The nature of phenomenographic research. In J. Bowden & E. Walsh (Eds.), *Phenomenographic research: Variations in method.* (pp.43-55). Melbourne: RMIT, Educational Quality Assurance, Research and Development Unit (EQARD).

Bowden, J. & Marton, F. (1998). *The university of learning: Beyond quality and competence*. London: Kogan Page.

Bowden, J. & Walsh, E. (Eds.) (2000). *Phenomenography*. Melbourne: RMIT University Press.

Bowden, J. & Walsh, E. (Eds.) (1994). *Phenomenographic research: Variations in the method*. Melbourne: RMIT, Educational Quality Assurance, Research and Development Unit (EQARD).

Bruce, C.S. (1999). Phenomenography: Opening a new territory for library and information science research. *The New Review of Information and Library Research, 5*, 31-47.

Bruce, C.S. (1997a). *The seven faces of information literacy*. Adelaide: Auslib Press.

Bruce, C.S. (1997b). *Seven faces of information literacy in higher education*. Retrieved 26 August 2004 from http://sky.fit.qut.edu.au/~bruce/inflit/faces/faces1.php

Bruce, C.S. & Gerber, R. (1995). *Phenomenographic research: An annotated bibliography*. Retrieved 26 August 2004 from http://sky.fit.qut.edu.au/~bruce/anabib/title.php

Cope, C. (2004). Ensuring validity and reliability in phenomenographic research using the analytical framework of a structure of awareness. *Qualitative Research Journal, 4*(2), 5-18.

Cope, C. (2000). *Educationally critical aspects of the experience of learning about the concept of an information system.* Unpublished PhD, La Trobe University, Bundoora, Vic.

Dahlgren, L. (Writer) (1993). Lars Dahlgren on phenomenography [Video]. In QUT (Producer), *Qualitative research – Phenomenography: Theory and applications.* Brisbane, QLD: Queensland University of Technology.

Edwards, S.L. (2006a). *Panning for gold: Information literacy and the Net Lenses model.* Adelaide: Auslib Press.

Edwards, S.L. (2006b). The *Net Lenses model: Focusing on web searching experiences.* Retrieved 21 August 2006 from http://www.netlenses.qut.edu.au/

Edwards, S.L. (2004). Web-based information searching: Understanding student experiences to enhance the development of this critical graduate attribute. In K. Appleton, C. Macpherson & D. Orr (Eds.), *3rd International Lifelong Learning Conference, 13th-16th June* (pp.106-115). Rydges Capricorn International Resort, Yeppoon, Australia: Central Queensland University.

Edwards, S.L. (2000). You have provided me with a new set of tools and taught me how to use them: Embedding generic skills within the IT curriculum. In K. Appleton, C. Macpherson & D. Orr (Eds.), *Lifelong Learning Conference: Inaugural International Lifelong Learning Conference, 17-19 July 2000* (pp.95-101). Yeppoon, Central Queensland, Australia: Lifelong Learning Conference Committee.

Edwards, S.L. & Bruce, C.S. (2006). Edwards, Sylvia L. & Bruce, C. S. (2006). Panning for gold: understanding students information searching experiences, in Bruce, C.S., Mohay, G., Smith, G., Stoodley, I., & Tweedale, R. (Eds.). (2006). *Transforming IT education: Promoting a culture of excellence* (pp.351-369). Santa Rosa, California: Informing Science Press.

Edwards, S.L. & Bruce, C.S. (2004). The assignment that triggered … change: Assessment and the relational learning model for generic capabilities. *Assessment & Evaluation in Higher Education, 29*(2 Special Issue), 141-157.

Edwards, S.L. & Bruce, C.S. (2002). Needles, haystacks, filters and me: The IT confidence dilemma. In K. Appleton, C. Macpherson & D. Orr (Eds.), *2nd International Lifelong Learning Conference: Building learning communities through education, 16-19 June 2002* (pp.165-171). Rydges Capricorn International Resort, Yeppoon: Central Queensland University Press.

Kirk, J. (2004). Tumble dryers and juggernauts: Information-use processes in organizations. In P.A. Danaher, C. Macpherson, F. Nouwens, & D. Orr (Eds.), *Lifelong learning: Whose responsibility and what is your contribution?* Refereed papers from the 3rd International Lifelong Learning Conference, 13-16 June 2004 (pp.192-197). Rockhampton, QLD: Central Queensland University Press.

Klaus, H. & Bruce, C. (1998). *Phenomenographic research: An annotated bibliography 1997 supplement.* Retrieved 26 August 2004 from http://sky.fit.qut.edu.au/~bruce/anabib/indexsup.php

Marton, F. (2000). The structure of awareness. In J. Bowden & E. Walsh (Eds.), *Phenomenography* (pp.102-116). Melbourne: RMIT University Press.

Marton, F. (1994). Phenomenography. In T. Husén & T.N. Postlethwaite (Eds.), *The international encyclopedia of education* (2nd ed., Vol.8, pp.4424-4429). Oxford, UK: Pergamon Press.

Marton, F. (1988). Phenomenography: Exploring different conceptions of reality. In D. Fetterman (Ed.), *Qualitative approaches to evaluation in education: The silent revolution* (pp.176-205). New York: Praeger.

Marton, F. (1986). Phenomenography – a research approach to investigating different understandings of reality. *Journal of Thought, 21*(3), 28-49.

Marton, F. & Booth, S. (1997). *Learning and awareness.* Mahwah, NJ: L. Erlbaum Associates.

Marton, F., Dall'Alba, G. & Beatty, E. (1993). Conceptions of learning. *International Journal of Educational Research, 19*(3), 277-300.

Pang, M.F. (2003). Two faces of variation: On continuity in the phenomenographic movement [1]. *Scandinavian Journal of Educational Research, 47*(2), 145-156.

Runesson, U. (1999, 24-28 August). *Teaching as constituting a space of variation.* Paper presented at the 8th EARLI Conference, Göteborg, Sweden.

Shulman, L. (1986). Paradigms and research programs in the study of teaching: A contemporary perspective. In M. Wittrock (Ed.), *Handbook of research on teaching.* New York: MacMillan.

Walsh, E. (2000). Phenomenographic analysis of interview transcripts. In J. Bowden & E. Walsh (Eds.), *Phenomenography* (pp.19-33). Melbourne: RMIT University Press.

Further reading

Pang, M.F. (2003). Two faces of variation: On continuity in the phenomenographic movement [1]. *Scandinavian Journal of Educational Research, 47*(2) 145-156.

Shulman, L. (1986). Paradigms and research programs in the study of teaching: A contemporary perspective. In M. Wittrock (Ed.), *Handbook of research on teaching.* New York: MacMillan.

Walsh, E. (2000). Phenomenographic analysis of interview transcripts. In J. Bowden & E. Walsh (Eds.), *Phenomenography* (pp.19-33). Melbourne: RMIT University Press.

CHAPTER 7
Action research

Karen Visser

The focus of this chapter is to provide an account of a research project conducted early in the online era. The aim of the project was to support a large Year 7 cohort at a school in Canberra, ACT to become information literate in information searching, information management and information technology. The method chosen to underpin this research was a modified Kemmis action research model (Henry & Kemmis 1985) as described in figure 7.1. While the information environments described in this chapter may now be different, action research remains a vital, valid and accessible method of research for those engaged in information support.

This chapter aims to provide an account of a research method which:

- is well suited to those attempting to carry out practical research projects while dealing with the maelstrom of a busy workday,
- can be used as a practical scaffold to harness the many information gathering opportunities provided within information environments,
- is predicated on the fact that meaningful change will take place when practitioners become researchers,
- embeds research in the environment in which the practitioner is totally engaged on a daily basis, and
- enables researchers to gather, review and reflect on the data and information gathered for a project.

Often large scale or longitudinal projects need to be broken into a number of small research spirals if they are to have any chance of completion. Action research allows for:

- the project to respond to the opportunities and challenges of emerging information and communication technologies,
- a number of people to continue with a project, regardless of staff changes, and
- a number of concurrent projects to be brought together into larger programs.

The general idea

Students develop broad-based critical information literacy (IL) competence most readily when their educational institution becomes a *learning community*, rather than a community of teachers and learners. New information and communication technologies do not just affect student learning, they affect everyone's learning and everyone's teaching. This research project began with a general idea of 'getting kids to engage more with their library assignments'. It quickly crystallised into a clear and succinct goal: To design, implement and evaluate an information access program which would introduce and then enhance critical literacy of both teachers and students.

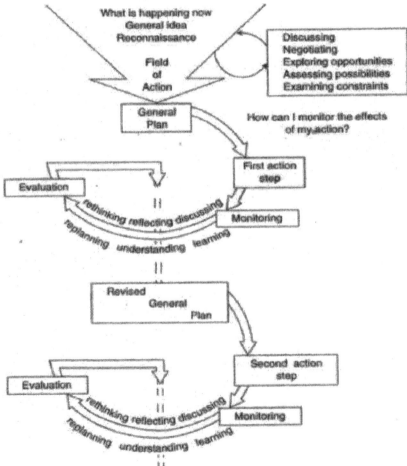

Figure 7.1 Lewin's action research cycle (Kemmis 1990)

Field of action

To be information literate, students and teachers need to be fluent across a range of competencies: information searching, information management, information technology and scholarly writing. Libraries and information environments offer a unique window of opportunity for researchers to build an understanding of how students of all ages interpret the task, gather information, decide on its relevance, manipulate and synthesise raw information into a response and then create their final assignment product.

The successive and relentless tidal waves of information and communication technologies washing into educational institutions and libraries had sharpened my awareness of how these new learning technologies have created a growing disparity between intended teaching objectives and actual learning outcomes. More important, teachers know well the interplay between learning technologies and IL but are occasionally at a loss as to how to incorporate these pedagogies into their raft of teaching, learning and assessment strategies. Information professionals have a unique perspective on the impact of these new technologies and are often a gateway for the infusion of these new technologies into the teaching process. At the time this project began, it had become obvious that teachers and students had vastly different understandings of the role information technologies played in resource-based learning and that there was increasing fragmentation of IL competencies. Some students were 'digital natives' but almost all teachers were 'digital immigrants' (Prensky 2001). It was clear that information professionals, such as teacher librarians, have a pivotal role in mediating or perhaps, 'translating', between these two groups.

There were three main outcomes expected for this action research project:

1. to create a cross-curricular information access program which would develop critical literacies in a variety of information formats for all Year 7 students *and their teachers,*
2. to develop a set of evaluation measures which would ensure the program remained relevant in successive years, and
3. to provide an opportunity to gather data and reflect on whether equipping teachers with IL skills makes a difference to student learning.

The general plan: a double helix

After several years of thinking, dithering, tinkering with solutions and experimenting with pilot programs, I began to see IL as a 'double helix'. It would only be successful if an IL development program for students was supported by an almost exact parallel program for teachers. This double helix concept reflects the fact that fragmented IL competencies of teachers and students prepare neither for effective, lifelong information literacy. The instant and widespread availability of online information means that students often plunge headlong into this rich and complex information world without considering the critical importance of ensuring the scholarly credence of their sources or the 'big picture' context offered through sequenced formats such as books. Teachers, however, often underestimate the importance of visual, graphical and interactive factors in the decision-making process when students define, locate, select, organise, present and evaluate information.

Assessing possibilities: choosing a research method

The problem and a goal were thus identified. Next a method was sought to find the solution or solutions. Action research was the key to moving from the goal to the changed situation.

Action research offers a stable framework which can be sustained over a long period of time. It is flexible enough to respond to rapidly changing information environments and can accommodate evolutionary responses to research findings as they emerge during the research process. One of the distinct attractions was that action research incorporates a concept of the researcher as part of the process – research is not at arm's length or bound in theory only. Action research is a simple, achievable scaffold which allows an individual or group to undertake self-reflective enquiry (Henry & Kemmis 1985) within their particular work organisation or occupational sector. The research outcome is to support practitioners to improve practice and reach specific goals.

Most practitioners have to manage their research while maintaining normal work duties and are seeking a workplace friendly model. The concept of formal documentation or publishing the results might never be part of the action research plan, in contrast to other research methods which may have contribution to the field of literature as the main outcome of research.

Defining action research

Since first developed by Kurt Lewin in the 1940s (Burns 1994), action research has acquired a reputation as a method that is particularly suited to building information literate communities of learning. Action research is sometimes simplistically depicted as a cycle where there is first an awareness of a problem, then some investigation, followed by action to remedy or minimise the situation, and after a time some evaluation to reassess the situation as it is after the change, before embarking on a new cycle. This view misses the most salient point of action research – that it is both a process of change (the action) and a process of learning (the research). Change not only occurs for the situation but also for the researcher. This new knowledge flows from *within* the action researcher through the change process to the organisation and hopefully, but not necessarily, beyond to contribute to the knowledge of the occupational sector.

The literature on action research reveals a number of core terms: 'cycle', 'reflective', 'practitioner as researcher', 'enquiry', 'process', 'learning'. These terms have a distinct attraction in that they imply a rigorous and energetic approach to problem owning and solving: 'I can achieve/change this' rather than 'This is a study on how this is done here'. It follows a cycle of planning, action, observation, reflection, change/modification/adaptation. The practitioner is integral to all phases of problem solving. Grundy (1982) refers to action research as a 'spiral of cycles' which an individual or an organisation can implement in order to effect incremental, manageable and sustainable educational, organisational or societal change.

Action research allows the researcher to carefully construct evaluations of change and opportunity. Henry and Kemmis (1985) list four main critical and self-critical records of improvement of:

1. changed practice,
2. how understandings about practice have changed,
3. changes to institutions, and
4. our understandings of action research practice.

These records can provide a reasoned construct of the largely unseen and misunderstood work undertaken by information professionals.

Action research must represent at least a triangulation of viewpoints: those of the broader educational umbrella (the institution or sector); the practitioner (action researcher); and the object of the change (in this case, staff and students). Other issues such as time, trust and expectations complicate the critical role of collegiate support in successful action research (Drennon 1994; Burns 1994). Practical or organisational change within educational institutions, even if directed inward via the self-reflective process of action research, cannot affect one person alone. Action research encourages reflection, review and evolution for all those involved as problems and possible solutions present themselves in different ways over time.

Over time, individual and institutional practice can become accepted and routine, with little critical reflection on what happens, why it happens or how outcomes are determined in reality. Action research offers a way to interrogate these well accepted practices with a view to turning 'normal practice' into 'exceptional practice'. This change process can extend over long or short time-frames, enabling the researcher to balance the demands of everyday priorities (their core activities) with research (a non-core activity).

Action research is perfectly suited to small- or large-scale projects. Individuals who see the need for change but may not have extensive resources or time to conduct a large research project can use the action research framework because the spiral of reflection can apply equally to a short-term, single-outcome project or a large, multifaceted project. The action research project described in this chapter may have consisted of just one spiral – that of the Year 7 IL project. It evolved into multiple spirals of reflection which combined to form a research roadmap for several complex multifaceted projects: the double helix.

In this action research project, three 'spirals' were used. Together they were a recognition that the IL competence of the whole learning community under consideration needed to be enhanced. This was a long-term project, involving multiple stakeholders who represented vertical and horizontal slices of the community (a spiral of spirals). In order to achieve the umbrella goal, a number of sub-projects (single spirals) were developed, lasting different periods over several years and starting at different times.

The spirals of figure 7.1 are flattened into columns in table 7.1 in order to easily add information about each step. It also acts as a quick visual planning tool. Each spiral was a separate piece of paper and was added to the planning board against a two-year calendar. It was easy to see the target dates for each stage of each spiral. If the target dates proved unrealistic, that flattened spiral was unglued from the planning board and simply moved down to the more achievable start date.

The outcome of the first spiral was to understand the strengths and challenges facing the library and to access the capabilities of its excellent staff. This understanding built the physical and intellectual scaffold to support the staff and students' programs which followed. The other two spirals reflected the concept of learning together as a community. The three spirals can be seen in table 7.1. While three spirals were used, this chapter will concentrate on the professional development spiral for the teachers.

Table 7.1 A triple helix

Spiral 1: the library	Spiral 2: the teachers	Spiral 3: the students
What is happening now? A well run, efficient, non teaching library General idea: prepare the physical and human resources to have teaching as the core business Field of action: library General plan: upskill library staff, review IT infrastructure and weed print resources 1st action step: determine age of collection and areas of weakness Monitoring, discussing, thinking, reflecting, learning: lack of balance between print and electronic resources Evaluating: purchase electronic resources to balance print Revising general plan: library staff needed upskilling with loading, using CD-ROMs 2nd action step: PD for library staff on IL competencies and technical skills associated with electronic literacy	What is happening now? Interest in incorporating IL and IT into teaching and assessment General idea: provide a range of IL and IT learning incidents Field of action: teachers of Year 7 English, Religious Education, Science and Social Science General plan: over 12 months develop skills needed to support the Year 7 IL program 1st action step: conduct whole school learning technologies survey Monitoring, discussing, thinking, reflecting, learning: whole school understanding of IL through whole school and department activities. PD program mapped against outcomes Evaluating: IL and IT are so interwoven they need to be taught as a double helix Revising general plan: need to provide different levels of training as wide range of competencies existed. 2nd action step: provide targeted PD for staff involved in Year 7 program	What is happening now? Year 7 not systematically exposed to the range of IL competencies General idea: develop a program which includes info searching, info technology, info management within subject context Field of action: Year 7 General plan: create a 4-term, 4-subject program of increasing complexity which develops info searching and info management skills for electronic and print sources 1st action step: Year 7 Science, science celebrities: target technical aspects of logging on, accessing cached internet, loading CDs, using table of contents and index in pre-selected books Monitoring, discussing, thinking, reflecting, learning: simplified questions, set up better record-keeping Evaluating: students and staff liked it Revising general plan: continue with program 2nd term but allow more time 2nd action step: Year 7 Social Science: target concept mapping and note taking from multiple formats and sources

Exploring opportunities and assessing possibilities: developing a successful professional development (PD) program

Radical, fundamental changes had to be implemented if teachers and students were to develop habitual critical information behaviours and high level IL competencies which were aligned with opportunities available through emergent information and communication technologies (ICTs). These changes could not be confined within the library walls. If information technologies were to be embedded in IL practice beyond the library walls and if this was to be permanent, pervasive and inculcated into normal classroom teaching practice, then it was vital that the theory underpinning the concepts of professional development and critical literacy be very clearly understood by all stakeholders before fine-tuning and launching the information access program.

'Knowledge management' is the term used to describe 'blending a company's internal and external information and turning it into actionable knowledge via a technology platform' (DiMattia & Oder 1997). How can this 'actionable knowledge' be fostered in teachers whose duties and priorities are increasingly demanding and diversified? Educational organisations, like their commercial counterparts, are recognising the value of having knowledge management principles in place to facilitate the growth of corporate knowledge and culture. In schools, the 'actionable knowledge' mentioned by DiMattia and Oder is of particular significance. Information technologies and the resultant changes in educational outcomes have forced teachers to re-evaluate and rethink both their pedagogy and their methodology. In-house PD with peer cohorts actively engaged in both teaching and learning about new uses for educational technologies is often a valuable, cost effective, quickly transferrable and easily implemented opportunity for change.

Reconnaissance: exploring the literature

The following section explores the body of literature related to professional development (PD) for teachers. Two aspects will be explored specifically, and these relate to how the theories of best practice in this field were applied to further the goal of a school-wide culture of IL in this particular project:

1. the broader educational contexts for PD, and
2. critical factors for successful transfer of theory to classroom practice.

Broader educational contexts for PD

Professional development is taken in the context of this chapter to be adult learning within a specific employment context and with outcomes relevant to those specific workplace goals. Professional development can be an opportunity to develop new attitudes and beliefs, which were not current during preservice education, and/or to augment ongoing practice.

During the past decade, the need for professional development in education has been driven largely by three factors:

1. the watershed impact of information technology,
2. the need to understand and enact reforms which promote new and more appropriate goals for education (Hixson & Tinzmann 1990), and
3. the pedagogical move from 'replication to reflection' (Reconceptualising professional teacher development 1995).

All three of these factors are fundamental to the development of IL for both teachers and students.

Critical factors for successful transfer of theory to classroom practice

This project sought to create a learning community, in which the responsibility for building IL sat with all staff and in all disciplines and was not seen as the province of the library. Change in classroom practice is most likely to occur after a PD program or session if one or more of the following factors are present:

- context fits the individual's situation and needs. For this project, it meant allowing time for skill development to become part of the teacher's personal routine and then part of classroom practice. Also, the skills and content introduced need to be applicable to the teacher's own class, and within the resources, restrictions and opportunities of their teaching space. The teachers' spiral began six months before the students' spiral and sessions were always conducted in the classrooms, computer labs and library which the staff would use in their work.
- concept fits into the broader educational goals of the institution. Showers et al. (1987, cited in Butler 1999) estimated that when dealing with complex methodologies or skills (such as for information literacy) teachers need 'about 25 teaching episodes' for real transference to take place. The enthusiastic, long-term support from the school executive was crucial. This support was part of the original library preparation spiral.
- content fits within the theory of adult learning. All sessions were constructivist, for example, the PD session 'How to turn the Evil House of Cheat into the

Temple of Learning' gave the theory of how to evaluate websites, then the teachers did an evaluation exercise using a topic from the 'Pole to Pole' Year 7 geography course, which was being taught two weeks after this exercise.

- pedagogical methods are clearly articulated. Teachers tend to discuss what they are teaching, but rarely how they are teaching it. Scheduling PD across subject groups or by staffrooms can spark the 'how'. In order to spark this conversation, the program and thus the PD was conducted across groups of kindred spirits – departments, staffrooms, circles of acquaintances – working through theory and practice.
- information processing draws upon existing knowledge and experience. Adults have a vast 'bank' of previous experiences and knowledge that can be called upon to create connections to reinforce new knowledge (Fournier 1996). Much of the subsequent success of this program came about because the preparation PD was centred on the experiences of the individual teacher and embedded within the ethos of the college culture.
- the ethics of action and enquiry are married together. Each preparation session started with the theory but moved quickly on to 'how can we, will we, could we do this in my classroom and the library today, tomorrow?'

Determining the best PD support for the Year 7 information access program

Several key factors needed to be woven into the fabric of the spiral to prepare the teachers who would be involved in the student IL program. The professional development activities and strategies took multiple forms and so they were referred to as 'incidents'. Each preparation incident was underpinned by one or more of the following factors:

Knowing your clientele

The college where this action research project took place is a school with a buoyant optimism for the future. Academic results are improving and the physical infrastructure is systematically being refurbished. Staff can see that IT is integral to the learning futures for the school and also that their own IT skills are in need of development. This created a positive atmosphere for PD which supports the integration of IT and literacy.

Ensuring executive support

The school executive allocated time and funding for presenters and materials and ensured that PD was given 'top down' credence, especially if the PD concerned IL or IT. Repeatedly raising the possibility of a whole-year program ensured that the executive were aware that up to twenty-eight teachers (more than one-third of the staff) would be learning to incorporate information technologies and IL into their classroom activities.

Choosing the best messenger

Rogers' model of change found that 'a person's choice to adopt some new tool is more dependent on who shares the news of the tool, than how well the tool can actually assist that non-user' (Rogers 1995, cited in Clarkson 1998). Interestingly, he also found that the 'opinions of the most innovative members of any social system are often not trusted by most of their peers'. Choosing a range of teachers, including change makers and traditionalists, to deliver PD was important if teachers were to be willing to risk new techniques. Including 'less stellar' peers to lead PD sessions often resulted in teachers feeling that 'OK, if my colleague took the risk, I can!' The program was couched in terms of a community of learners on a learning journey.

Choosing the best song

Rogers (1995) found that, regardless of the employment context, similar proportions of people fall into categories of readiness to take on innovations. Table 7.2 compares Rogers' findings with my findings from a survey conducted in the College to determine the competency levels for simple IT skills of the College teachers. This was vital because having a clear idea of the individual practices of staff using various applications and understanding their fears would inform any future decisions about how to structure the PD outcomes and program. The data were gathered using a short learning technologies survey completed by 104 staff at the end of a regular whole-of-staff meeting.

Rogers' criteria were adapted to suit the College environment. For example, those who would equate to Rogers 'innovators' criteria were determined by them self identifying that they would be prepared to help other teachers learn IL skills. The 'innovators' group responded positively to the statement: 'I will lead a PD session in [e.g., word-processing.]'. The premise was that if they were comfortable and knowledgeable enough to teach these skills to their peers, this group had already explored the possibilities of these applications and hence were likely to be innovators in their use of such technologies. Similarly, those in Rogers' 'laggards' category equated to those who identified themselves as never having used common applications such as word-processing, internet or email. While these categories reflect adaptations of technologies available early in the era of mass availability of educational technologies, the same remains true today. The categories would be the same but the instruments used to classify users into Rogers' criteria would perhaps include: writing a blog, contributing to a wiki, creating static/interactive websites, using GPS and so on. Column 1 in table 7.2 shows Rogers' original criteria with column 2 showing how these criteria were renamed for the survey. Columns 5-8 illustrate the range of ICT adoption by teachers.

Table 7.2 Comparison between Rogers' criteria and College survey

Column 1	Column 2	Column 3	Column 4	Column 5	Column 6	Column 7	Column 8
Rogers' criteria	College survey criteria	Rogers' average	Teacher average	Word-processing	Using CD encyclopedias	Using the internet	Using email
Innovators	Will lead PD	2.5%	8%	12%	6%	7%	6%
Early adopters	Use in classroom	13.5%	13%	26%	11%	12%	2%
Early majority	Personally skilled	34%	34%	40%	31%	29%	37%
Late majority	Basic skills	34%	32%	18%	38%	37%	34%
Laggards	Never used	16%	12%	3%	13%	14%	19%

It is interesting to note that Rogers' results (column 3) are strikingly similar to those of the averages revealed in the College's learning technologies survey (column 4). This confirmed Rogers' idea that any population is made up of people with different levels of skill, but, more important, with different levels of adoption. It was thus necessary to provide a range of PD sessions. Sessions were offered for different levels, with titles such as: 'Putting your toe in the water with Google' for new users, up to 'The Google lifesavers certificate' for those with significant experience in using the internet. These sessions aimed to inform and to review how teachers can challenge their students to refine search strategies and critically evaluate the information students retrieve when searching the internet.

Changing the tune
Sparks and Loucks-Horsley (1989; cited in Butler 1999) identify that there are five different staff development models for teachers. In some way all these models were called into play in preparation for the program.

- school development process – the principal initiated an IT working group early in this action research project. The PD IT working subgroup has a brief to find a number of ways in which the IT benchmark level of skills for the college could be increased. This was a wonderful opportunity to dovetail the IL program with wider school initiatives.
- training – several early PD sessions were designed to develop often simple but widely applicable IT skills, such as techniques for efficient file storage and retrieval for groups.
- mentors – the teacher librarian models the information process with students in the classroom before they come to the library. The teacher is not a passive observer but the lesson runs as a duet, or partnership.
- self-determination of needs – as their skills developed, teachers were asked to take a more proactive role in the IT component, such as moving with the same group of students as they rotated through the four resource formats (print, CD, video and internet), rather than staying with print resources as the groups rotated.
- inquiry such as action research – three fellow teachers involved in the program were engaged in Masters' degrees, one by project work. This has created a sense of 'camaraderie in adversity' and generated much discussion around the role of information and communication technologies in teaching and learning.

First action step: creating IL PD programs for teachers

Once the theoretical framework for the PD program was understood, the next part of the action research model was to begin the first action step. Even though it may appear that this is one 'loop' of the action research spiral, in reality each PD session and interaction with the classes formed a mini-loop, in that each interaction was planned > delivered > evaluated > modified before the next session took place.

Each PD session fused IT and IL and this meant that it had to take into account several overarching factors. Each session:

1. introduced or incorporated different learning situations,
2. involved long-term and complex change which was backed by teachers learning new theories and new practices, and
3. recognised that for many teachers at that stage IT was the stumbling block to the adoption of IL into their classroom strategies.

Incorporating different learning situations

Information literacy will only be accepted as integral to research-based learning if it is seen as part of a general schema which caters for many learning situations. According to Butler (1999), there are three types of learning situations and his schema adapts perfectly to IL. Table 7.3 shows how the program mirrored a variety of learning situations.

Table 7.3 Product, process and function of learning

Learning situation	i.e.	e.g.	PD session
where the emphasis is on the *product* of learning	where the outcomes are described in terms of acquiring skills or knowledge	navigating the library catalogue – balancing print and virtual collections: *This is your life*, English term 4	Getting more out of the library catalogue
where the emphasis is on the *process* of learning	where the outcomes are described in terms of how learners solve their information needs	understanding how each of the six steps in the information process can be used to create a framework for meeting many information needs: *Discovering the dreaming*, term 2	Computers, research and students
where the emphasis is on the *function* of learning	where the outcomes are described in terms of learner motivation	applying different learning theories to achieve lifelong learning: *The book and how to use it*, RE term 3	Each teacher developed their own assignment task in response to the target IL skills

Learning: using new theories and practices

In order that these new theories become practice the PD should:

- be grounded in sound, no-fad theory – the consistency of a six-step information process model commonly used across several Australian states adds credence to the permanence of IL as an integral component in developing critical thinking as an overarching outcome in all educational institutions.
- build a skill base so the use of learning technologies becomes routine and teachers have a toolkit of strategies to get it working. These skills include

locating appropriate online resources with ease – a complex but endlessly repeated task in teaching.
- be constructed so that the teacher experiences the learning technologies as a learner either before the unit starts or during learning with their students – preparation sessions were held where the program would take place: computer lab, library, and so on.
- recognise the fears and phobias of those less technically able. Clarkson gives three options – resistance, renaissance or retirement (Clarkson 1998) – as the only choices open when weighing up response to technology. All sessions were sequenced to have renaissance as the preferred outcome!
- locate the point in the learning technologies cycle. Learning technologies are introduced in phases, not as a smooth progression. The first phase is the introduction, then adoption by one or two enthusiasts, followed by leadership by a coordinator. This can lead to changes in the curriculum and finally the infusion of the learning technology throughout the organisation. The same phased approach can be applied to IL, in that the first spiral was the introductory phase, the second and third spirals the consolidation and transfer phases.

Removing the IT stumbling block

Many teachers were successful in their own education because they were able to follow the *define, locate, select, organise, present and evaluate* model (or some other) of IL without even recognising that they had these skills. For many teachers the information process part is easy. It is the overlay of IT that is the problem. Butler (1999) devised a list of factors critical to the successful integration of IT into teaching:

1. the focus is school improvement rather than personal professional development. In our case, after a six-year trial the school formally committed to the optional laptop program and therefore all teachers were now engaged in teaching classes which had easy access to the vast plethora of online information within the walls of the classroom.
2. content is concrete and aimed at developing specific skills rather than just introducing new concepts. Subject content is simple so that students can concentrate on developing specific IL competence rather than struggling with unfamiliar content.
3. the theoretical basis or rationale is part of the content about new skills. Specifying the theory behind IL (i.e., the information process and the impact of

information technology) puts the new skills in context of both a continuum and the subject.

4. professional development focuses on job – or program – related tasks faced by teachers. All IL work is within a framework of subject-related tasks.
5. there are clear, specific goals and objectives related to implementation. All teachers and students are aware of the goals, because teachers determine the outcomes and students transcribe them into their own words or must self-evaluate.
6. content is research-based and is tied to student performance. Student performance is assessed on each research task.
7. the use of new behaviours is made very clear, and applicability to individuals' home situations is understood. Individual access to IT (if the student has their own laptop, no/personal/shared computer at home, no/dial-up/broadband internet access at home) is factored into each IL skills development experience.
8. between-workshop content, such as observation, visitation and discussion, is included to facilitate implementation. During the PD training before each program one item for discussion is how teachers can reinforce IL before, during and after the program.

Evaluation: keeping on course

The type of evaluation which accompanies most PD for teachers is usually a 'tick and flick' form at the end of the session. Often the evaluation is verbal and anecdotal or simply not done. In this action research project, both summative and formative evaluation techniques were intensively used over the second and third spirals. They were administered in a number of different ways: formal and informal, verbal and written, anonymous and named. Formative evaluation is most effective when taken at the point of delivery. This type of formative feedback allows for immediate adjustment of content, delivery mode and/or venue if the outcomes are not being reached. After the first class it was clear that the questions were beyond the scope of the group and the questions were modified for the following classes.

A number of different evaluation pro formas were used during the teachers' PD spiral. The questions below are taken from an evaluation form used throughout the last part of the spiral where IL was being transferred to the responsibility of the classroom teachers. The use of this form over four terms with four different subjects and twenty-two teachers gave a valuable longitudinal study. This form included both quantitative tick boxes and qualitative free text responses. Examples of qualitative questions appear in tables 7.4 and 7.5.

Table 7.4 Reflective evaluation for teachers

Qualitative questions for teachers
1.   What was the most successful aspect of this program for you as a teacher?
2.   What wasn't successful? Please give an indication why it didn't work for you.
3.   Did you follow up what we did in the library with any activities in the classroom? If so, what sort of things did you do? If not, can you tell us why the work didn't transfer to the classroom?

Table 7.5 Triangulation of reflection

Students, teachers and the action researcher responded to qualitative questions such as appear after each spiral: Asking the same evaluation questions to all three groups enabled triangulation of the research.
1.   How well do you feel you (your class, this class) achieved the outcomes of this assignment?
2.   Since the start of year, when I (my class, this class) do assignments I have improved most in …
3.   When I have to do assignments one thing I (my class, this class) find hard to do is …

Regardless of where it was used in the spiral, each different *pro forma* was designed to meet a range of criteria, drawn from the reflective process of action research. As the project evolved, practical applications became evident from a growing understanding of theories and research of the literature. These criteria are 'home-grown' from experiences gained through the evaluative process at the end of each spiral:

- extend over time – this gives time for the participant to practise, reflect and internalise the theory. Summative evaluation, taken either immediately at the end of a course or after a period of time, may result in the whole course being redesigned.

- zoom out to the big picture – teachers are more likely to proceed with new practices if they see positive results in their students through increases in scores and better quality portfolios.
- include both statistics and free text – outcomes need to be measurable in concrete terms but also need qualitative data. Statistics will give feedback only within the outcomes determined by the designer of the evaluation form. Participants also need to be given the opportunity to express concerns and raise issues which are part of their agenda.
- be tied to the organisational context – research shows that organisational climate strongly influences both initial and continued use of an innovation (Cook & Fine 1997).
- have easy to see goal posts – participants need to be able readily to identify outcomes and standards at the outset of any PD session or program.

Evaluation: multiple perspectives

If evaluation of professional development is to be valid and robust it must be constructed to take into account several perspectives. These perspectives should include the user, the instructor, the administrator and the organisation (Recker & Greenwood 1995). In this case, the triangulation of perspectives was gained by reflections from:

1. the user (i.e., the teachers learning new theories and practices in PD sessions and students of those teachers who were involved in the project);
2. the administrator/instructor (i.e., the action researcher and teachers using the theories and practices learnt in the PD sessions); and
3. the organisation (i.e., the PD committee and executive).

Regardless of the perspective, the evaluation instruments all conformed to the following:

- they were quick and easy to use;
- they provided a number of opportunities for free text responses;.
- anonymity and/or confidentiality were assured;
- They were flexible in design and able to be changed easily as the project evolved. This was especially important as the project moved from teacher focus to student focus;
- questions were aligned closely with the intended learning outcomes of the activity;

- responses were sought on multiple perspectives: personal, philosophical, pedagogical;
- evaluations were administered without substantial overhead in either cost or time (careful formatting allowed speedy tabulation and data entry, results were stored on spreadsheets); and
- a standard core of questions allowed for comparisons over time and so different contexts, perspectives and content could be compared.

The results of the surveys built up a picture of substantial change in the use of technology in teaching and learning over the period of the project. The results were tabled and discussed at executive, subject coordinators and general staff meetings.

Reflecting: the core of action research

Action research proved a remarkably efficient way to scaffold this two-year journey into IL. The core terms of action research are: 'cycle', 'practitioner as researcher', 'enquiry', 'process', 'learning' and 'reflective'. The following section summarises how, by the end of the project, a deep understanding of these core terms led to a new level of awareness, in both the action researcher and the learning community, of how to effectively build an information literate learning community.

Cycle – the cyclic concept of action research meant that there was a mechanism to design, implement, evaluate, 'mend or discard' and redesign each phase of the journey before moving on to the next action step. Since the evaluation was thorough and immediate, potential difficulties were limited and not repeated. Each spiral took us closer to our goal.

Practitioner as researcher – blending the roles of researcher and practitioner strengthens both components. The researcher role enforces academic rigor and can provide the framework to bring the project to fruition. The practitioner knows the research setting intimately and can create and capitalise on research opportunities. Action research grounds academia in reality.

Enquiry –in action research enquiry has two meanings: conducting a formal literature review and encouraging a questioning of the status quo. Reading widely and deeply in the literature surrounding IL cemented the underpinning theories of professional development for teachers from the instructor's point of view, rather than the consumer's. The approach was enlightening and has been used extensively in subsequent positions and projects. Each spiral begins with constructing a goal and in order to do this effectively careful questioning of outcomes and current practice is needed.

Process – action research provides an easily accessible process for the researcher to follow. The outcomes and evaluations were analysed and remedial action taken. Problems were solved or minimised, corrections were made, and subsequent outcomes were clarified. The process of action research has become a habitual scaffold or guide for consequent minor and major projects.

Learning – the most important part of this action research project was the intense learner/researcher-centered focus of the spirals. It was a truly enlightening process to reflect on managing priorities and goals, accepting that change was not as fast as I wanted it to be, building a solid support base for change, calling for help, researching at work while working at research, learning to write in a way which maximised the impact of research findings, asking questions and challenging the norm, and finally celebrating the successes and keeping the disappointments in perspective.

Reflective – the action research method requires reflection and review at the end of each spiral. These repeated opportunities to think deeply about the complex interrelationships between teaching, learning, IL and information technologies, meant that the nature of those connections became more evident with each spiral. It is empowering to be confident about what you have done, exactly how and why you did it, and knowing how to effectively construct and evaluate the effects of future initiatives.

Does action research work for information environments?

The steps of the action research spirals fit well within information environments, which offer a plethora of opportunities for formal and informal observation, reflection of effectiveness through assessment instruments, statistical analysis and predictable yearly rhythms which can be used to time the start of the next spiral. Educational settings combine well with information environments because modifications to the original plan can be quickly implemented for the next cohort of a multiple group, such as the seven Year 7 classes engaged in each aspect of this action research project.

A key aspect of action research is the literature review which underpins the theoretical strength of projects. Since action research is a method with a fifty-year track record, there is a readily accessible and strong body of literature to which the practitioner/research can refer. Much of the literature can be quickly located through freely available scholarly publications as well as simple or advanced web searches.

Action research is an intensely personal quest. Those working in education and information environments are often passionate about what they do and the quest for excellence is strong.

The practitioner/researcher designs the project and adapts the action research method, implements the actions and evaluates the resulting change and improvement. The aim of action research is to effect change in practice – through modifying individual practice, intensifying small group interactions, value-adding peer workflows or even enhancing the teaching and learning culture of whole learning communities. This action research project was a wonderful affirmation of theory in practice. Every step and activity had a place in the research schema and a purpose. It worked.

Understanding: the end of the project

By the end of the project a number of the initial goals had been reached. The language and actions of effective critical literacy were beginning to be clearly in evidence across both teaching and learning. The students, particularly Year 7, were showing growing competence in a range of information literacies: information searching, information management and information technology. Teachers were increasingly willing risk takers in adapting and using ICTs in their teaching and learning strategies. By the close of the second year of the project, upon observing a Year 7 class at the end of Term 3 on a Friday afternoon in the library and totally engrossed in their task – some with headsets at the videos, some on the computers, others with books, all note-taking – a visiting teacher librarian asked ...

> 'How did you get them to do that?'
> 'Well', I said. 'We...., they....., I ...... It's a long story.'

References

Burns, R. (1994). *Introduction to research methods* (2nd ed.). Melbourne: Longman Cheshire.

Butler, J.A. (1999). Research you can use. School Improvement Research Series (SIRS). Accessed 9 May 1999, http://www.nwrel.org/scpd/sirs/6/cu12.html

Clarkson, B. (1998). I've never enjoyed teaching so much: Continuing turning teachers on learning technologies. In *Planning for progress, partnership and profit*. Proceedings EdTech'98. Perth. Australian Society for Education Technology. Accessed 16 March 1999, http://cleo.murdoch.edu.au/gen/aset/confs/edtech98/pubs/articles/abcd/clarkson.html

Cook, C.J. & Fine, C.S. (1997). Critical issue: Evaluation professional growth and development. North Central Regional Education Laboratory. Retreived from http://www.ncrel.org/sdrs/areas/issues/educatrs/profdev/pd500.htm

DiMattia, S. & Oder, N. (1997). Knowledge management: Hope, hype or harbinger? *Library Journal, 122*(15), 33-35.

Drennon, C. (1994). Adult literacy practitioners as researchers. ERIC digest, ED372663 [online]. Accessed 24 April 1999.

Fournier, J.F. (1996). Information overload and technology education. University of Arkansas. Accessed 21 October 1998, http://www.coe.uh.edu/insite/elec_pub/html1996/07course.html

Grundy, S. (1982). Three modes of action research. *Curriculum Perspectives, 2*(3), 23-34.

Henry, C. & Kemmis, S. (1985). A point by point guide to action research for teachers. *The Australian Administrator, 6*(4), 1-4.

Hixson, J. & Tinzmann, M.B. (1990). Who are the at-risk students of the 1990s? Accessed 21 May 2000, http://www.ncrel.org/sdrs/areas/rpl_esys/equity.htm#d=29

Kemmis, S. (1990). Action research in retrospect and prospect. Melbourne: Deakin University Press.

Prensky, M. (2001). Digital natives, digital immigrants. *On the Horizon, 9*(5). Accessed 21 May 2000, http://www.marcprensky.com/writing/Prensky%20-%20Digital%20Natives,%20Digital%20Immigrants%20-%20Part1.pdf

Recker, M. & Greenwood, J. (1995). An interactive student evaluation system. Conference Paper at AUUG'95 and Asia-Pacific WWW'95 Conference Program. 19-20 September 1995 Accessed 24 July 2000, http://www.csu.edu.au/special/conference/apwww95/papers95/mrecker/mrecker.html

Reconceptualising professional teacher development. (1995). ERIC Digest ED 38695, June 1995. Washington, DC: ERIC Clearinghouse on Teaching and Teacher Education.

Rogers, E.M. (1995). *Diffusion of innovations* (4th ed.). New York: The Free Press.

Showers, B., Joyce, B. & Bennett, B. (1987). Synthesis of research on staff development: A framework for future study and a state-of-the-art analysis. *Educational Leadership, 45*(3), 77-87.

Sparks, D. & Loucks-Horsley, S. (1989). Five models of staff development for teachers. *Journal of Staff Development,* 10(4), 40-57.

CHAPTER 8
Using focus groups in a mixed method approach to evaluate student learning in an information literacy embedding project

Lesley Procter and Richard Wartho

In 2004 and 2005, a collaborative research project was conducted at the University of Otago to evaluate the impact of embedding information literacy (IL) concepts into the sociology programme. This impact was evaluated by the use of two surveys and a number of focus groups. This chapter examines the use of focus groups as a research method in this project. The relevance of the focus group method for an evidence-based research approach involving IL is also discussed.

Information literacy and sociology at Otago

The term 'information literacy' is commonly used to refer to a learning outcome focusing on the lifelong ability to recognise the need for, locate, evaluate, and effectively use information (American Library Association 1989).[1] IL issues have been widely debated during a worldwide shift in the philosophy of education from an emphasis on teaching styles, to one focusing more on student-centred learning (Kuh & Gonyea 2003). In an 'information society' all students need to be information literate if they are to stay up-to-date with developments in a particular subject (Breivik 1998).

Embedding IL into the curriculum has now become widely accepted (De Jager & Nassimbeni 2002) and many university-based librarians work in conjunction with academic staff towards this goal. In relation to IL, the term 'embedding' refers to the process of aligning IL objectives with the learning outcomes of an academic course or programme; '[t]he embedding of information skills into a subject integrates it into the content, learning activities and delivery modes of the subject'

---

[1] See Bawden (2001) and Armstrong et al. (2005) for detailed reviews of various definitions of IL.

(Hine et al. 2002). It is desirable because students are much more likely to retain IL skills and hence develop into lifelong learners if IL is presented as integrated with a subject rather than as a 'clip-on' (Bruce 2000). Evidence-based research should also be integrated into the curriculum. Evidence should, Todd argues, emerge out of the range of assessment tasks that students undertake (Todd 2002a).

Sociology at Otago is taught as a separate academic programme in the Department of Anthropology, Gender and Sociology within the Division of Humanities. It was first offered as a minor in 2002, and by 2004 courses were offered at all three undergraduate levels, with undergraduates being permitted to take a major in sociology from 2005. Various IL skills and concepts have been incorporated into the sociology programme from the outset, maximising students' interaction with information and their utilisation of that information as part of the learning process for knowledge construction (Todd 2001). Such skills are an integral part of both the delivery and assessment in most of the courses that make up the major. For example, sociology students at the University of Otago commonly begin their courses with a tutorial introducing the University Library's sociology holdings, discipline specific databases and search strategies. These tutorials are matched to the particular course requirements and IL level. We agree with Todd (2001) that learning is developmental and that learners' competence accrues over time – processes which may be tracked using evidence-based research techniques of trial, test, review and reflect.

By the end of 2003, it was apparent that a more structured and formalised approach to embedding IL was necessary as the programme developed into a major. Academic and library staff involved with the programme needed to know if the embedding strategies used thus far were actually working as we intended. And, of course, we wanted to improve on them wherever possible. These desired outcomes are emphasised by Hargreaves' (1997) assertion in support of evidence-based practice that teachers are pragmatic professionals, primarily interested in what works and in 'best practice' derived from tradition and personal experience, but also keen to have this practical wisdom underpinned by evidence tested through research. Underpinning these requirements was the additional need to base our future decisions on evidence drawn from the students themselves rather than solely from theoretical supposition. For us, as for Hargreaves (1997), research transforms individual tinkering into public knowledge with increased validity. We decided to undertake an evidence-based research project with first- and third-year students. Our choice of level at which to assess was dictated by a need to have the greatest degree of comparison between students possible, and by the fact that the academic staff involved in the project were not due to teach second-year students until the second semester in 2004.

Assisted by funding from the University of Otago's Committee for the Advancement of Learning and Teaching (CALT), our project involved two academic staff members from the sociology programme and a librarian for whom sociology is a specific IL responsibility. Such collaboration between teachers and teacher librarians is integral to students' achievement of IL-based learning outcomes. Libraries, Todd argues, offer tangible contributions to student learning (Todd 2002a). Collaborative research between library and teaching staff ensured that the library's contribution was both explained to the students and reinforced to the wider University academic community.

Our project evaluated the effectiveness of embedding IL skills into the discipline and academic assessment requirements in the two target sociology courses. It sought to answer the following questions:

- how did the assessment tasks assist with specific IL skill uptake?
- to what extent (if any) were students' IL skills improved?
- to what extent were students' discipline-specific competencies increased?

These questions would not only provide evidence of the effectiveness of the current embedding programme, but would also indicate areas where improvements and/or modifications might be made. In these respects, our project combined the element of evaluation of an intervention (what works) with a concern for how it could be made to work better, introducing the element of evidence-based *practice* – or what the online *Guide to evidence-based research* refers to as evaluating a service-level intervention with a view to potential changes to the way services are delivered or organised (http://www.hip.on.ca/EvidenceBasedGuide/ GuideMain.htm). In our project, 'service' refers to the IL embedding.

An integrated approach to IL and classroom teaching has been demonstrably effective at both secondary and tertiary level. See, for example, the studies noted by Young and Von Seggern (2001). But existing evaluative research in this area primarily examines foundation courses, seldom extending to IL embedding across whole academic programmes. We were faced, therefore, with the problem of designing a project to evaluate not only the relatively well-documented format for IL achievement, but also the relatively unexplored terrain of assessing discipline-based learning outcomes delivered alongside IL skills. We chose a multi-method approach, in which a focus group–survey/questionnaire nexus played a central part, for two primary reasons. First, we hoped that combining quantitative and qualitative methods would minimise the risk of self-reported biases. Second, whereas quantitative methods typically utilise top-of-the-mind responses, qualitative methods frequently allow for a more considered response. The primary unit of analysis for our project is the learner, making it a micro-level project in Todd's (2002b) categorisation.

Using focus group interviews, individual interviews and whole class surveys, our project provided both qualitative and quantitative data relating to students' acquisition of IL skills and to their evaluation of the embedding approach. Two separate populations were studied – a large first-year class and a smaller third-year class. For each target group an identical survey was administered at the beginning and end of semester. This survey was based on the Information Skills Survey (ISS) which was developed by the Council of Australian University Librarians (CAUL).

For the first-year class (total roll 197) 145 and 135 responses were received to these surveys. In the third-year class (total roll 11) 11 responses were received. In addition to the whole-class surveys, focus group participants in each target population were asked to complete a survey to determine study habits. The objective of this was to provide a point of comparison to the ISS-generated responses. By utilising the ISS we have been able to firmly ground our assessment of 'effective' in students' achievement of clearly identified learning outcomes.

A major component of the project involved student volunteers participating in focus group sessions in which they discussed their understandings of what the assessment involved for them in terms of time, research, writing and knowledge; their planned approach to the assessment tasks; and where they thought any difficulties arose. In each group, academic assessment involved a series of incremental, skill-based tasks. Part of the early tasks involved IL and generic academic skills combined within a subject-specific context. (See Procter 2006 for a fuller discussion of this assessment policy.) Incorporating and discussing lessons learnt from, and comparisons with, previous assessment was possible as the semester progressed. This chapter concentrates on the focus group component of our project and discusses some results from the first-year group.

The focus group method and evidence-based research

The focus group is 'focused' – that is the interview is limited to a small number of relevant issues. It revolves around the 'group' – that is a number of interacting individuals having a community of interest. The use of focus groups as a qualitative research method has been traced to Bogardus's 1926 description of group interviews (Morgan 1997), but the method is generally held to originate with the 1941 collaboration between Paul Lazarsfeld and Robert Merton at Columbia

University. Merton's work *The focused interview* (Merton et al. 1956) has become the seminal text on focus groups (Stewart & Shamdasani 1990; Morgan 1997). Focus group method showed phenomenal growth in the 1980s and 1990s and is now common in all social science applications (Morgan 1997).

The method provides 'depth' by seeking information that is more profound than can usually be accessed at the level of interpersonal relationships in the research setting. Burton and Chapman (2004) argue that some of what they call evidence-based orthodoxy has resulted in 'a strategy of simplification' and a 'drive for quantification and control of variables'. Both results create a winnowing down of information to a few key numbers, ignoring the 'processes by which participants come together, construct or negotiate meaning, and create expectations for change (Burton & Chapman 2004, pp.59-60).

Our decision to use focus groups as a method was based on two assumptions identified by Lederman (1990). First, an individual's ability to articulate thoughts and feelings makes them an important source of information. We wanted to gain first-hand insight into the way our students felt about the assessment task we set them and understand how they went about using IL skills in their completion. As already mentioned, beginning with the learner at the micro level helps to identify and understand the specific dynamics of their engagement with, and use of, IL (Todd 2002b). Second, the dynamics of the group itself not only bring out more and better information than could be obtained in individual interviews, but the dynamics also ensure the validity of the information contributed (Lederman 1990).

Considerable debate exists about the precise definition of the focus group as a method. Table 8.1 defines both 'focus group' characteristics in general and the specific groups used in this research.

Glitz (1998) defines the focus group as a method for generating data or information from small groups. When analysed, such data assist with planning, decision-making, evaluation, developing models or theories; enriching both the findings from other research methods and the construction of questionnaires for further data gathering. The focus group is therefore an excellent way of meeting the necessary requirements of an evidence-based approach: to challenge the imposition of unproved practices, to solve problems and avoid harmful procedures, and to create improvements that lead to more effective learning. Our choice to use this method was influenced by our need to make specific decisions about how we assessed and how we incorporated IL into that assessment. It also helped to 'enrich' the quantitative information gathered from whole class surveys.

Table 8.1 Focus group characteristics

	General characteristics	Specific characteristics
The group		
Number of participants	• six – twelve • fewer than six inhibits discussion and may allow one or two participants to dominate • more than twelve can be difficult to manage	• between three and six – fluctuations experienced in successive group meetings • numbers did not affect quality of discussion
Membership of group	• community of interest • members share knowledge and/or experience(s)	• community of interest (enrolled students) • group shared experience(s) of academic assessment in papers under discussion
The researcher/moderator		
Role of researcher(s)/ moderator(s)	• moderator leads discussions, records interaction • generally well-trained or experienced in group facilitation and interviewing techniques • exact role determined by broader research agenda	• moderator's role was to facilitate group sessions and organise participants contact and follow-up • moderator asked questions and recorded answers in audio-tape and note format • moderator had previous experience with methodology
The interview session		
Style of interaction	• group interaction is encouraged • non-directive style of questioning • discussion allowed to flow naturally as long as it remains within the topic of interest • amount of direction provided will influence the type and quality of data collected • formality of session depends on researcher's goals, nature of research setting and likely reaction of group participants	• participants interacted • questioning was non-directive • no problems were experienced keeping participants 'on track' • moderator used very little direction • sessions were relatively informal
Style of questions	• open-ended	• open-ended
Length of interview session	• one and a half – two and a half hours	•
Venue	• various • usually easily accessible for participants, or close to where large numbers of people gather • often purpose-built • use of teleconferencing and internet focus groups is increasing	• group study room in University library • sound proof room

Equipment required	• any or all of:
	  - note-taking facilities
	  - one-way mirrors
	  - viewing rooms
	  - audio and visual recording equipment
	  - 'bug in the ear' transmitter for moderator
		• audio-recording equipment
		• note-taking facilities
		• table and whiteboard

Our data fits within the category of 'good practice' evidence. That is, it provides examples of what worked (or did not) within a particular context. Due to its qualitative nature, the focus group enables the researcher to interpret results rather than merely measuring them. As such it provides an answer to the question, 'Where is the evidence?' by exploring 'the relationship between practice and outcomes' (Burton & Chapman 2004, p.56).

Morgan (1997) suggests three ways to utilise the focus group: as a self-contained method, as a supplementary source of data, and in multi-method studies. In our project, the focus group was a supplementary method, providing additional data for the method with which we combined it – the survey. Using the focus group as a supplement in this way requires that it provide follow-up data to assist the primary method, to augment partially understood results or to evaluate the outcome of the program or intervention. We were able to utilise the focus group data to 'flesh out' what sometimes were ambiguous responses to our surveys. Because the first survey was undertaken before the focus groups, we used some of the survey questions to generate discussion in the group.

Advantages and disadvantages

From an evidence-based approach, the focus-group method has the following advantages:

- it allows data to be acquired quickly, facilitating rapid response to necessities for delivery changes;
- it does not require complex sampling techniques and reduces the cost of data acquisition;
- it is flexible and adaptable to a wide range of research situations; and
- it is one of the few methods available for obtaining data from children or persons with limited literacy skills.

These are particularly useful characteristics for a method to examine IL situations across a wide variety of learning contexts. Less advantageously, however, the focus group sample is not randomly selected and generalisation from small focus group to larger population is problematic – many groups may be needed to make any kind of projections from results because individual groups represent too small a number of people. Convenience of access may mean that an unrepresentative sample of the target population is used – that is, those who are 'handy' may not be representative in terms of compliance or deference for example. These disadvantages are less important, however, where micro-research is undertaken because in this case the local is all important and representability less so.[2]

The focus-group process works well with a socially oriented research procedure, direct interaction with respondents and increased opportunities for clarification, follow-up and probing. Related, but unanticipated, topics may be explored as they present themselves, providing maximum responsiveness to student groups in local settings. The focus-group process is less helpful when interaction between respondents and between respondents and researcher(s) becomes undesirable for two reasons. One is because responses from members of group are not independent of each other and therefore generalisability is restricted; the other is because results obtained may be biased by a very dominant or opinionated member and more reserved respondents may be reluctant to talk. The researcher may also have less control in the group interview than in an individual interview or may inadvertently 'cue' particular group responses.

Data obtained from focus groups has high face validity since the open response format ensures large, rich data sources in respondents' own words, allowing for the possibility of deeper-level meaning and subtle nuances in expression and meaning. Results are easy to understand in comparison to some other methods, which may employ complex statistical analyses. But there are disadvantages associated with focus-group data. The live and immediate nature of method may lead the researcher to place greater reliance on the data gathered than it would otherwise warrant. Culturally, more credibility may be attached to the spoken word, leading to results obtained being privileged over results obtained through other methods. Open-ended responses sometimes make summarisation and interpretation difficult.

Ethical issues in focus group research

In general terms, ethical issues for focus groups remain the same as those for other methods of social research (Gibbs 1997; Bloor et al. 2001; Morgan & Krueger 1993), and are relevant to all stages of design, implementation and presentation (Kitzinger & Barbour 1999).

We were required to complete a request for clearance to proceed from the University of Otago Human Ethics Committee for Ethical Approval of a Research

---

[2] Burton and Chapman (2004) identify three levels of research evidence: micro level evidence deriving from practice with individual people or small groups; meso level evidence deriving from local studies, evaluations and audits; and macro level evidence deriving from published literature. Our project combines the micro and meso elements.

or Teaching Proposal Involving Human Participants. Gaining such clearance requires researchers to provide information about the population to be involved in the project; the nature of the task required of participants and the various precautionary measures to be taken to avoid harm or discomfort if appropriate, and the measures taken to collect, store, code and eventually dispose of personal information collected.

As an institution that supports the principles of the Treaty of Waitangi between the Crown and Māori as Tangata Whenua[3], the University of Otago also requires that information on ethnicity should not normally be collected unless it is required to adequately describe the sample population, for example, if the researchers are drawing comparisons or conclusions between ethnic groups or the nature of the project is such that there are clear potential implications of direct interest to Māori. Where such information is collected for the purposes of drawing comparisons or conclusions between Māori and other ethnic groups, or the project has clear implications of direct interest to Māori, consultation should be undertaken in accordance with the University's Policy for Research Consultation with Māori. This did not apply to our project but due to the nature of ethnic identity in New Zealand, it is not always possible to outwardly determine ethnicity. For this reason ethically it is wise to undertake research consultation with the University's Facilitator Research (Māori).

The University of Otago Ethics Committee also requires copies of information and consent sheets to be attached to the application. Such requirements observe the generic requirements of ethical research behaviour. At recruitment time, researchers should be meticulous about providing full information about the purpose and uses of participants' contributions; keeping participants informed about the expectations of the group and the topic; not pressurising participants to speak (Gibbs 1997); and ensuring that participants are fully aware of their right to withdraw from the research at any time.

Focus groups have specific requirements for confidentiality, both within the group and during the analysis process. Because the focus group is, by definition, composed of multiple individuals it is impossible to preserve the absolute anonymity of participants (Gibbs 1997; Bloor et al. 2001). For this reason moderators must set clear ground rules (Kitzinger & Barbour 1999) which emphasise the principle of respect for the beliefs, attitudes, wishes and rights (including the right to refuse to participate) of participants (Vaughn et al. 1996) and

[3] This term loosely translates to 'people of the land' and is commonly used to refer to the indigenous inhabitants of Aotearoa/New Zealand.

which apply both to moderator/researcher *and* participants. Responsible researchers keep confidential any identifying information about participants (Bloor et al. 2001) and handle all sensitive material with care, especially where participants are drawn from within a social circle or other pre-existing group. Potential participants should be made aware that others will hear their responses and that absolute confidentiality cannot be guaranteed due to the possibility of other participants 'gossiping' or of vicarious disclosure taking place within the group (Kitzinger & Barbour 1999). Participants should be reminded that they must keep confidential what they hear within the group and that researchers will make data from the group anonymous (Gibbs 1997). Such issues were particularly relevant to our project because all members of the group were drawn from the same class and would see each other two or three times a week in addition to the focus-group sessions. Part of our consent form outlined the researchers' responsibilities in regard to anonymity. This is another requirement of the University ethics committee.

By observing the basic principle of social research – do no harm to the participant – the focus group researcher can militate against ethical abuses, especially if care is taken to examine the research environment and protocol from the *perspective of the participant* (Vaughn et al. 1996). Additionally, however, the focus group environment itself will assist in this endeavour. Although concerns expressed about power differentials in one-to-one interviews do not simply disappear in a focus-group situation, the group environment considerably reduces the researcher/moderator's power and influence. Group participants are more likely to take control of the questions and topics than are individuals in one-on-one interviews, since sheer weight of numbers counter-balances many differentials in social power.

An ethical power issue did surface in our project. The moderator was also a tutor in the paper and one participant was streamed to be in her tutorial. With the participant's permission, we solved the potential dilemma of having the moderator mark this person's work by getting the course coordinator to mark these assessments instead.

Researchers should beware, however, the potential for power differentials to reappear during the analysis and writing-up stages (Wilkinson 1998). As we choose which parts of the transcripts to include as 'examples' in our report it becomes clear where the potential for further 'gate keeping' exists. Ethically, the temptation to omit remarks that challenge assumptions, or otherwise have the potential to complicate results must be avoided.

Focus group participants are a vulnerable population, especially stigmatised groups and groups occurring in conflicted or hierarchical settings (Morgan & Krueger 1993). The latter raises the issue of academic staff using students as research subjects. Although the research team members did not mark participant's internal assessment, one of the team was responsible for marking examination answers. Three strategies militated against the potential for bias here. First, the individual marking the exam was not the focus group moderator. Second, we decided not to transcribe the focus group interviews until after the exam had been marked. Third, the University policy of 'blind' marking prevented individual students being identified. The potential for such bias remains a possibility that researchers should be aware of, however. Specifically, researchers should keep in mind that participants may be put at risk by researchers' need to gather information about their opinions and experiences (Morgan & Krueger 1993).

Another factor in the greater potential vulnerability of some focus group participants is the potential for misinformation to be shared within the group and unintentionally validated by the presence of the researcher/moderator. In such cases it is the moderator's responsibility to provide accurate information during the discussion's debriefing stage. Some recruitment ethics may also be affected by over-zealous contacts maximising group participation by providing partial or misleading information (Kitzinger & Barbour, 1999). This project avoided this particular danger by calling for volunteers during lectures. Interested students could email for further information thus avoiding the necessity to identify themselves before the class population. Full information was then provided before interested persons were asked to consent to join the project, including their right to withdraw at any time throughout the research.

Results/findings

The full presentation of our research findings is beyond the scope of this chapter[4]. Quantitative data suggested that our initiatives were successful, supporting our hypothesis that 'embedding IL skills into the course assessment would improve students' IL skill levels'. Qualitative results from focus group interviews, however, provided more detail and some explanations for this apparent improvement.

The data from focus groups provided a more comprehensive and detailed understanding of the results of quantitative research (from the ISS). For example, in the end-of-semester survey, to identify study habits among the groups surveyed

[4] See Procter et al. (2005) and Procter (2006) for more detailed analyses.

in the ISS, 46.7 per cent of respondents began their essay a week or more before it was due. This result contradicts a common perception held by academic teaching staff that poor essays result from insufficient preparation. Reasons for this unexpectedly organised approach were supplied by focus groups participants, one of whom said that having to submit the plan two weeks before the essay was due encouraged thinking about the assignment much earlier than they usually did. These results support the supposition that better preparation might be encouraged by cumulative assessment tasks. Another focus group participant revealed that having to get organised to do the essay plan and having already started the research some weeks before meant that the task of writing the essay itself was less daunting.

Interpreting ISS results was greatly facilitated by the responses to focus group questions. The percentage of 'Always' responses to the ISS statement 'I use a combination of search tools' decreased by 14.4 per cent between the two ISS surveys. One focus group participant remarked, 'I always find it quite a pain to try and reference the websites and things and I'm not sure still how you reference it within an essay. It's really difficult because sometimes you haven't even got an author. That puts me off using them [internet resources] and the authenticity of them as well.' This opinion provides a possible explanation for the ISS data, indicating a skill component that should be better presented to students.

Data from the end-of-semester survey shows that 45.7 per cent of respondents used at least one journal article for their summary exercises, while a further 57.8 per cent used a book or book chapter. These statistics and the 50.8 per cent affirmative response to the question 'Do you think this paper has helped you to be a better researcher?' indicate that the embedded IL strategies were successful in their aim to foster constructive academic behaviour patterns. Focus group responses supported this assumption. One participant commented favourably on the IL component: 'This information literacy though, it's fabulous, I can't speak highly enough of it because those kids that are coming straight from school, you know, obviously they're the clever ones but for people who haven't done it before or taken much interest in it, it must be pretty hard to know where to start.' S/he felt that there had been an increase in confidence in using IL skills: 'I'm getting a lot more confident using journals now whereas before it was pretty hit and miss whether I found things.'

Such improvement was not shown in every ISS category. For example, Survey 2 responses to ANZIIL Standard 5 ISS statement #15 ('I present the information in a medium that suits the audience') were slightly fewer in the 'Always' category, suggesting that students were less sure of their abilities in this respect at the end of semester than they had been at the beginning. This may have been the result of confusing messages from teaching staff or simply a result of the students themselves realising that they were not as good at this as they thought they were at the start of semester.

Although focus group data did not specifically help to explain this result, focus group interviews did identify some problems with the assessment instructions, enabling immediate adjustments to be made to assessment tasks as the course unfolded. From this feedback it was apparent that instructions about assignments had not been as clear as intended. Students indicated a number of aspects of the assessment could be delivered more appropriately. The library tutorial, for example, was conducted by four different library staff who emphasised sociological perspectives to varying degrees. Feedback from the focus group meeting held after this tutorial indicated that the lack of consistency was problematic for some students. As a result of such feedback, the library tutorial in 2005 was conducted by only two library staff, both of whom were academically experienced in sociology. Other more comprehensive changes to both the assessment profile and IL embedding were consequently made to the paper in 2005.

In general, however, trends across each set of responses to individual ISS questions showed an increase in 'often' and 'always' responses and a corresponding decrease in the 'never' and 'seldom' responses, in the second survey. Positive results were also observable in respect to ANZIIL Standard 4, where significantly more students in Survey 2 felt confident about their abilities to keep records of research results. This trend is also noticeable with respect to Standard 5, where deep learning improvements are shown in the abilities to compare new with existing information and information processing by explanation. Standard 6, particularly in website referencing abilities, was also markedly improved by the end of the semester.

Focus group data also helped the research team to understand features of the initiative that were beyond the scope of the ISS. One participant thought that although some students might not like the structured nature of the first-year assessment, 'they got round to it and thought 'this really helped me in the essay'. Another said, 'The idea is so that you can get feedback from the first [assignment] so that you can improve the second. It gave you confidence to go onto the essay.' In response to questions about the assessment structure, one participant replied: 'I guess it gave you kind of a structured way of approaching the whole essay-writing thing and researching and everything. If you don't do that people just sort of go about their own way of doing it. It was good having the structure.' When asked what s/he thought of having to do two summary exercises with different resources, this respondent said that 'it was actually reasonably good because often you got quite different perspectives from your two sources and if you'd done one you would probably focus your essay on that one resource and like one point of view or you'd be likely to. So I thought it was kind of good.' Such responses indicate that the structured approach successfully engaged the students in the essay-writing process and that they viewed the sequential assessment tasks as helpful in a number of respects.

One particularly pleasing set of results in both quantitative and qualitative data was the improvement shown in students for whom 2004 was their first year at University. For example, in all responses to ISS questions relating to ANZIIL Standard 2 and 5, percentages of those who checked the 'Always' category significantly increased in Survey 2, indicating that by the end of the semester students were more aware of the need to deploy IL skills when undertaking their research. These results demonstrate a successful academic socialisation process during the semester and are supported across all data sets for this group.

Conclusion

In our research, the focus group method was extremely successful in challenging the imposition of unproved practices. Using focus groups allowed the research team to meet the necessary requirements of evidence-based approaches to research in general and to research into IL in particular. In conjunction with quantitative methods, the focus groups enabled assessment practices to be evaluated and improvements made which led to more effective learning. All of this successfully helped the research team to identify what worked and, crucially, how it might be improved upon in the future.

References

American Library Association (ALA). (1989). *American Library Association Presidential Commission on Information Literacy. Final Report.* American Library Association. (Available at http://www.ala.org/ala/acrl/acrlpubs/whitepapers/presidential.htm26. Accessed January 2004).

Armstrong, C., Boden, D., Town, S., Woolley, M., Webber, S. & Abell, A. (2005). Defining information literacy for the UK. *Library and Information Update.* 4(1-2), 22-25.

Bawden, D. (2001). Information and digital literacies: A review of concepts. *Journal of Documentation, 57*(2), 218-259.

Bloor, M., Frankland, J., Thomas, M. & Robson, K. (2001). *Focus groups in social research*. London: Sage.

Breivik, P.S. (1998). *Student learning in the information age*. Phoenix, AZ: Oryx Press.

Bruce, C. (2000). Information literacy research: Dimensions of emerging collective consciousness. *Australian Academic and Research Libraries, 31*(2), 91-109.

Burton, M. & Chapman, M.J. (2004). Problems of evidence-based practice in community based services. *Journal of Learning Disabilities, 8*(1), 56-70.

De Jager, K. & Nassimbeni, M. (2002). Institutionalizing information literacy in tertiary education: Lessons learned from South African programs. *Library Trends, 51*(2), 167-184.

Gibbs, A. (1997). Focus groups. *Social Research Update. 19.*. Accessed 14 October 2002, http://www.soc.surrey.ac.uk/sru/SRU19.html

Glitz, B. (1998). *Focus groups for libraries and librarians*. New York: Forbes Custom Publishing for Medical Library Association.

Guide to evidence-based research. Accessed 28 April 2005, http://www.hip.on.ca/EvidenceBasedGuide/GuideMain.html

Hargreaves, D.H. (1997). In defense of research for evidence-based teaching: A rejoinder to Martyn Hammersley. *British Educational Research Journal, 23*(4), 405-419.

Hine, A., Gollin, S., Ozols, A., Hill, F. & Scoufis, M. (2002). Embedding information literacy in a university subject through collaborative partnerships. *Psychology Learning and Teaching, 2*(2), 102-107.

Kitzinger, J. & Barbour, R.S. (1999). Introduction: The challenge and promise of focus groups. In R.S. Barbour & J. Kitzinger (Eds.), *Developing focus group research: Politics, theory and practice*. London: Sage.

Kuh, G.D. & Gonyea, R.M. (2003). The role of the academic library in promoting student engagement in learning. *College & Research Libraries, 64*(4), 256-282.

Lederman, L.C. (1990). Assessing educational effectiveness: The focus group interview as a technique for data collection. *Community Education, 39*(2), 117-127.

Merton, R.K., Fiske, M. & Kendall, P.L. (1956). *The focused interview*. New York: The Free Press.

Morgan, D.L. (1997). *Focus groups as qualitative research* (2nd ed., Vol.16). Thousand Oaks, CA: Sage.

Morgan, D.L. & Krueger, R.A. (1993). When to use focus groups and why. In D.L. Morgan (Ed.), *Successful focus groups: Advancing the state of the art* (pp.3-19). Newbury Park, CA: Sage.

Procter, L.J. (2006). Supporting legitimate peripheral participation: Challenges for teaching and learning in a first year sociology course. *International Review of Modern Sociology, 32*(1), 75-101.

Procter, L., Wartho, R. & Anderson, M. (2005). Embedding information literacy in the sociology programme at the University of Otago. *Australian Academic and Research Libraries 6,*(4), 153-168.

Stewart, D.W. & Shamdasani, P.N. (1990). *Focus groups: Theory and practice.* Thousand Oaks, CA: Sage.

Todd, R. (2002a). Evidence-based practice II: Getting into the action. *Scan, 21*(2), 1-8.

Todd, R. (2002b). Evidence-based practice: The sustainable future for teacher-librarians. *Scan, 21*(1), 1-8.

Todd, R. (2001). *Transitions for preferred futures of school libraries: Knowledge space, not information place. Connections, not collections. Actions, not positions. Evidence, not advocacy.* Paper presented at International Association of School Librarianship Conference, Auckland New Zealand, 2001.

Vaughn, S., Schumm, J. S. & Sinagub, J. (1996). *Focus group interviews in education and psychology.* Thousand Oaks, CA: Sage.

Wilkinson, S. (1998). Focus groups in feminist research: Power, interaction, and the co-construction of meaning. *Women's Studies International Forum, 21*(1), 111-125.

Young, N. & Von Seggern, M. (2001). General information seeking in changing times: A focus group study. *Reference and User Services Quarterly, 41*(2), 159-169.

CHAPTER 9
Evidence-based practice and information literacy

Helen Partridge and Gillian Hallam

Introduction

Evidence-based practice (EBP) has recently emerged as a topic of discussion among professionals within the library and information services (LIS) industry. Simply stated, EBP is the process of using formal research skills and methods to assist in decision making and establishing best practice. The emerging interest in EBP within the library context serves to remind the library profession that research skills and methods can help ensure that the library industry remains current and relevant in changing times. The LIS sector faces ongoing challenges in terms of the expectation that financial and human resources will be managed efficiently, particularly if library budgets are reduced and accountability to the principal stakeholders is increased. Library managers are charged with the responsibility to deliver relevant and cost effective services, in an environment characterised by rapidly changing models of information provision, information access and user behaviours. Consequently they are called upon not only to justify the services they provide, or plan to introduce, but also to measure the effectiveness of these services and to evaluate the impact on the communities they serve. The imperative for innovation in and enhancements to library practice is accompanied by the need for a strong understanding of the processes of review, measurement, assessment and evaluation.

In 2001, the Centre for Information Research was commissioned by the Chartered Institute of Library and Information Professionals (CILIP) in the UK to conduct an examination into the research landscape for library and information science. The examination concluded that research is 'important for the LIS domain in a number of ways' (McNicol & Nankivell 2001, p.77). At the professional level, research can inform practice, assist in the future planning of the profession, raise the profile of the discipline, and indeed the reputation and standing of the library and information service itself. At the personal level, research can 'broaden horizons and offer individuals development opportunities' (McNicol & Nankivell 2001, p.77). The study recommended that 'research should be promoted as a valuable professional activity for practitioners to engage in' (McNicol & Nankivell 2001, p.82).

This chapter will consider the role of EBP within the library profession. A brief review of key literature in the area is provided. The review considers issues of definition and terminology, highlights the importance of research in professional practice and outlines the research approaches that underpin EBP. The chapter concludes with a consideration of the specific application of EBP within the dynamic and evolving field of information literacy (IL).

EBP and the library and information profession?

The concept of EBP is derived from the domain of evidence-based medicine, which has been described as 'an approach to decision making in which the clinician uses the best evidence available in consultation with a patient to decide upon the option which suits the patient best' (Gray 2001, p.17). EBP is based on the premise that 'practice should be based on up-to-date, valid and reliable research' (Brice & Hill 2004, p.13). In her inaugural speech as incoming president of the Medical Library Association (MLA) in 1997, Rachael Anderson suggested that librarians needed to develop their own version of EBP (Anderson 1998). In the same year, the term 'evidence-based librarianship' (EBL) was first introduced into the library and information profession's vocabulary by Jonathan Eldredge (1997).

The first attempt to define EBL was made by Andrew Booth. In 2000 he adapted a pre-existing definition of EBP. Booth noted that this modified definition has the 'advantage of being coined by a librarian, Anne McKibbon from McMaster University' (Booth & Brice 2004, p.7).

> Evidence-based librarianship (EBL) is an approach to information science that promotes the collection, interpretation, and integration of valid, important and applicable user reported, librarian observed, and research derived evidence. The best available evidence moderated by user needs and preferences is applied to improve the quality of professional judgements (cited in Booth 2002, p.53).

In 2002, Eldredge offered his definition of EBL:

> Evidence-based librarianship (EBL) seeks to improve library practice by utilising the best available evidence in conjunction with a pragmatic perspective developed from working experiences in librarianship. The

best available evidence might be produced from either quantitative or qualitative research designs, depending upon the EBL question posed, although EBL encourages using more rigorous forms over less rigorous forms of evidence when making decisions (p.72).

Having noted that the existing definitions of EBL were overly theoretical, Crumley and Koufogiannakis offered a more 'practical definition for everyday referral' (p.62). EBL was described as:

> a means to improve the profession of librarianship by asking questions as well as finding, critically appraising and incorporating research evidence from library science (and other disciplines) into daily practice. It also involves encouraging librarians to conduct high quality qualitative and quantitative research (Crumley & Koufogiannakis 2002, p.62).

This last definition places a greater emphasis on 'the improvement of professional practice together with the addition of the librarian as practitioner–researcher' (Booth 2002, p.54). In reviewing definitions of EBL, Booth compiled the following list of 'consensually-based' defining characteristics of EBL:

- a context of day to day decision making,
- an emphasis on improving the quality of the professional practice,
- a pragmatic focus on the 'best available evidence',
- incorporation of the user perspective,
- acceptance of a broad range of quantitative and qualitative designs, and
- access to the (process of) EBP and its products (Booth 2002, p.54).

Booth also noted one significant omission from the list, and by consequence from existing definitions of EBL: 'a preoccupation with obtaining best value services for available resources' (Booth 2002, p.54). Booth argued that this characteristic must be included as recognition that the 'pragmatic real world thrust of EBL, coupled with its emphasis on decision making, requires that all decisions be taken in the context of finite resources' (Booth 2002, p.54). In 2006, Eldredge offered a revised version of his 2002 definition:

> Evidence-based librarianship (EBL) provides a process for integrating the best available scientifically-generated evidence into making important decisions. EBL seeks to combine the use of the best available research evidence with a pragmatic perspective developed from working experiences in librarianship. EBL actively supports increasing the proportion of more rigorous applied research studies so the results can be available for making informed decisions.

The revised definition introduces EBL as a *process* for decision making and places greater emphasis on the need for *scientifically-generated* evidence in research that can be *made available* or used by others in their own decision making.

In recent years there has been a shift from the term 'evidence-based librarianship' to the terms 'evidence-based information practice' or 'evidence-based library and information practice' (EBLIP). Booth (2006) provided three reasons for this shift. First, the shift represented a need to broaden the concept away from the narrow confines of 'librarianship'. The newer terms provided a more inclusive acknowledgement of the wider context of library and information practice (Booth & Brice 2004, p.8). For example, where EBL focused on the librarian and their use of EBP, EBLIP focused more on the application of EBP within the broader library and information context generally (i.e., by the library technician, the librarian, or other allied professionals). Second, the change arose out of the positive desire to embrace the related fields of information systems, informatics and IL. This is an interesting point given the context of the current chapter. The relationship between EBP and IL is one worthy of further consideration. It could be argued that when an information professional (or indeed any professional) engages in, or applies EBP within their work practice, they are in effect engaging in IL constructs within their workplace. It is interesting to compare the EBP process (as outlined below) to the many frameworks or standards of IL, for example, the Australian and New Zealand Institute for Information Literacy (ANZIIL) framework (2004) or the Society of College, National and University Libraries (SCONUL) and Seven Pillars of Information Literacy (SCONUL 2007). Third, the introduction of the word 'practice' helped to emphasise more explicitly the conceptual connection between the overarching paradigm of EBP and IL.

Why is EBP important?

The arguments for EBP within the LIS profession have been widely discussed within the literature. In 2002, Williamson proposed that 'research can play a very valuable role in the practice of information professionals' (p.12). Six key reasons were identified to underscore the value of research to professional practice:

1. to assist in understanding the problems and issues which arise in the workplace;
2. to add to knowledge in the field and/or provide solutions to problems;
3. to maintain dynamic and appropriate services;

4. to meet requirements of accountability – research is important in the age of accountability as it can assist in policy formulation and provide data to justify present funding or increased funding;

5. to maintain and improve professional status; and

6. to provide a body of research findings and theory to inform practitioners (Williamson 2002, p.12).

Juznic and Urbanija (2003) observed that 'research ... [helps] LIS professionals to learn more about their work, perform better and offer a higher level of service to their clientele and users ... [the] research findings provide further motivation, guidance, and input to the successful services' (p. 325). This idea was supported by Lowe (cited in Williamson 2002) who contended that research allows information professionals to add value to their work practices. This view was further developed through the proposition that the use of research in practice clearly differentiated between '[those] professionals who maintain the status quo without question and those who strive to develop their work practices through continual evaluation and investigation' (cited in Williamson 2002, p.12). Harvey (2002) built upon this idea by arguing that 'research and professional practice are inextricably linked' (p.xiii) and, as such, 'research skills are a *prerequisite* [italics added] for those who want to work successfully in information environments' (p.xiii). He postulated that research skills represented an 'essential set of tools which enable information *workers* to become information *professionals*' (p.xiii). According to Harvey (2002), 'change and its ramifications' have made research a core part of being an information professional. He contended that the inevitable processes of change in society were leading to changes in the services and products that library and information professionals designed and offered. Consequently, the 'work of information professionals is being transformed' (Harvey, 2002, p.xii), meaning that information professionals could not be effective unless they had a working knowledge of research and its many tools and techniques.

In 2001, the Special Libraries Association (SLA) released its revised Research Statement in which the role of EBP within current library and information work was strongly advocated. In a commentary on the research statement, the SLA Research Committee and Joanne Gard Marshall (2003) suggested that the health and future of any profession depended on the members' ability to evaluate both themselves and their professional practice. Therefore, the development of strategies to undertake EBP could well prove to be an invaluable opportunity to improve and refine our own professional activities.

In further support of these views, the SLA Research Statement (2001) itself noted that 'these are challenging times for professionals in all areas of practice' (p.2). It was time for special librarians to recognise the need for increased competence and accountability and therefore the value of EBP. Ultimately it was EBP that would 'set information and library professionals apart in an increasingly competitive world of information service providers' (p.2).

Juznic and Urbanija (2003) encouraged the LIS profession to use research to 'create new knowledge and thereby contribute to the growth of LIS as a profession or discipline. If research is absent, non existent or even scarce, there is no profession, but only an occupation grounded in techniques, routine and common sense' (p.325). Crumley and Koufogiannakis (2002) observed that 'in our profession we help our patrons make decisions by leading them to research evidence. It is vital that we follow the same model: we should consult our own literature when we have questions about best practices in our field' (p.112). Indeed they proposed that 'when a librarian encounters a workplace problem or question to which there is no answer, conducting research to answer that question benefits the entire profession' (p.112). Ritchie (1999) also noted that, given our role as managers of the literature of research, library and information professionals were uniquely placed 'to model the principles of EBP, not only as they apply to other disciplines which we serve, but also as they apply to our own professional practice – 'if you are not modelling what you are teaching you are teaching something else' (Ritchie, 1999, para. 6). Ultimately, library and information professionals should 'practice what they preach'.

How is EBP undertaken?

Discussion continues within the LIS literature on the best process or method for applying EBP within the LIS profession. In recent years, a growing number of studies have been conducted and published which illustrate how EBP is being applied in the profession. These studies have demonstrated the different evidence-based approaches and strategies that can be used within the broad spectrum of LIS work (i.e., systems, client services, virtual). Eldredge (2000; 2006) provided one of the few 'generic models' for engaging in EBP within the LIS profession. His five-step process forms the basis for the current chapter's discussion on how to undertake EBP. It should be noted that this five-step process is offered merely as guide; it is acknowledged that the EBP process will vary depending on the issue or problem to be explored and the context in which the exploration is taking place. Eldredge viewed the EBP process in EBL as being analogous to the scientific method in science. Library professionals were encouraged to conceptualise the following five steps:

1. *formulate* a clearly-defined, relevant, and answerable question;
2. *search* for an answer in both the published and unpublished literature, plus any other authoritative resources, for the best available evidence;
3. critically *appraise* the evidence;
4. assess the relative value of expected *benefits* and costs of any decided upon action plan; and
5. *evaluate* the effectiveness of the action plan (Eldredge 2006, p.342).

The first and most important step is to develop a well-structured question. Eldredge (2006) noted that 'time taken at the outset to formulate a question appropriately produces in the end more closely matched answers' (p.344). The following practical suggestions were offered to LIS professionals in order to help them identify, formulate and refine answerable EBLIP questions:

1. *cultivate* the habit of recognizing and recording questions related to our profession.
2. *capture* – recognize questions as they arise and, before they are forgotten, record them immediately, no matter how vague or in need of further refinement.
3. *refine* your question during a quiet moment – ask colleagues for assistance in helping you refine and clarify what you really want to know.
4. *reframe* – is there really another question behind your initial question? Experience suggests that the question you initially ask rarely continues to be the question you eventually pursue.
5. *prioritize* – determine how important this question is to you, your institution, or the profession; further determine the immediacy of the need to know an answer: today, tomorrow, or just some day? Clearly, not all questions that we formulate can deserve our full attention. Yet, when making important decisions, our emphasizing the EBL process increases the probability of yielding a high-quality answer.
6. *courage* – Great discoveries are made when someone asks a new question rather than provides a new answer (p.344).

The next step in the EBLIP process is to search the literature relevant to the question being investigated. Crumley and Koufogiannakis (2002) suggested that the EBLIP questions can be assigned to one of six domains or general areas of librarianship. An awareness of these domains can assist in managing the search for information. The six areas are:

- reference/enquiries: providing service and access to information that meets the needs of library users.
- education: finding teaching methods and strategies to educate users about library resources and how to improve their research skills.
- collections: building a high-quality collection of print and electronic materials that is useful, cost-effective and meets the users' needs.
- management: managing people and resources within an organization.
- information access and retrieval – creating better systems and methods for information retrieval and access.
- marketing/promotion: promoting the profession, the library and its services to both users and non-users (Crumley & Koufogiannakis 2006, p.63).

Crumley and Koufogiannakis (2002) and Eldredge (2006) reminded LIS practitioners that the profession was multi-faceted and multi-disciplinary in nature. Therefore the 'evidence base will be contained in multiple and varied information resources' (Winning 2004, p.71), which must then be included in the literature search that is undertaken. For example, Eldredge (2006) observed that a significant part of the LIS knowledge base was located in grey literature such as conference papers and posters. He also noted the important role of oral histories within workplaces. While the LIS literature was often criticised for being overly 'anecdotal' in nature, Brophy (2007) advocated the need to acknowledge and value workplace 'narrative' (i.e., those experiences that were shared in the corridor or the stories swapped over a drink in the conference bar). He contended that narrative could be a powerful addition to the evidence base upon which LIS professionals could rely when making decisions. He called for the development of 'narrative based practice' within the LIS field.

Once the literature relevant to the investigation has been obtained, the third step in the process, critical appraisal, can take place. The aim of critical appraisal is two-fold: first, to look at a piece of research in an objective and structured way in order to determine the validity or reliability of the research findings, and, second, to determine whether or not the findings could be applied to the decision making or problem solving at hand. Booth and Brice (2004) have provided a checklist (CriSTAL) to guide the critical appraisal of LIS literature (see table 9.1).

More recently, and of greater relevance to the concept of IL, is the ReLIANT instrument produced by Koufogiannakis et al. (2006). ReLIANT was developed via a systematic review of studies in the area of information skills training. Presented in table 9.2, the instrument provided a solid foundation for critically appraising literature in the field of IL. However, the instrument was limited by its failure to explicitly include a focus on IL theories and learning theories. While a user of the

ReLIANT instrument was required to consider 'learning outcomes', 'teaching methods' and 'IL competence' when appraising a study, the checklist could be improved by including the following more overt questions:

1. what IL theory or model (or human information behaviour theory or model) is being used to inform the design and delivery of the instruction or intervention? Why? Is this theory or model appropriate?
2. what learning theory is being used to inform the design and delivery of the instruction? Why? Is this theory appropriate?

Table 9.1 CriSTAL – critical appraisal checklist (Booth & Brice 2004)

Is the study a close representation of the truth?	
	Does the focus address a clearly focused issue?
	Does the study position itself in the context of other studies?
	Is there a direct comparison that provides an additional frame of reference?
	Were those involved in the collection of data also involved in delivering a service to the user group?
	Were the methods used in selecting the users appropriately and clearly described?
	Was the planned sample of users representative of all users (actual and eligible) who might be included in the study?
Are the results credible and repeatable?	
	What was the response rate and how representative was it of the population under study?
	Are the results complete and have they been analysed in an easily interpretable way?
	Are any limitations in the methodology (that might have influenced results) identified and discussed?
Will the results help me in my own information practice?	
	Can the results be applied to your local population?
	What are the implications of your study to practice?
	- in terms of current employment of services?
	- in terms of costs?
	- in terms of the expectations and attitudes of your users?
	What additional information do you need to obtain locally to assist you in responding to the findings of the study?

Table 9.2 The ReLIANT instrument (Koufogiannakis et al. 2006, pp.49-50)

I Study design
Is the objective of the study clearly stated? Is the reason for the study apparent?
Is the population described in detail? Is the number of study participants clearly stated? Is there a description of participants (gender, age, race, academic level, level of previous library experience, and so on)? Is the loss of any of the participants explained? Are participants required to participate in the course, or is their participation voluntary?
Are groups of participants that are receiving different educational interventions similar in their size and population characteristics? Other than the difference of the intervention, are the groups treated equally throughout the research process?
What research method was used? Was the research methodology clearly stated? Is it appropriate for the question being asked? Does the method attempt to avoid bias via randomisations, blinding and so on, when possible?
When were the learning outcomes measured? Is this a study looking at short term, intermediate or long term effects?
Is the research instrument described in detail? What questions were asked? What level of learning is the study addressing? Was the research instrument validated?
II Educational context
In what type of learning environments does the instruction take place (e.g., university, college, secondary school, public library, special library, hospital and so on)?
What teaching method was used? Is there a clearly outlined philosophy, or theoretical basis behind the instruction?
What mode of delivery was used (e.g., lecture, web-based tutorial, hands-on computer lab, videoconference and so on)?
Is the instructional topic clearly described? What was taught?
Are learning objectives stated?
How much instructional contact time was involved?
What learning outcomes were measured (e.g., cognitive, affective, behavioural learning outcomes)?
III Results
Are the results of the study clearly explained?
Do the results address the original research question?
Are the data presented in a clear manner, giving true numbers?
Were appropriate tests for statistical significance carried out and reported?
Was the reported outcome positive or negative in respect to the intervention?
Does the reported data support the author's conclusions?
Are potential problems with the research design presented?

IV Relevance
Is the study population similar to my own user/teaching population?
What IL competencies does this study address? Are those learning needs the same as those of my students?
Are the practice implications of the research reported?
Can the results of this study be directly transferred to my own situation, or what aspects of this study can I use to inform my practice?

A recent publication by Bruce et al. (2006) noted that 'people see information literacy, learning and teaching differently' (p.1) and as such 'ways of seeing IL and ways of seeing teaching and learning are likely influences on our approaches to, and experiences of, IL education' (p.2). Therefore, a critical appraisal checklist for literature in the area of IL education or instruction should also consider the way IL, learning and teaching have been defined and subsequently used to inform the educational design or intervention that is being explored within the study itself.

'The six frames for information literacy education' (Bruce et al. 2006) was developed to provide a tool for reflecting on and analysing the varying implicit or explicit theoretical influences on a particular educational or instructional context. The six frames are: (i) the content frame, (ii) the competency frame, (iii) the learning to learn frame, (iv) the personal relevance frame, (v) the social impact frame, and (vi) the relational frame. Each frame brings with it a particular view of IL, information, curriculum focus, learning and teaching, content and assessment. No one frame is better than the other. The six frames are presented in table 9.3. While the six frames model is not offered as a tool for critical appraisal per se, it can be viewed as an excellent supplement to the ReLIANT instrument.

The ultimate aim of critical appraisal is to determine whether the findings of a study being reviewed provide valid and reliable 'evidence' to inform the decision making or problem-solving process. What constitutes 'quality' evidence is therefore an important issue to consider. Existing definitions of EBL within the LIS profession (see above) acknowledge that the 'best available evidence' to make a decision or solve a problem might be either quantitative or qualitative. However, commentators have noted that the role and value of qualitative evidence within EBP in the LIS profession is being marginalised as 'less rigorous forms of evidence' when compared with quantitative evidence (Brophy 2007; Given 2006). For example, Eldredge (2002) provided a medical-based model for the levels of EBL evidence, with systematic reviews and randomised controlled trials (RCTs) placed at the top of the hierarchy. He pointed out that as 'most research evidence from the LIS field occupies the lowest levels of evidence', the LIS profession should be encouraged to 'use more rigorous forms over less rigorous forms of evidence when making decisions' (Eldredge 2002).

Given (2006) observed that the poor status placed on qualitative evidence in the LIS field was the result of 'confusion' and 'uncertainty' over the 'value of qualitative results for informing practice'. The LIS profession (like so many other

Table 9.3 The six frames for IL education (Bruce et al. 2006)

(1) Content frame	(2) Competency frame	(3) Learning to learn frame	(4) Personal relevance frame
Information exists apart from the user; can be transmitted.	Information contributes to the performance of the relevant capability.	Information is subjective – internalised and constructed by learners.	Valuable information is useful to the learners
What should learners know about the subject and IL?	What should learners be able to do?	What does it mean to think like an (IL) professional in the relevant field?	What good is IL to me?
Teacher is expert – transmits knowledge.	Teachers analyse tasks into knowledge and skills.	Teachers facilitate collaborative learning.	Teaching focuses on helping learners find motivation.
Learning is a change in how much is known.	Learners achieve competence by following pre-determined pathways	Learners develop conceptual structure and ways of thinking and reasoning.	Learning is about finding personal relevance and meaning
What needs to be known has primacy. All relevant content must be covered.	Content derived from observation of skilful practitioners.	Content chosen for mastering important concepts and fostering reflective practice.	Problems, cases, scenarios selected by learners to reveal relevance and meaning.
Assessment is objective. Measures how much has been learned; ranks student via exams.	Assessment determines what level of skill has been achieved.	Complex, contextual problems are proposed. Self or peer assessment is encouraged.	Typically portfolio based – learners self assess.
IL is knowledge about the work of information.	IL is a set of competencies or skills.	IL is a way of learning.	IL is learned in context and different for different people/groups.

professions) needed to learn to value each type of evidence and to acknowledge that the best type of evidence required will invariably depend on the nature of the question being answered or the decision being made. In short, the LIS profession should adopt a pluralistic approach to EBP. A pluralistic approach is grounded in the belief that no one research paradigm (positivist, interpretivist, critical theory) or research method (quantitative or qualitative) was superior, and that each focused

Table 9.3   The six frames for IL education (Bruce et al. 2006)

(5) Social impact frame	(6) Relational frame	Frame orientation
Information is viewed within social contexts.	Information may be experienced as objective, subjective or transformational.	View of information.
How does IL impact society?	What are the critical ways of seeing IL?	Curriculum focus.
Teachers' role is to challenge the status quo.	Teachers bring about particular ways of seeing specific phenomena.	View of teaching.
Learning is about adopting perspectives that will encourage social change.	Learning is coming to see the world differently.	View of learning.
Reveals how IL can inform widespread or important social issues or problems.	Examples selected to help students discover new ways of seeing. Critical phenomena for learning must be identified.	View of content.
Designed to encourage experience of the impact of IL.	Designed to reveal ways of experiencing.	View of assessment.
IL issues are important to society.	IL is a complex of different ways of interacting with information.	View of IL.

attention on different aspects of the situation or phenomenon being studied (Mingers 2001). Similarly, Robey (1996) argued that a diversity of research methods within a discipline was a positive source of strength. This was primarily because different methods focus attention on the diverse aspects of the situation or phenomenon being studied. Consequently, multi-method research was required to deal effectively with the full richness and complexity of the individual situations or phenomena.

The fourth step in the process is to assess the relative value of expected benefits and costs of the proposed plan of action. Eldredge (2006) warned against being too restrictive and only viewing the 'costs' and 'benefits' in purely economic terms. As a guide, he advocated the work of Clark and Wilson's (1961), whereby the costs and benefits within the context of organisational incentives were placed into three categories:

1. *material incentives* – that is, tangible rewards that have a monetary value or can easily be translated into ones that have. This most closely matches the traditional concepts of costs and benefits.
2. *solidary incentives* – that is, derived from associating, including rewards such as socializing, congeniality, the sense of group membership and identification.
3. *purposive incentives* – that is, principally derived from the stated ends of the association; the incentive is provided by belief in the organization's purposes (Eldredge 2006, p.348).

Eldredge (2006) proposed that 'this expanded concept of costs and benefits … keeps librarians attuned to local social or cultural contexts, which might need to be factored into the decision-making processes' (p. 348). This point was also noted by Koufogiannakis and Crumley (2004) who observed that even the most sound analyses of the best available evidence might be in vain if a prudent political strategy did not accompany and possibly modulate the diffusion of these results into the immediate cultural or social context.

The fifth and final step of the process involves evaluating the effectiveness of the action taken. This evaluation should take place at three levels: the practitioner level, the institutional level and the professional level. At the practitioner level the library professional engaged in the research needs to evaluate the process critically and, if at all possible, 'voice concerns about the integrity of that process in the course of discussions among co-workers' (Eldredge 2006, p. 349). Eldredge (2006) suggests the individual practitioner should reflect upon questions such as:

- are they cultivating the habit of identifying the many questions that occur in everyday practice?

- are they helping to identify the most answerable and important questions to be investigated in their institution?
- are they identifying the most comprehensive and effective strategies for searching for the needed evidence?
- are they alert to their own individual biases, the biases of other individuals, or the biases of the group?

At the institutional level the focus is on evaluating the project or program outcomes. It is at this point that the practitioner needs to return to the first step of the process and examine whether the question posed has in fact been answered. Beyond this, at the professional level, the evaluation needs to consider how well the profession is able to articulate the most relevant questions to the field, employ the most appropriate methodologies to answer these questions and make the necessary distinctions between different forms of evidence.

The five-step process described here offers a framework for making important decisions that were based upon the best available evidence. According to Eldredge (2006), 'each of the five steps in the process requires librarians to integrate their professional experience in judging the relevance and appropriateness of the best evidence' (p.351). He also suggested that while 'wide consensus surrounds the steps of the process' (p.351), there may be factors in the local external environment that impacted upon the actual application of the steps in different library contexts.

Eldredge's (2006) five-step process is presented as a useful tool for LIS professionals interested in EBLIP. It is interesting to note, however, that the primary focus of the process is on the gathering and critical appraisal of 'secondary' evidence (i.e., using the existing literature or research conducted by others) to inform practice. The process does not provide steps or guidance to LIS professionals interested in gathering 'primary' evidence (i.e., designing and conducting research to gather their own data) to meet their evidence-based needs in decision making and problem solving. Indeed the authors find this an intriguing omission. Eldredge acknowledged that his definition and discussion on EBP in the LIS profession was focused on the professionals who both 'consume' the results of research in making decisions and who strive to 'produce' their own research evidence. From the authors' point of view it is the latter point – producing one's own research – that is at the heart of EBL, to create new information that was relevant to the practitioner's own situation and could feed into the evolving knowledge base for the profession as a whole. The authors therefore recommend that in addition to the five-step process outlined above, LIS professionals should also consult work on the research methods and the research processes that would guide them in the design and implementation of EBL projects which are specifically aimed at gathering 'primary' evidence. There is a range of texts to support this (Creswell & Plano Clark 2007; Leedy & Ormrod 2005; Moore 2006) and for the LIS profession specifically (Gorman & Clayton 2005; Matthews 2007; Powell 2004; Williamson 2002).

How has EBP been applied to IL?

EBP has been used to explore, make decisions and solve problems in a number of different areas in the LIS profession including customer service (Abbott 2005) website usability (Cotter et al. 2005), collection development (Koufogiannakis 2007) and student library use (Nagata et al. 2007). In recent years, EBP has also been applied to the field of IL. Three examples are offered to illustrate how EBP is being used in the field. These examples are presented not as instances of 'best practice' but rather as illustrations of the different approaches through which EBP can be applied to provide insight into an array of IL issues and problems. The studies have been chosen as exemplars of three different types of evidence production that might be used within the IL field: a systematic review, a validation of an instrument and results of a survey. While detailed discussion on each example is not provided, further information on the research background and the key findings for each example can be found in the referenced papers.

The first example was a study conducted by Clark and Catts (2007) that explored the Information Skills Survey (ISS) (Catts 2003). The ISS is a standardised twenty item self-reporting measure to explore IL skills. It was developed using students in the fields of law, education and social sciences and currently exists in two forms, a generic form and a law discipline-specific form. Clark and Catts (2007) undertook an investigation to test the suitability of the generic form for use with medical students. Eighty-six first-year and 120 fourth-year medical students completed the inventory. Statistical analysis was used to explore the validity and reliability of the inventory for the two cohorts. The inventory was found to be reliable when used with both first- and fourth-year students. Content validity of the inventory was established with the first-year students but not the fourth year. Clark and Catts (2007) recommended further research to validate a discipline-specific version of the inventory. They concluded that the study findings were consistent with the situated (that is, both discipline and year of study can impact on IL development) nature of IL within higher education. The ISS is a tool that can assist library and information professionals in two ways: to help assess IL development in students during the course of their studies; and to help ensure that IL education programmes are being designed and subsequently re-designed in order to be more effective in the goal of developing student IL skill and knowledge.

The second example was a systematic review of the existing library research literature undertaken by Koufogiannakis and Weibe (2006). The objective of the review was to assess which library instruction methods were most effective for improving the information skills of students at the introductory undergraduate level, based on cognitive outcomes. Koufogiannakis and Weibe (2006) noted that librarians were constantly looking to improve the methods by which they teach information skills to undergraduate students and that most librarians have their own stories of success or failure to share with colleagues. The goal of the research was to help librarians who teach IL to undergraduate students at academic institutions to make more informed decisions about their teaching methods. Fifteen databases were searched to locate relevant articles. A total of 4356 potential articles were identified. There were 122 unique studies that met the inclusion criteria and were subjected to an extensive data extraction and critical appraisal process. Selection was made based on three criteria: (i) the instruction class or session had to be given by a librarian or library assistant (or part of a teaching team), (ii) the population had to be undergraduate students at a post-secondary academic institution, and (iii) the published article had to include an evaluative component that measured the cognitive effect of instruction on student learning via some test of IL. Of the 122 studies, fifty-five met the researchers' defined quality criteria to provide information on the effectiveness of different teaching methods. From this review there was a final group of sixteen studies with sufficient information to support a meta-analysis. The elements for critically appraising the articles were based upon the checklist developed by Morrison et al. (1999) and included the teaching evaluation used, learning objective and contact time. The study concluded that there was sufficient evidence to suggest that computer-assisted instruction was as effective as traditional instruction. Evidence also suggested that both traditional instruction and self-directed independent learning were more effective than no instruction. Koufogiannakis and Weibe (2006) noted that additional comparative research was required across different teaching methods and that studies comparing active learning, computer-assisted learning and self-directed independent learning would greatly enrich the research literature.

The third and final example was a study conducted by Bertulis and Lord (2005). The study aimed to explore the information needs of nurses and other health professionals by the Royal College of Nursing (RCN) library and information service. Seventeen hundred and fifteen (1715) participants completed a self-administered survey. The survey gathered data on issues such as access to computers and the internet, access to the local health library, awareness and use of different information resources, use of information services and perceived training needs. The results from the survey provided insight for the RCN in terms of how it could improve the service it provided to more effectively meet the information needs of its clients. For example, it was noted that more information skills training at all levels, basic to advanced, was required. A blended service was preferred, that is, physical library which incorporated hardcopy resources and the opportunity to speak with a librarian, in conjunction with a virtual library that offered access to electronic resources and online services. Bertulis and Lord (2005) noted that their findings could be used to help ensure better information provision and support for nurses which would hopefully lead to better patient care.

The three studies presented here reveal some of the diverse ways in which EBP can be applied within the field of IL. Each of the studies had different goals, focus, participants, approaches and impact. However, each study also illustrated clearly how EBP could, and should, be used to advance our knowledge base, make decisions, solve problems and improve our professional practice.

Conclusion

EBP has progressively become an important topic of discussion within the library and information literature. Booth and Brice (2007) prepared a 'mid-term report card' to consider the progress made in the actualisation of EBP in the LIS sector. They indicated that it was 'time to use the EBP process to produce real and transferable solutions to important practical problems' in libraries and information services and that there was 'an urgent need to consider the adoption of EBP as a core personal, professional and organisational responsibility'.The ongoing dialogue within the profession has clearly established that 'research can and does play a vital role in professional practice' (Harvey 2002, p.viii), indeed, 'it is more important than ever to build our knowledge base and to use evaluation research methods to constantly monitor and improve the quality of the services provided' (SLA Research Committee & Gard Marshall 2003, p.40). EBP therefore can and should have a significant role to play in many areas of library and information practice, but there are many particular opportunities in the area of IL education and practice.

References

Abbott, W. (2005). Persuasive evidence: Improving customer service through evidence-based librarianship. 3rd International Evidence Based Librarianship Conference, Brisbane, Australia, 16-19 October 2005. Retrieved 11 August 2007, http://conferences.alia.org.au/ebl2005/Abbott.pdf

Anderson, R.K. (1998). Inaugural address in *Proceedings of the Ninety-seventh annual meeting*, Medical Library Association, Seattle, USA, May 23-28, 1997. *Bulletin of the Medical Library Association, 86*(1), 117-143.

Bertulis, R. & Lord, J. (2005). Where there's a way there's a will! The Royal College of Nursing's information needs survey of nurses and health professionals. 3rd International Evidence Based Librarianship Conference, Brisbane, Australia, 16-19 October 2005. Retrieved 11 August 2007, http://conferences.alia.org.au/ebl2005/Bertulis.pdf

Booth, A. (2006). Counting what counts: Performance measurement and evidence-based practice. *Performance Measurement and Metrics, 7*(2), 63-74.

Booth, A. (2002). From EBM to EBL: Two steps forward or one step back? *Medical Reference Services Quarterly, 21*(3): 51-64.

Booth, A. & Brice, A. (2007). Prediction is difficult, especially the future. A progress report. *Evidence Based Library and Information Practice, 2*(1), 89-106. Retrieved 14 February 2008, http://ejournals.library.ualberta.ca/index.php/EBLIP/article/view/99/242

Booth, A. & Brice, A. (Eds.). (2004). *Evidence-based practice for information professionals: A handbook.* London: Facet.

Brice, A. & Hill, A. (2004). A brief history of evidence-based practice. In A. Booth & A. Brice (Eds.). *Evidence-based practice for information professionals: A handbook.* London: Facet. pp.13-23.

Brophy, P. (2007). Narrative based practice. *Evidence Based Library and Information Practice, 2*(1), 149- 158. Retrieved 14 December 2007, http://ejournals.library.ualberta.ca/index.php/EBLIP/article/view/137/248

Bruce, C., Edwards, S.L., & Lupton, M. (2006). Six frames for information literacy education: A conceptual framework for interpreting the relationships between theory and practice. *ITALICS, 5*(1), 1-18. Retrieved 14 December 2007, http://www.ics.heacademy.ac.uk/italics/vol5-1/pdf/sixframes_final%20_1_.pdf

Bundy, A. (Ed.) (2004). *Australian and New Zealand Information Literacy Framework* (2nd ed.). Adelaide: Australian and New Zealand Institute for Information Literacy (ANZIIL). Retrieved 14 February 2008, http://www.anziil.org/resources/Info%20lit%202nd%20edition.pdf

Catts, R. (2003). *Information skills survey for assessment of information literacy in higher education: Administration manual.* Canberra: Council of Australian University Librarians (CAUL).

Clark, C. & Catts, R. (2007). Information skills survey: Its application to a medical course, *Evidence Based Library and Information Practice, 2*(3), 3-26. Retrieved 15 September 2007, http://ejournals.library.ualberta.ca/index.php/EBLIP/article/view/51/529

Cotter, L., Harije, L., Lewis, S. & Tonnison, I. (2005). Adding SPICE to our library intranet site: A recipe to enhance usability. 3rd International Evidence Based Librarianship Conference, Brisbane, Australia, 16-19 October 2005. Retrieved 11 August 2007, http://conferences.alia.org.au/ebl2005/Cotter.pdf

Creswell, J.W. & Plano Clark, V.L. (2007). *Designing and conducting mixed methods research.* Thousand Oaks, CA: Sage.

Crumley, E. & Koufogiannakis, D. (2002). Developing evidence-based librarianship: Practical steps for implementation. *Health Information and Libraries Journal, 19*, 61-70.

Eldredge, J.D. (2006). Evidence-based librarianship: The EBL process. *Library Hi Tech, 24*(3), 341-354.

Eldredge, J.D. (2002). Evidence-based librarianship: What might we expect in the years ahead? *Health Information and Libraries Journal, 19*(2), 71-77.

Eldredge, J.D. (2000). Evidence based librarianship: an overview. *Bulletin of the Medical Library Association, 88*(4), 282–302.

Eldredge, J.D. (1997). Evidence-based librarianship: A commentary for *Hypothesis. Hypothesis, 11*(3), 4-7

Given, L. (2006). Qualitative research in evidence-based practice: A valuable partnership. *Library Hi Tech, 24*(3), 376-386.

Gorman, G.E. & Clayton, P. (2005). *Qualitative research for the information professional: A practical handbook.* London: Facet.

Gray, J.A.M. (2001). *Evidence-based health care* (2nd ed.). London: Churchill Livingstone.

Harvey, R. (2002). Introduction. In K. Williamson, *Research methods for students, academics and professionals: Information management and systems* (2nd ed., pp.xiii-xvii). Wagga Wagga, NSW: Centre for Information Studies, Charles Sturt University.

Juznic, P. & Urbanija, J. (2003). Developing research skills in library and information studies. *Library Management, 24*(6/7), 324-31.

Koufogiannakis, D. (2007). Establishing a model for evidence-based collection management. 4th International Evidence Based Library and Information Conference, Chapel Hill-Durham, USA, 6-11 May 2007. Retrieved 11 August 2007, http://www.eblip4.unc.edu/papers/Koufogiannakis.pdf

Koufogiannakis, D., Booth, A. & Brettle, A. (2006). ReLIANT: Reader's guide to the literature on interventions addressing the need for education and training. *Library and Information Research, 94*, 44-55.

Koufogiannakis, D. & Crumley, E. (2004). Applying evidence to your everyday practice. In A. Booth & A. Brice (Eds.), *Evidence-based practice for information professionals*, London: Facet. pp.119-126.

Koufogiannakis, D. & Wiebe, N. (2006). Effective methods for teaching information literacy skills to undergraduate students : A systematic review and meta-analysis. *Evidence Based Library and Information Practice 1*(3), 3-43. Retrieved 14 February 2008, http://ejournals.library.ualberta.ca/index.php/EBLIP/article/view/76/153

Leedy, R.D. & Ormrod, J.E. (2005*). Practical research: Planning and design* (8th ed.) Upper Saddle River, NJ: Prentice Hall.

McNicol, S. & Nankivell, C. (2001). The LIS research landscape: A review and prognosis. Center for Information Research, Retrieved 1 May 2005, http://www.ebase.uce.ac.uk/cirtarchive/projects/past/LISlandscape_final%20report.pdf

Matthews, J.R. (2007). *The evaluation and measurement of library services*. Westport, CT: Libraries Unlimited.

Mingers, J. (2001). Combining IS research methods: Towards a pluralist methodology. *Information Systems Research, 12*(3), 240-259.

Moore, N. (2006) . *How to do research. A practical guide to designing and managing research projects* (3rd ed. rev.) London: Facet.

Nagata, H., Toda, T. & Kytomaki, P. (2007). Students' patterns of library use and their learning outcomes. 4th International Evidence Based Library and Information Conference, Chapel Hill-Durham, USA, 6-11 May 2007. Retrieved 15 September 2007, http://www.eblip4.unc.edu/papers/Nagata.pdf

Powell, R.R. (2004). *Basic research methods for librarians*. Westport, CT. Libraries Unlimited.

Ritchie, A. (1999). Evidence-based decision making. *InCite, 12*. Retrieved 10 May 2005, http://www.alia.org.au/publishing/incite/1999/12/appraisal.html

Robey, D. (1996) Diversity in information systems research: Threat, promise and responsibility. *Information Systems Research, 7*(4), 400-408.

SLA. (2001). Putting OUR knowledge to work: A new SLA research statement. June 2001. The role of research in special librarianship. Retrieved 11 August 2007, http://www.sla.org/content/resources/research/rsrchstatement.cfm

SLA Research Committee & Gard Marshall, J. (2003). Influencing our professional practice by putting our knowledge to work. *Information Outlook, 7*(1), 40-44.

Society of College, National and University Libraries (SCONUL) (2007). The seven pillars of information literacy. Retrieved 14 February 2008, http://www.sconul.ac.uk/groups/information_literacy/seven_pillars.html

Williamson, K. (2002). *Research methods for students, academics and professionals: Information management and systems* (2nd ed.). Wagga Wagga, NSW: Center for Information Studies, Charles Sturt University.

Winning, A. (2004). Identifying sources of evidence. In A. Booth, & A. Brice (Eds.), *Evidence-based practice for information professionals*, London: Facet, pp.71-88.

Further reading

Beck, S.E. (2007). *Practical research methods for librarians and information professionals*. New York: Neal-Schuman.

Booth, A. & Brice, A. (Eds). (2004). *Evidence-based practice for information professionals: A handbook*. London: Facet.

Evidence Based Library and Information Practice Journal http://ejournals.library.ualberta.ca/index.php/EBLIP

Powell, R.R. (2004). *Basic research methods for librarians*. Westport, CT: Libraries Unlimited

Williamson, K. (2002). Introduction to research in relation to professional practice. In K. Williamson, *Research methods for students, academics and professionals: Information management and systems* (2nd ed., pp.5-23). Wagga Wagga, NSW: Centre for Information Studies, Charles Sturt University.

CHAPTER 10
The evidence-based model of information literacy research: a critique

Melanie Lazarow

This chapter unravels the multifaceted ways that evidence can be interpreted and used. It takes a position that the questions asked and the answers given are inextricably intertwined in a changing social, historical and political framework, where researchers and the researched are actors in the process.

That evidence is useful goes without saying. However, the evidence-based (EB) model competes with other models, which also use evidence but in different ways. Depending on the model, different questions are asked, different strategies are used, different answers are found and different ways forward are proposed.

The EB model for information literacy (EBIL) is new. *Evidence Based Library and Information Practice* (EBLIP), an open access, peer-reviewed journal, began publication in 2006 and *Evidence-based Practice for Information Professionals: A Handbook* (Booth & Brice), the first book published of its kind, came out in 2004. Speaking of her own approach, Denise Koufogiannakis, one of the co-founders of EBLIP, explains that:

> her goal is to improve library services to users. She encourages librarians to find research to support their day-to-day strategies and decisions. Where such evidence does not yet exist, she urges librarians to 'incorporate research into the new services or products they are developing' (Koufogiannakis 2007).

In the context of evidence and decision making, this chapter also looks at those who implement decisions and those who are affected by decisions, as part of an intertwined picture.

Using good evidence to answer questions seems, on the surface, so undeniable that to critique the model seems contrary. However, there is debate about the model that draws in questions of qualitative versus quantitative research, how cultural meaning is produced, what constitutes evidence and the way the paradigm is used politically.

In 2003, Todd pointed to the success of EB models stating that 'evidence-based practice – the process of carefully documenting – is key to being recognized' (Todd 2003). But what does recognition mean and who is recognising whom? In an earlier article, Todd's research into the use of heroin information by a small group of teenage girls illustrated that they 'were not passive, robot-like processors of information, merely absorbing information indiscriminately … [but] were active creators of knowledge, manipulating information selectively and creatively to develop revised pictures' (Todd 1999, p.21). The acknowledgement that the social sciences are engaged with creative actors, who play a part in the outcome of their world environment, is important in understanding evidence. This chapter emphasises the importance of not seeing evidence as a static entity.

The influence of the medical model

The origins of the EB model in information literacy stem from the dominance of the EB medical model. EB medicine (EBM) is mainly attributed to Archie Cochrane, an epidemiologist who argued that different kinds of evidence could be ranked according to the strength of their freedom from bias, the best form of evidence coming from randomised, double-blind, placebo-controlled trials. Cochrane's premises were that because resources would always be limited they should be used only where they have been shown to be effective (Cochrane 1972). It is important not to take diminishing resources as a given. The Iraq war has consumed disproportional resources, while health, welfare and education have received ongoing reductions.[1] The core concepts of EBM are based in work done in the 1970s and 1980s addressing Cochrane's accusation that many of the treatments, tests and procedures used in medicine had no evidence to demonstrate their effectiveness, and may in fact be doing more harm than good (Hill 2000, p.1190).

A definition of EBM often cited is:

> Evidence-based medicine is the conscientious, explicit, and judicious use of current best evidence in making decisions about the care of individual patients. The practice of evidence-based medicine means integrating individual clinical expertise with the best available external clinical evidence from systematic research (Sackett et al. 2007, p.71).

---

[1] The striking feature of modern war is its expense. The cost of the war in Iraq is estimated at $US 2.3 trillion (Stephen 2007). 'The cost of the Iraq war to Australian taxpayers is approaching $3 billion and is rising at a faster pace as the conflict has reached its fourth anniversary' (Davis & Coorey 2007).

From another angle, Hollway (2001) questions the reductive definition of what counts as evidence. Particularly from the 'caring' professions perspective, Hollway wonders whether scientific evidence epitomised in EB practice compromises the helping professions by threatening 'to impose reductive and standardised interventions' (Hollway 2001, p.10).

EBM concepts were taken up by library and information professionals interested in information literacy (IL). However, where EBM is primarily concerned with encouraging practitioners to make more use of the research evidence that is already available, EBIL is more concerned with filling the gap of too little quality research. What it means to be information literate depends on the framework one is using for understanding. The intertwining of what evidence is, whether the EB model is used, and what IL means to the researcher all combine to make the terrain of evidence far more rich and complex than first meets the eye.

Evidence-based librarianship (EBL)

Eldredge (2000a) puts forward a seven-part conceptual framework for EBL outlining that 'EBL seeks to improve library practice by utilizing the best-available evidence combined with a pragmatic perspective developed from working experiences in librarianship' (p.291). His framework acknowledges the distinct body of knowledge that has been accumulated throughout the history of librarianship. Like others, he encourages librarians to collect information and evidence where there are gaps.

> In clinical medicine, these research methods are intended to establish causal relationships while minimizing systematic or human biases. Until recently, health sciences librarianship has been largely influenced by research designs developed in the social, behavioral, and management sciences. Theoretical approaches developed in humanities disciplines, such as history or philosophy, have also influenced the field. EBL now seeks to adapt rigorously tested research designs from the health sciences, particularly clinical medicine (Eldredge 2000a).

Clyde (2005) in a paper delivered to IFLA in 2005 expands on one of the EBL threads explaining that evaluating research goes beyond research questions and/or hypotheses, descriptions of methodology and discussions of results. Her research touches on the value-laden nature of evaluation procedures. Investigating article-ranking, she identifies that 'value perceptions' are important. One group says empirical research is most important, another stressed factors external to the research itself. Yet another stressed the ethical issues and the value of the research to the profession, while a fourth group was most interested in whether research was set within the context of the literature. She concluded that there are problems with evaluating the quality of research because quality means different things to different people. This is a rather inconvenient finding for those who believe citations and or impact factors are reliable and meaningful. It is outside the scope of this paper to talk about the world phenomenon of government control and demand on universities for utilising questionable, and perhaps irrelevant, research frameworks (that are tied in many ways to an EB ideology).

A recent stock-taking report on EBL stressed 'that, as evidence-based practitioners, we have learned not to conflate increased inputs and outputs with increased impact' (Booth & Brice 2007, p.90). EB practice in librarianship is still largely focused on health; in fact in 2006 only 9 per cent of *LISA (Library and Information Science Abstracts)* citations, containing the words 'evidence-based', fell outside health librarianship. They hope that the use of evidence will become so widespread that there will no longer be a need for international organisations and journals to promote its use (Booth & Brice 2007, p.102).

Beneath the surface

Kirsty Williamson, in her introductory chapter to this book, gives an overview of positivist and interpretivist approaches, attempting to unravel some of the meanings of the philosophical and methodological concepts underpinning evidence. Her overview indicates the rich variety of ways of undertaking research, each starting from different premises and ending with different results.

This chapter acknowledges that evidence in the form of sense-experience must be the basis of understanding processes of becoming information literate. However, evidence cannot always be taken at face value; to give a simple example, it does not appear that the earth is moving yet it is. Collecting evidence should combine the systematic record of what is directly observable with the discovery of underlying causes. Evidence within the empiricist theoretical account is a restricted method of thought, which views the world as a collection of facts. It is wrong to emphasise observation at the expense of theory, and to treat evidential concepts and theories only as convenient mechanisms for relating isolated facts rather than as a way to illuminate the whole picture. An example is a study of 1,097 nurses across the US, researching whether they have the skills to engage in clinical decision making. Even though they have access to the internet, the nurses mainly get their information from colleagues or peers. This finding causes the authors to conclude that the nurses do not value or understand research (Pravikoff, et al.

2005). A fundamental understanding about learning as a social phenomenon is missed by this EB study.

Marx noted that 'all science would be superfluous if the outward appearance and the essence of things directly coincided' (Marx & Engels 1967, p.817). It is important not to unquestioningly adopt the language and the premises of EB without asking underlying questions about its philosophical, social and historical roots. For example, Forrest (2007) says 'As library and information professionals involved in teaching and learning, we need to ensure that our teaching methods and actions follow "best practice" and are "evidence-based"' (p.222). She does not say why.

The Evidence-based Medicine Working Group (1992) defined EB medicine as a new paradigm for clinical practice. Even though some have called EBM a paradigm, the debate and argument about its veracity put into doubt its paradigmatic status.

Statistics and neutrality

EB models often use statistical methods to test hypotheses (Hjorland 2005). In many of the EB articles there are only correlations between variables, with no questions about causes. A dialectical model of information/data-evidence-cause is more multi-faceted. Take Jones's (2007) example:

> In real life, creativity and innovation overlap, with a profound and complex interaction, in which cause and effect are inextricably linked: touch a cause, and it changes the effect, which then changes the cause, and so on.

EBM and EBL embody faith in neutral observations and deductions. Is there real space for traditions which emphasise cultural influence, class interests and the theory-laden nature of knowledge in the model? Government representatives in the UK argue that statistically-based, experimental research is to be preferred by EB practitioners since it is less biased by the interests of the researcher. However, experimental researchers, even those looking through a microscope are very capable of making mistakes or finding what they want to find. Statisticians well know that statistics can be used to 'prove' almost anything.

What EB is demanding is that all professional decisions are based on documented evidence. This demand sounds reasonable, even common sense. The question has, however, been asked: If evidence-based medicine is a new trend within medicine, 'what on earth was medicine based on before?' (Worrall 2002, p.S316).

There has been opposition to the EB movement because it is seen as a modern empiricist/positivist movement that is opposed to, for example, more interpretative tendencies (Davies 2003; de Leeuw 2005; Fowler & Lee 2007; Hill 2000; Hjorland 2005; Lipu 2005; Little 2003; Rodwin 2001; Rogers 2004). Evidence is not neutral, it is always ideologically situated. Evidence is shaped by power and in turn shapes those who use it.

Asking questions

Proponents of EB tell us that the first stage in the EB process is to get the question right (Booth 2006; Eldredge 2000b; Van Biervliet 2007). 'Evidence-Based Librarianship begins with the simple act of asking an answerable, practical question' (Eldredge 2000b, p.74). Eldredge gives four examples of questions which are pragmatic and cost-related: the cost of one database versus another, evaluating cost effectiveness of print versus electronic journals, online tutorials effectiveness versus face-to-face teaching, and determining when to weed a collection. To be more precise, he points to the need for questions to have a noun, verb and object as part of their sentence structure. In a recent article, Booth said that EBL 'involves asking answerable questions, finding, critically appraising and then utilising research evidence' (Booth 2004, p.65).

Is there a tendency for the questions that are posed as a starting point for gathering evidence in the EB model to be simplistic rather than simple? Pragmatism allows for this but pragmatism is not a philosophy which challenges or pushes boundaries. How often does the EB project ask questions that do not imply cost-saving endeavours? Are EB practitioners interested in questioning whether increased nurse/patient ratios could be good for hospitals, or that more teachers could be good for schools? Paradigms which construct IL as social and cultural practice imply an embodied interchange and attention to individuals combining collectively with others to make knowledge, not just to receive it or to understand it in isolation.

Davies (2003), Rogers (2004) and de Leeuw (2005) all question the assumptions of the pragmatism of asking questions which assume a western or managerialist bias. Lipu (2005) uses a feminist approach to discuss IL. She talks about Papua New Guinean women and blends IL with sociology, psychology and education to get a greater depth in answers to questions which include 'Who says so and what will it mean for women?'.

In 2005, de Leeuw considered the 125 scientific questions and problems yet to be resolved which the journal *Science* had examined in that year. All the health questions were political questions, and in de Leeuw's view 'the next stage of the evidence debate will have to address (these) far more astutely' (p.211). Looking at feminism and 'new managerialism', Davies unpacks evidence with a Foucaultian tinge. Not mincing her words she says:

> To this end, the language of managerialism cleverly cannibalises the liberal humanist terms in vogue during the period of high modernity that seem, on the face of it, indisputably virtuous and desirable. Take 'literacy', for example. Who can dispute the desirability of every child achieving a minimum standard of literacy and thus achieving not only the potential to be active citizens but also the potential to survive in the new information technology driven world? The means of achieving this may actually be at the expense of the teaching strategies through which critical literacy or any other critical/analytical skills are taught. They also may draw massive resources away from teaching itself and into the bureaucracy that stages and evaluates the testing and other strategies through which the 'new' objectives are to be achieved ... Resistance may well position you as one of those whom the system are supposedly designed to catch out (Davies 2003, p.98).

The importance of context

Undoubtedly there is enormous danger in looking at evidence out of its political and socio-historical context. 'Twenty-five years after AIDS was first identified, programs to fight disease continue to be undermined by conservative ideologies and moralistic approaches', says Joe Amon, director of the HIV/AIDS program at Human Rights Watch (2006). 'Evidence' proves that informing citizens about the transmission of AIDS, and providing condoms, is the best way forward 'in sub-Saharan Africa [where] a majority of young adults lack adequate knowledge of HIV transmission. Yet some governments emphasize 'abstinence-only' approaches'. In fact in some countries condoms are restricted and virginity parades are held (Human Rights Watch 2006). This is an example where AIDS/HIV evidence cannot be fenced away from problems of economic crises, the rich-poor divide, and long standing colonialism.

Asking the 'right' question might involve a process of engagement where some wrong questions eventually lead to some right ones, but where cultural sensitivity and non-paternalism override the initial correctness of the question.

For constructivist theorist Vygotsky, the object of study and the method of study are practical. Here he does not mean pragmatic; he means 'useful'. Practical-critical activity are 'simultaneously prerequisite and product' (Vygotsky 1986, p.86). The linear cause/effect process involves both looking at cause, looking at effect and then also looking at how they interlink and influence each other. 'Evidence' is always tied to the history of the question asked, how the question is answered and how the answers determine future questions. But questions and answers do not occur separately; they happen interactively and at the same time. Using the AIDS example, a socio-cultural framework would have to ask multiple questions relating not only to the health problem itself, but also to the context and historical political situation surrounding health funding, schooling, food and basic needs. The distribution of wealth and privilege are important considerations for significant answers.

Power, privilege and bureaucratic control

Power as a central concern in EB models and particularly EBM is taken up by many writers:

> Thus EBM, from being a 'solution' to the problem of indeterminacy (and therefore a professionalizing strategy) gives what are essentially 'political' decisions an illusion of objectivity while shifting the indeterminacy into the policy arena (Armstrong 2007, p.82).

and

> EBM is not simply a new way of doing medical research or clinical work … EBM has operated in the problem space of professionalism, indeterminacy and medical dangers. It has functioned at the interface between professionalizing strategies (the promise of effective medicine) and the new dangers from medical intervention (the promise of safe medicine). And, by increasing the precision by which uncertainty is known, it has moved the problem of indeterminacy into a new arena of power (Armstrong 2007, p.83).

EBM has changed the balance of power to give bureaucratic control over doctors and patients. Yet as Rodwin (2001, p.441) points out: 'Policy making, by its nature, requires making choices that are not value free or reducible to technical issues over which there is little controversy. It is not possible to purge issues of value, or politics from public policy.' Lupton (2002) pleads with us to utilise the most complex of the IL standards, faces or facets: information wisdom. Like others quoted, she recognises that wisdom involves using knowledge in a reflective way, acknowledging personal values for the benefits of others.

In the case of EBIL, an important consideration is what IL is. Information literacy is understood variously as a teaching method, process, concept, behaviour or framework. To superimpose a structured EB model on the many interpretations of IL is problematic. Most important, if the EB model is primarily constructed for digestible results for policy makers the wisdom facet will be undermined.

Lloyd (2007) and Fowler and Lee (2007) explore discursive analysis and break the linear nexus of cause-effect questioning. These studies look at evidence and IL as more than a development of skills. Lloyd describes IL as acknowledging the person as embodied, bringing physical and emotional sensations together as sources of information passed to them from their 'community of practice'. In her investigation of how firefighters gain information literacy, Lloyd gives an example of a method which goes beyond the uni-linear. She shows how 'participants' beliefs, values and ideologies and information accessed through sensory, experiential or social domains is unpredictable until experienced' (Lloyd 2007, p.197). Fowler and Lee use discursive analysis by looking at one case study, a woman learning to breastfeed her first baby. They examine the complex and contradictory dynamics of this mother's knowing and learning, situated in relation to formal knowledge about breastfeeding, in order to explore and elaborate an argument for more complex cultural and relational understandings of knowing and learning than that offered by the statistical EB model. Fowler and Lee acknowledge that the 'conceptualization of learning is often unnecessarily narrow, valuing knowledge gained from formal education settings as more important than informal learning gained from experience' (Fowler & Lee 2007, p.190).

Lloyd (2005; 2007) and Davies (2003) both in their own way point to 'authentic' practice. Davies says that 'the first and necessary step in counteracting the force of any discourse is to recognise its constitutive power, its capacity to become hegemonic'. Lloyd draws attention to learning as a complex process where the 'learning environment may be considered informal or unstructured, and where learning is constituted through collective practices and focused on the development of collective competence as opposed to individual competence.' Lloyd talks about the experience of firefighters becoming 'enculturalised' and suggests that evidence interpretation 'may be facilitated through access to authentic practices in the context of supportive communities who share a common discourse that focuses on the central meanings of practice and profession' (Lloyd 2005).

Conclusion

Steven Rose, neurologist, humanist, anti-war activist and director of the Brain and Behavior Research group, spent a lifetime in neurobiology only to have his work used to develop 'sonic booms' high-powered millimetre microwaves which affect pain receptors in the skin, causing intense unbearable burning sensations (Rose 2005). Like Robert Oppenheimer before him (one of the developers of the atomic bomb), Rose has been caught in the nexus between evidence, research and use.

There is no argument that evidence is important. However, if IL seriously includes the reflective element and the critical element, then how evidence is used must be a priority in our theory building.

In conclusion, some of the problems with the EB model are that despite all the fervency with which the idea of evidence-based policy is being advocated it is not really new but has its antecedents in many other philosophical movements. If the EB movement is a fashion, the encouragement it gives to IL practitioners to start looking and enquiring should be endorsed, but its ideological component must not be ignored. In this 'risk society' where fear is constantly manufactured, the management of evidence is as important as evidence itself. The strangle-hold of the EB model as it tightens on information literacy may close off dynamic ways of knowing rather than open them up, unless we demand that evidence is seen in a complex, caring way. By all means let us all enquire and gather evidence, but let us also understand that 'evidence' is much more than it seems.

References

Armstrong, D. (2007). Professionalism, indeterminacy and the EBM project. *BioSocieties*, *2*, 73-84.

Booth, A. (2006). Clear and present questions: Formulating questions for evidence-based practice. *Library Hi Tech, 24*(3), 355-368.

Booth, A. (2004). Formulating answerable questions. In A. Booth & A. Brice (Eds.). *Evidence-based practice for information professionals: A handbook* (pp.61-70). London: Facet.

Booth, A. & Brice, A. (2007). Prediction is difficult, especially the future: A progress report. *Evidence Based Library and Information Practice, 2*(1), 89-105.

Booth, A. & Brice, A. (Eds.) (2004). *Evidence-based practice for information professionals:A handbook*. London: Facet.

Clyde, A. (2005). The basis for evidence-based practice: Evaluating the research evidence. Paper presented at the World Library and Information Congress: 71th IFLA General Conference and Council. Retrieved 8 May 2007 from http://www.ifla.org/IV/ifla71/Programme.htm

Cochrane, A.L. (1972). *Effectiveness and efficiency: Random reflections on health services*. London: Nuffield Provincial Hospitals Trust.

Davies, B. (2003). Death to critique and dissent? The policies and practices of new managerialism and of evidence-based practice. *Gender and Education, 15*(1), 91-103.

Davis, M. & Coorey, P. (2007). $3b and rising rapidly: Cost of the war to Australian taxpayers. *Sydney Morning Herald*, from www.smh.com.au/news/national/3b-and-rising-rapidly-cost-of-iraq-war/2007/03/20/1174153066804.html

de Leeuw, E. (2005). Who gets what: Politics, evidence, and health promotion [Electronic Version]. *Health Promotion International, 20*, 211-212. Retrieved 1 September 2005 from http://heapro.oxfordjournals.org

Eldredge, J.D. (2000a). Evidence-based librarianship: An overview [Electronic Version]. *Bulletin of the Medical Library Association, 88*(4), 289-302. Retrieved from http://www.pubmedcentral.nih.gov/articlerender.fcgi?artid=35250

Eldredge, J.D. (2000b). Evidence-based librarianship: Formulating EBL questions. *Bibliotheca Medica Canadiana, 22*(2), 74-77.

Evidence-based Medicine Working Group. (1992). Evidence-based medicine: A new approach to teaching the practice of medicine. *Journal of the American Medical Association, 268*(17), 2420-2425.

Forrest, M. (2007). Learning and teaching in action. *Health Information and Library Journal, 24*, 222-226.

Fowler, C. & Lee, A. (2007). Knowing how to know: Questioning 'knowledge transfer' as a model for knowing and learning in health. *Studies in Continuing Education, 29*(2), 181-193.

Hill, G.B. (2000). Archie Cochrane and his legacy – an internal challenge to physicians' autonomy? Commentary. *Journal of Clinical Epidemiology, 53*(12), 1189-1192.

Hjorland, B. (2005). Empiricism, rationalism and positivism in libary and information science. *Journal of Documentation, 61*(1), 130-155.

Hollway, W. (2001). The psycho-social subject in 'evidence-based practice'. *Journal of Social Work Practice, 15*(1), 9-22.

Human Rights Watch. (2006). World AIDS Day 2006: Ideology trumps action as epidemic worsens. Retrieved 15 October 2007 from http://www.hrw.org/english/docs/2006/12/01/global14688.htm

Jones, B. (2007). Advancing knowledge: Pushing boundaries. Paper presented at the Educause Australasia Conference April 29-May 2. Retrieved from http://www.caudit.edu.au/educauseaustralasia07/authors_papers/Barry-Jones.pdf

Koufogiannakis, D. (2007). Where's the evidence? [Electronic Version]. *Library Journal*. Retrieved 14 June 2007 from http://www.libraryjournal.com/article/CA6423397.html

Lipu, S. (2005). Measuring the immeasurable. 33rd Australian and New Zealand Comparative and International Education Society (ANZCIES) Conference

'Questioning "Best Practice' in Education: Benefits and Disadvantages, Debates and Dilemmas', 2-4 December, Coffs Harbour.

Little, M. (2003). 'Better than numbers' … a gentle critique of evidence-based medicine. *ANJ Journal of Surgery, 73*, 177-182.

Lloyd, A. (2007). Learning to put out the red stuff: Becoming information literate through discursive practice. (Special Issue on Discursive Approaches to Information Seeking in Context) (Case study). *Library Quarterly, 77*(2), 181-198.

Lloyd, A. (2005). No man (or woman) is an island: Information literacy, affordances and communities of practice [Electronic Version]. *Australian Library Journal, 54*, from http://www.alia.org.au/publishing/alj/54.3/full.text/lloyd.html

Lupton, M. (2002). The getting of wisdom: Reflections of a teaching librarian [Electronic Version]. *Australian Academic and Research Libraries, 33*. Retrieved 30 October 2007 from http://alia.org.au/publishing/aarl/33.2/full.text/lupton.html

Marx, K. & Engels, F. (1967). *Capital: A critique of political economy*. New York: International Publishers.

Pravikoff, D., Tanner, A. & Pierce, S. (2005). Readiness of US nurses for evidence-based practice. *American Journal of Nursing, 10*(9), 40-51.

Rodwin, M.A. (2001). The politics of evidence-based medicine. *Journal of Health Politics, Policy and Law, 26*(2), 439-446.

Rogers, W. (2004). Evidence-based medicine and women: Do the principles and practice of EBM further women's health? *Bioethics, 18*(1), 50-71.

Rose, S. (2005). *The 21st-century brain: Explaining, mending and manipulating the mind*. London: Vintage Books.

Sackett, D.L., Rosenberg, W.M.C., Gray, J.A.M., Haynes, R.B. & Richardson, W.S. (2007). Evidence-based medicine: What it is and what it isn't (reprinted from *BMJ*, vol.312, pp.71-72, 1996). *Clinical Orthopaedics and Related Research* (455), 3-5.

Stephen, A. (2007). Iraq: The hidden cost of war [Electronic Version]. *New Statesman*. Retrieved 12 March 2007 from http://www.newstatesman.com/200703120024

Todd, R. (2003). Irrefutable evidence: How to prove you boost student achievement [Electronic Version]. *School Library Journal*. Retrieved 14 June 2007 from http://www.schoollibraryjournal.com/article/CA287119.html

Todd, R. (1999). Utilization of heroin information by adolescent girls in Australia: A cognitive analysis. *Journal of the American Society for Information Science, 50*(1), 14-23.

Van Biervliet, J. (2007). An evidence-based approach to clinical questions in the practice of equine neurology. *Veterinary Clinics of North America-Equine Practice, 23*(2), 317-328.

Vygotsky, L.S. (1986). *Thought and language*, revised and edited by A. Kozulin, Cambridge, MA: MIT Press.

Worrall, J. (2002). What evidence in evidence-based medicine? *Philosophy of Science* *69*(S3), S316–S330.

CHAPTER 11
Alternative methods in information literacy research in Australasia

Suzanne Lipu

Introduction

This book has presented a range of approaches that Australasian practitioners and researchers have used to explore their information literacy (IL) research questions. This chapter is about encouraging future IL researchers – both in scope and depth of understanding about IL – to use other research methods. This will help foster a greater consistency in the use of terminology that may lead to shared dialogue, deeper engagement with the research field and a growing ability to convey the significance of IL for society and the twenty-first century workplace.

Research methods

Research methods are the approaches employed by researchers to perform their study. These methods originate from broader theoretical frameworks (see figure 11.1). I believe that the range of methods used in IL research is still somewhat limited and that positivist methods can offer only limited contributions to the under-theorised IL arena, where models have not yet been rigorously debated. Several methods have therefore been selected for discussion here as alternative methods for consideration by researchers for their relevance to IL. These are:

- narrative research methods,
- feminist research methods, and
- cross-cultural research methods.

Each of these is rooted in interpretivist frameworks. These frameworks were introduced earlier in this book in Williamson's Chapter 1. As she points out, interpretive frameworks are based on the notion of people constructing individual, and highly personal, realities (including their experiences of IL). The appeal of these frameworks lies in the acceptance of multiple perspectives. There is no promotion or advocacy for *one* 'reality' or 'truth', which is particularly significant and relevant to IL research since we have only scratched the surface of IL so far.

Furthermore, those, like me, who take a critical research stance (in terms of social justice, equity and human rights) can also recognise an easy 'fit' under the interpretivist umbrella. A range of suitable methods and techniques can be utilised to help a researcher delve deep into people's experiences with information, encourage the voices of the researched to emerge, and help reveal multiple personal and cultural perspectives. They have the potential to greatly enrich our current understandings of the IL phenomenon and inspire greater attention to it by those outside the information profession.

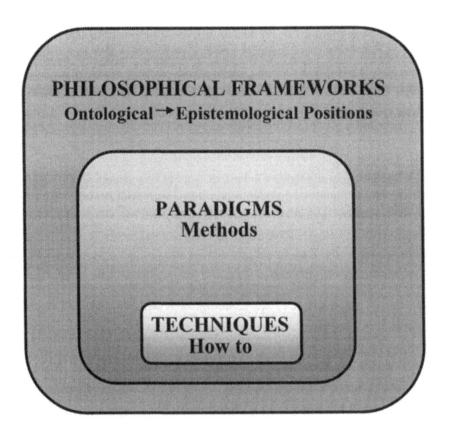

Figure 11.1 Philosophical frameworks of research methods

Narrative research methods

Hinchman and Hinchman (1997, p.xvi) provided this definition of narrative:

> Narratives (stories) in the human sciences should be defined provisionally as discourses with a clear sequential order that connect events in a meaningful way for a definite audience and thus offer insights about the world and/or people's experiences of it (cited in Elliot 2005, p.3).

For the last decade, narrative inquiry (as narrative research method is often called) has been popular among social science researchers. Connelly and Clandinin (1999, p.132) say that narrative researchers are those who 'believe that human experience is basically storied experience: that humans live out stories and are story-telling organisms'.

Using narrative as a method can involve exploring written stories, gathering stories through conversations and/or interviews, or writing up research data as narratives. The method requires a researcher to make many decisions throughout the research about the data gathering, interpretation and presentation of the stories. Despite the richness narratives can offer, some complexities can arise. For example, capturing the essence of an experience can be difficult – both for the person telling their story and for the researcher re-telling it. Some critics question the ability of people to reliably use memory to construct their stories. Furthermore, not everything that a person says to a researcher is a 'story'.

What then is a story in research terms? In their research with African-American families with seriously ill or disabled children, Mattingly and Lawlor (2000) tackle this issue of defining what a story is:

> Stories concern action, more specifically human action, and particularly social interaction. Stories have plots. They have a beginning, middle and end, so that while they unfold in time, the order is more than mere sequence ... Stories show how human actors do things in the world, how their actions shape events and instigate responses in other actors, changing the world (and often the actors themselves) in some way ... stories explore the complex motives that drive individuals to act in some ways rather than others and they also reveal the constraints of environment, of body, of social contexts that delimit a person's possibilities for actions (p.6).

Then there are attempts to define narrative research itself. For example, Cottle (2002) describes narrative research as an invitation for interaction. Stories and narrative research could provide answers to critics of existing IL research about being text-based (text-bound). Researchers from countries such as Africa and Papua New Guinea have pointed out the need for greater attention to oral-based cultures and experiences with information (see Obi 2002, Aiyepeku et al. 2002). Stories are a powerful source of communication and information within such cultures. Using them in narrative inquiry therefore offers the opportunity to include much broader conceptualisations of IL, thus filling gaps which several recent literature reviews of the field have revealed (Hughes et al 2005, Virkus 2003).

Furthermore, narrative research opens up the possibility for IL researchers to collect rich and unique accounts of people's experiences with information. By actively facilitating the voices of information users rather than the privileged ones of 'information experts' we may find directions and needs to guide IL educational practice and interaction with users in a variety of settings. In such a small field, narratives could also provide fertile ground for future investigations about issues or themes.

Feminist research methods

Feminist research methods have originated from a range of highly contested feminist theoretical perspectives. No single feminist theoretical perspective exists and feminist researchers – like other researchers – often identify with several theoretical frameworks. Their 'commonality' lies within the concept that feminist research 'aims to make women's lives and experiences central and seeks to uncover oppression and inequity in everyday experiences' (Garrett 1999, n.p.) regardless of whether they consider themselves a postcolonial feminist, post-structural feminist or critical feminist, for example.

Another commonly shared belief among feminists is that Western knowledge, at least, is typically gendered knowledge. That is, that knowledge frameworks have been constructed primarily from male perspectives and dominant discourses in the same way that Western frameworks have long (overtly or covertly) silenced non-Western 'ways of knowing'. Feminists typically seek to disrupt the dominant frameworks.

Feminist researchers often consider the following as critical to their research:

- reflexivity,
- careful use of language throughout the research process, and
- consciousness of power relations.

Reflexivity

McMullen (2006, p.39) says that reflexivity:

> forces us to come to terms with why we have chosen a particular research
> problem, how we engage with our research participants and the
> implications of bringing and enacting our own biographies in a research
> setting. Taking a reflexive stance means that we examine and question
> both our behaviour and that of our participants in a research setting.

This highlights a very important point about reflexivity – that it is an *ongoing*
activity or process required of a researcher throughout a research study. At all
phases the researcher is required to reflect – *and act* – on their design, data
collection, presentation of data.

Furthermore, feminist researchers acknowledge:

> Because the people who construct and articulate the research
> findings inevitably shape knowledge, feminist researchers must
> reflect upon and be explicit about their subjective role during the
> research. This 'reflexivity' is particularly the case with respect to biases,
> values, and experiences ... because the researcher's identity and life
> experiences are used as assets and tools for interpretation.(Broido &
> Manning 2002, p.442).

One of the ways in which feminist researchers employ reflexivity is when they
position themselves. This may involve telling their own story in relation to the
research questions, or identifying their background or values that may influence the
design, collection and/or presentation of data. Brayton (1997) refers to this as
'locating' oneself within a research study. Doing this can then be helpful in a
variety of ways such as: building rapport with participants, establishing credibility
with the scholarly audience, prompting researchers to distinguish between their
interpretations of the participants' responses and their own personal perspectives or
assumptions. The ongoing process of reflexivity can also help ensure that the
research retains its integrity in relation to the philosophical underpinnings of
feminist research.

Use of language

The focus on language in feminist research is about the researcher paying great
attention to aspects of language throughout the *entire* research project. Language is
recognised as a powerful tool in the oppression of women. The language of
academe – and research – is highly influenced by the Western males who have
largely dominated the construction of research practice and the language involved

with it. The feminist researcher's goal is not to perpetuate this but to increase the opportunities for women's voices to come to the fore and be recognised.

Power relations

In using these methods, feminist researchers are usually attempting to actively disrupt power relations between the researcher and the researched (as much as is possible since power relations shift frequently and often imperceptibly). This should be of significance to IL researchers because much of the IL research thus far has come from 'information experts'. Admittedly this label is value-laden, but it is meant to indicate that the existing research has largely been carried out by librarians and library educators (so called 'experts'). The 'danger' of such limitation is that we run the risk of working in our own small universe, becoming oblivious to the needs/demands/wishes of those with whom we are meant to be working. If we want to foster increased awareness of IL with governments, cultural leaders and the community then we need to be representing them rather than speaking for them. As Nagar observed in 2003, it is one thing to bring knowledge to the fore but another to co-produce knowledge that speaks the political and theoretical languages of communities beyond the academy (p.65).

Power relations, even when women research women, however, are not always clear. There has been much research literature dedicated to exploring the desire of feminist researchers to be conscious of hierarchy during interviews, for example. However, as Tang (2002) discovered in her own comparative research of academic mothers in China and the UK, there are many factors (class, race, language, personal histories, cultural backgrounds and more) that impact on interviews in the field. Assuming some similarities between herself and the interviewees would ensure equal power, there were nevertheless times she was surprised by other factors influencing the interviews when she became the one in the position of less power in the research. She also aptly points out that, in assuming that the researched need to be given more power is the inherent assumption that the researcher is more powerful to begin with.

There have been some studies that focus on women. For example, in Africa, Mooko (2005) focused on the information-seeking behaviour of Botswanan women and used the snowball sampling technique, involving one participant suggesting another suitable participant who in turn suggested more suitable participants for as long as was necessary, eventually obtaining participants from three village areas and conducting interviews and focus groups about their information needs. She conducted the research partly because there is so little knowledge about how women access and use information in rural areas in non-industrialised countries.

Her findings showed the various reasons women sought information: health, work, family violence, financial information and basic needs. Mooko also identified sixteen sources of information that the women used to fulfil their information needs including medical practitioners, nurses, village chiefs, community welfare office, church members, spiritual healers and government officials. Printed sources were also used but to a much lesser extent. There is some debate about whether information seeking is or is not part of IL research. Because I believe that both deal with peoples' experiences with information this example has been included.

Feminist research does not just mean focusing on women as subjects. Rather it is about encouraging their perspectives to be heard and presented. Brayton (1997) quotes Lather (1988, p.571) as saying: 'The overt ideological goal of feminist research in the human sciences is to correct both the *invisibility* and *distortion* of female experience'. She then goes on to say: 'Feminist research takes women's situations, concerns, experiences and perspectives as the basis for research. It embodies women's experiences in their social world from their own interpretation and using their own language' (n.p.).

Despite the possibly unique role women have with information, feminist methods and techniques have scarcely been applied in IL research thus far. This situation needs to be rectified through consideration by researchers to use it within their studies. The scope, and possibilities, for feminist IL research are very exciting. Aside from the large gap in research focusing solely on women's experiences of IL, there lies the potential for feminist research in the field to decide, change, or disrupt the ways in which IL is currently explored and debated. For example, consider recent attempts to prove the worth of IL education in terms of measured outcomes. Is this really possible, or even desirable? *Why* are we trying to measure it? Feminist researchers could create significant new knowledge for the field by taking a step back and exploring IL issues identified by women as important to know. They could design and implement research designs and techniques that are not bound within existing discourses, potentially broadening research approaches to those issues. Furthermore, in taking into consideration the issues covered in this section – reflexivity, language and power – they could contribute new 'ways of knowing' as yet undiscovered in this burgeoning field.

Cross-cultural research methods

Like feminist research, cross-cultural research is rooted in deep theory from decades of anthropological, sociological and other research. There are many gaps in IL research in terms of cultural IL contexts and engagements with IL. It is not within the scope of this chapter, however, to explore the theoretical constructs or topic gaps of this type of research. Rather, it is to illuminate the *methods* that may be of interest to potential and existing IL researchers. It should be noted that these methods are not exclusive to cross-cultural research. It is more that they are ones that have informed many research projects of a cross-cultural nature.

Cross-cultural methods to be discussed here for their relevance to IL research are:

- ethnography/participant observation,
- participatory research, and
- collaborative research.

Ethnography/participant observation

As a key anthropological research method, originally ethnography involved a researcher being immersed in a location and culture, taking field notes, making observations and then writing up the research. This process was also called 'participant observation'. Fine (2006) says that: 'Participant observation involves the active engagement of the researcher with the members of the community he or she wishes to study' (p.11073). She adds:

> Adler and Adler (1987) divide participant observation methods according to the extent of participation: peripheral membership, active membership, and complete membership. In general, the peripheral member observes as an outsider to the group and its culture, the active member is directly engaged in the life of the group, while making it clear to the group that she or he does not fully belong and is conducting research. In the model of the Adlers, the complete observer essentially engages in ethnographic immersion, sometimes informing the group of the research goals (p.11076).

'Ethnography' and 'participant observation' are often interchangeable terms and the method is now used in a variety of settings by researchers in different disciplines. There is no longer the common acceptance of what constitutes 'culture', or how an ethnographer should collect – or represent – data (Agar 2006, pp.4857-4862).

The value of such a method to IL research can partly be found in Bow's (2002) statement that: 'If your interest is to learn about certain characteristics, behaviours, or opinions of your research participants in depth, then ethnography may be a good choice' (p.271).

Each of these represent aspects of IL we still do not know enough about. Using ethnography provides a researcher with flexible and adaptive techniques, such as the use of interviewing, focus groups and observations to varying degrees depending on the needs within different settings and with different issues. Choosing one or more of these techniques could help us gain closer insight into, and understanding about how individuals of certain cultural, social and other groups experience IL. Participatory and collaborative research methods also offer these opportunities.

Participatory research

While there are some similarities between participatory research and action research in terms of both revealing locally identified priorities and problems, participatory research focuses on equity. It is not the same as a researcher participating in a project. Participatory research is much more about participants being involved in a project to the extent that they may even determine the research problem, how the research is conducted and data analysed. The level of 'control' that they have may vary throughout the history of a research project (Cornwall & Jewkes 1995). Regardless, it is particularly important in cross-cultural research that the participants' agenda or needs are not lost or replaced in favour of the researcher's agenda.

Collaborative research

Collaborative research aims to demystify the research process, and involve others in the research. Using collaborative research methods is highly desirable in cross-cultural research especially where many communities have been previously exploited by privileged researchers (such as by researchers whose race dominates the other politically). This can result in skewed knowledge being put forth and accurate representations of people's experiences being affected. As Mertens (1998) says:

> Cross-cultural ethical principles require collaboration between the researcher and the host community... [she advocates that] the researcher communicate the intended research agenda, design, activity, and reports with members of the host community. The research should be designed in a way as to bring benefit to the host community (1998, p.27).

Such collaboration is not just a feel-good measure. The researcher's capacity to relinquish some of the control over a research project by encouraging collaboration with participants can mean that significant issues are not overlooked. As McMullen (2006) points out, 'The narrative structures that we use to organise our life are not of our own making – they are socially embedded and culturally transmitted' (p.39). If a researcher is an 'outsider' to a community (culturally or otherwise) then they may not be aware of, or privy to, information about practice or beliefs within it. Collaboration with 'insiders' could provide invaluable insights and dimensions to a research issue that the researcher may not have considered or know about. In IL research this seems particularly pertinent. We have yet to understand IL enough within specific communities, or across different cross-cultural settings. Collaborative research with those groups may help overcome this.

Collaborative research could be said to differ from participatory research in that collaborative research is more likely to have originated from the researcher, followed by some level of involvement from the participants – perhaps in the research design phase, or through channelling data analysis back and forth to them for validation. The *overlap* between participatory and collaborative methods of research resides perhaps in the notion that they are both *inclusive*; the research participants are co-constructors of knowledge. They are methods that are usually chosen because of a researcher's overt ethical concerns not to want to exert power over the researched; rather they are concerned with engaging with the communities they are researching. They are also methods that are particularly relevant to cross-cultural studies given the unique perspectives involved, and they complement narrative and feminist research methods.

Participatory and collaborative methods have been successfully used in information research (e.g., Penzhorn's 2002 research on information needs of disadvantaged South African women). In Australasia there is noticeable absence in the use of these methods despite them having been brought to our attention by indigenous researchers (see Huggins 1998, Nakata 2004). It would be refreshing to see these methods being explored by IL researchers to see if they will help our field of research become one that fosters scholarly debate and growth while simultaneously bringing to the fore significant issues in IL that we have yet to understand.

Conclusion

The aim of this chapter, and this book, has been to discuss the use of various research methods in the field of IL. It has not advocated one method over another, nor has it proclaimed that one single method should dominate future IL research. Further, it has not exhaustively covered *every* research method. Rather, it has attempted to show how different methods have, and could be, used in the field. Fundamentally, researchers need to consider paradigms of most importance and the most appropriate method for the question/s they are asking. While the questions needing to be investigated in the field remain diverse at this stage, greater understanding of the methods already used, and the experimentation in ones that are new to the field, will help researchers develop the IL field further.

References

Agar, M.H. (2006). Ethnography. In *International encyclopedia of the social & behavioral sciences* (pp.4857-4862). Amsterdam: Elsevier.

Aiyepeku, W., Atinmo, M. & Aderinoye, R. (2002). Towards a Functional Infoliteracy Campaign in African States. White paper prepared for UNESCO, the US National Commission on Libraries and Information Science, and the National Forum on Information Literacy, for use at the Information Literacy Meeting of Experts, Prague, The Czech Republic, July 2002.

Bow, A. (2002). Ethnographic techniques. In K. Williamson, *Research methods for students, academics and professionals: Information management and systems* (2nd ed., pp.265-279). Wagga Wagga, NSW: Centre for Information Studies, Charles Sturt University.

Brayton, J. (1997). What makes feminist research feminist? The Structure of Feminist Research within the Social Sciences, 2005. Retrieved 16 September 2007 from http://www.unb.ca/PAR-L/win/feminmethod.htm

Broido, E.M. & Manning, K. (2002). Philosophical foundations and current theoretical perspectives in qualitative research. *Journal of College Student Development 43*(4): 434-445.

Clandinin, D.J., Pushor, D. & Orr, A.M. (2007). Navigating sites for narrative inquiry. *Journal of Teacher Education, 58*(1), 21-35.

Connelly, F.M. & Clandinin, D.J. (1999). Narrative enquiry. In J.P. Keeves & G. Lakomski, *Issues in Educational Research* (pp.132-140). Amsterdam: Pergamon.

Cornwall, A. & Jewkes, R. (1995). What is participatory research? *Social Science & Medicine, 41* (12): 1667-1676.

Cottle, T.J. (2002). On narratives and the sense of self. *Qualitative Inquiry 8*(5), 535-549.

Elliot, J. (2005). Using narrative in social research: Qualitative and quantitative approaches. Thousand Oaks, CA: Sage.

Fine, G.A. (2006). Participant observation. In *International encyclopedia of the social & behavioral sciences* (pp.11073-11078), Amsterdam: Elsevier.

Garrett, R. (1999). Feminist Research Dilemmas in How Young Women Move. Paper presented at the Australian Association for Research in Education Conference. Melbourne: AARE.

Huggins, J. (1998). *Sister Girl*. Brisbane: University of Queensland Press.

Hughes, H., Middleton, M., Edwards, S., Bruce, C. & McAllister, L. (2005). Information literacy research in Australia 2000-2005. A preprint in English of the paper, which after translation by Oristelle Bonis, appeared as: Hughes, H., Middleton, M., Edwards, S.L., Bruce, C. & McAllister, L. (2005). La recherche australienne en maîtrise de l'information 2000-2005. *Bulletin des Bibliothèques de France, 50*(6), 45-55.

McMullen, C. (2006). Weaving a research story: Agendas of the researcher and the researched. In *Voice, identity and reflexivity*, Proceedings of the Second RIPPLE Qualitative Research as Interpretive Practice Conference held at Charles Sturt University, Albury Campus 22-23 September 2005. G. Whiteford (Ed.). Bathurst, NSW: Centre for Research into Professional Practice, Leaning and Education (RIPPLE), pp.36-45.

Mattingly, C. & Lawlor, M. (2000). Learning from stories: Narrative interviewing in cross-cultural research. *Scandinavian Journal of Occupational Therapy, 7*(1), 4-14.

Mertens, D.M. (1998) *Research methods in education and psychology: Integrating diversity with quantitative and qualitative approaches.* Thousand Oaks, CA: Sage.

Mooko, N.P. (2005). The information behaviors of women in Botswana. *Library & Information Science Research, 27*, 115-127.

Nagar, R. (2003). Collaboration across borders: Moving beyond positionality. *Singapore Journal of Tropical Geography, 24*(3), 356-372.

Nakata, M. (2004). Indigenous knowledge and the cultural interface: Underlying issues at the intersection of knowledge and information systems. In. A. Hickling-Hudson, J. Matthews & A. Woods, *Disrupting preconceptions: Postcolonialism and education.* Flaxton, Qld: Post Pressed, pp.19-38.

Obi, M.J. (2002). The Changing Face of Librarianship in Papua New Guinea: Libraries for Life in the Papua New Guinea Information Society. Paper presented at the 68th IFLA Council and General Conference. Glasgow: IFLA.

Penzhorn, C. (2002). The use of participatory research as an alternative approach for information needs research. *ASLIB Proceedings, 54*(4), 240-250.

Tang, N. (2002). Interviewer and interviewee relationships between women. *Sociology, 36*(3), 703-721.

Tuonminen, K., Savolainen, R. & Talja, S. (2005). Information literacy as a sociotechnical practice. *The Library Quarterly, 75*(3), 329-345.

Virkus, S. (2003). Information literacy in Europe: A literature review. *Information Research, 8*(4).

Watt, D. (2007). On becoming a qualitative researcher: The value of reflexivity. *The Qualitative Report, 12*(1), 82-101.

Printed and bound by CPI Group (UK) Ltd, Croydon, CR0 4YY

08/05/2025

01864975-0003